Mastering Uncertainty

in

Leadership, Innovation and Strategy

S. P. Reid

Mike
Hope you enjoy my
3rd Book. See you soon?
Best Wishes
Stephen

For my

father Frank

D1420009

Published by 1_Permillion,

a division of Spring Business Innovation Ltd.

Registered office:

11 High Street,

Ruddington, Nottingham

NG11 6DT England

Tel: 0115 921 4035. Fax: 0115 921 4037

First published in Great Britain in 2012

13-digit ISBN Code 978-0-9552700-1-7

British Library Cataloguing-in-Publication Data.
A CIP record for this book is available from the British Library

The Kogs illustrations of PolyKog, MonoKog, D Kog and C Kog are by Jessica Congdon and are based on a concise brief by the author. All copyright to these illustrations as well as the concept narrative and format belong to Stephen Reid © 2011.

Cover design in collaboration with Redesign

Typeset by Andrew Welsh

Proofread by Wendy Smith

Printed by Henry Ling Ltd, The Dorset Press, DT1 1HD

Disclaimers
Where possible I have made contact with authors and practitioners to gain direct permission to quote or paraphrase their ideas or their work. If you believe your work is represented here in some way and I have not provided the correct citation, please contact me and I will amend future editions as appropriate.

A variety of people doing demanding jobs have generously offered practical comments regarding their personal experiences. Their views are personal to them and should be read as the opinion of an individual and do not necessarily reflect, nor should be read as representative of, the collective views of the organisation that employs them. For the more widely accepted opinions, values, norms and accepted principles of any organisations mentioned, you should refer directly to their company websites for further information.

A variety of Internet sites are suggested, however, the author and 1_Permillion take no responsibility whatsoever for the content of any of these sites.

About the author

Stephen Reid is a management consultant who works with large international organisations developing leadership innovation strategy. A lot of the issues that arise involve ambiguity, uncertainty and complex problems. Over the years, he has developed a variety of ideas, beliefs and models into pragmatic thinking patterns and decision-making tools to deal with some of the more complicated issues in business and life.

He is a faculty member of the UK Chartered Institute of Marketing and a member of Duke Corporate Education's global learning-resource network. Stephen is the author of two other books, *How To Think* and *High Performance Thinking Skills*.

He has lived and worked in the UK, Scandinavia, Saudi Arabia and Dubai. Stephen has a solid prior track record of running successful operations to managing director level.

Contact and further information

Email: spreid1@gmail.com
If you have any constructive comments I would be glad to hear from you.

Linkages

LinkedIn: look for SP Reid, Nottingham

Facebook: search for 'Mastering Uncertainty in Leadership Innovation and Strategy' or use the bit.ly short link: http://on.fb.me/qleMuD

Twitter: SP Reid (@spreid1) or look for SP Reid Nottingham

Website: www.spreid.com

Thanks to

John Chambers, Director of Applications at a large UK IT service provider.

Colin Harris, Head of Infrastructure UK, Middle East and Africa at Arup.

Joe Garner, HSBC's Deputy Chief Executive, UK retail banking.

Andrew McLaren, Head of Risk, HSBC Bermuda.

Eric Peeters, Business Vice-President Solar, Dow Corning Corporation.

Niall FitzGerald for permission to quote his story.

Robert Nuttall VP Strategic Marketing at Rolls Royce

Several individuals at IBM.

Professor George Ainslie, Veterans Affairs Medical Center and University of Cape Town.

Phil Hodgson, Ashridge Business School.

Narendra Laljani, Ashridge Business School.

Randall White, Executive Development Group and Faculty Member at Duke Corporate Education.

Fons Trompenaars, Amsterdam.

Charles Hampden-Turner, Cambridge.

Peter Woolliams, East Anglia.

GertJan Hofstede, The Netherlands.

John Kearon for helpful suggestions.

Trevor Long, for enlightenment.

Special thank you to:

Tony Kemmer, former director at Boots The Chemist.

Tim Last.

Carol O'Connor.

Contents

Introduction

A new way forward

The keys to success in a complex world involve your thinking pattern, aligned to what you believe to be true or certain as well as the extent to which you can tolerate uncertainty and withstand impulsive desires to act to resolve a tension. If you and others wish to operate consistently well when faced with complex uncertainty, you will need to employ 'always on awareness', feelings AND smart thinking.

This book provides useful guidelines, thinking models, tips and practitioner commentary. It is divided into four unequal parts:

An overview

This section provides a broad approach to the starting points, a new way forward and key models to consider. It provides the business case for why you need to embrace uncertainty and see it as normal as opposed to something to be resisted or avoided.

A variety of contexts are provided to help you visualise the important parts of a foggy ecology. A simple A B C model provides the outline structure to the rest of the book.

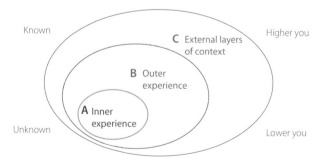

Part A: Inner uncertainties

The ancient advice to first know and conquer your self has never been more appropriate. If you are uncertain about yourself, how will you be able to cope in your external, volatile, real world? This section uses a small number of macro-models to describe quite different access points to your inner workings so that you can upgrade your ability to engage higher levels of uncertainty in an increasingly complex world.

Part B: Your outer experiences

Your 'focus of attention' is progressively shaped by your varied experiences, your expectations and by several of your other inner resources. Your fundamental orientation towards certainty and uncertainty or the extent to which you feel safe in different circumstances also shapes your experiences, interactions and results. The way you behave determines how other people see you and the extent to which they will offer or deny collaboration and support. To that extent your behaviours shape your character and the level of available resilience.

Part C: The wider contexts and real world application

This section constitutes more than half the book and is given over to the practical aspects of dealing more effectively with uncertainty and ambiguity as a leader, in innovation and in developing long-term strategy. To enrich the content I have added first-hand experiences and comments from practitioners from a variety of organisations plus a selection of useful references.

Taken together, the ideas and experiences covered here will provide essential elements to your successful navigation through volatile and uncertain times.

Overview

Chapter 1: Reasons to engage the fog of uncertainty

Chapter 2: Understanding the journey

Chapter 3: Lighting the way

This first part of the book is about how you think and how your beliefs and experiences shape your behaviour. Understanding any inner uncertainty before you tackle outer ambiguities helps you better understand your options and your experiences when life gets really foggy and uncertain.

Bear in mind that when faced with complex uncertainty there may be no absolutely 'right way'. In this respect, there can be no single perfect model, no prescription and no ready-made solution to your uncertainty. The aim of this book is to get you to think, to find your own truth.

This section describes why you need to embrace uncertainty and see it as normal as opposed to something to be resisted. I have approached the subject from several different directions and created some unusual contexts to help you visualise the important parts of a foggy ecology.

Chapter 1

Reasons to engage the fog of uncertainty

The reasons why you should consider embracing ambiguity and mastering uncertainty might include a wish to have a richer life story to tell, to be successful at work, to turn your organisation around, to lead effectively or to innovate. With this in mind this book will focus on your performance at work, teamwork, your leadership, innovation and strategic capabilities.

Teamwork, leadership, innovation and strategy share a core theme, namely complex uncertainty and ambiguity. It therefore makes sense to understand uncertainty. Several professors think embracing ambiguity and uncertainty is a good commercial idea, and successful global organisations agree.

The ambiguity ceiling

There is an important boundary point of uncertainty where many people struggle with their thinking. I call it **the ambiguity ceiling**. Beyond this boundary, new skills and experiences are needed that are rarely made explicit or taught. Some people have problems reaching above the ambiguity ceiling into the foggy zone of uncertainty whilst others have problems reaching below it to locate clarity. Here I pay attention to the idea of reaching into the fog of uncertainty and finding some sort of 'sense' AND then getting to a point where you can take a useful decision, if you choose to.

The ambiguity ceiling is not the gender barrier otherwise known as the 'glass ceiling' but it **is** a barrier to better paid jobs that require energy, intellectual dexterity and tolerance to prolonged uncertainty. Overcoming this particular barrier can lead to a deeper understanding of the complexity of life, business politics and relationships.

ambiguity and uncertainty will shape your life story

Your route forward doesn't involve avoiding the tension of uncertainty. Selectively embracing chosen uncertainties supported by a range of skills and beliefs can create advantage. In order to do this you need to be capable of working above the ambiguity ceiling. (See Chapter 3.)

A rich life story

Create and live a richer life story. As life gets increasingly complex you can be certain that you will encounter more ambiguity and increasing uncertainty. How you deal with ambiguity and uncertainty in multiple roles will shape your life story.

Uncertainty, ambiguity, contradiction and dilemmas are pervasive. They are the very essence and flavour of real living. Ambiguity is where fun, love, joy AND the sorrow of life abide. Great literature, poetry, children's stories and movies would be dead without uncertainty, ambiguity, dilemmas and contradiction. These are the essential elements of enjoyment, seduction, tension, energy and the thrill of life. They are virtually impossible to avoid if you expect to embrace life in the fullest sense.

we enjoy being surprised, yet many of us actively avoid uncertainty

Collectively our species spends vast amounts of effort and billions of dollars generating entertaining, blockbuster, audio-visual stimuli that embrace uncertainty in order to excite us. We enjoy being surprised, yet many of us actively avoid uncertainty. Contradictions can be a source of uncertainty for some. Learning to accommodate seemingly contradictory subjects requires an ability to reconcile, balance and sustain alternate logical AND emotional positions.

Embracing uncertainty requires us to open the door to our passions, not just individually but collectively too. A Dow Corning executive charged with leading innovation at a global organisation identified a useful working contradiction of 'passion AND patience' as one of their key success factors. He offers many more first-hand insights. (See Chapter 11.)

Success at work

Knowing how to add value at work and to one's career whilst avoiding getting left behind is becoming increasingly ambiguous and uncertain. Talent is increasingly globally resourced and outsourced.

Familiar ways of working are being uprooted. The increased uncertainty produces opportunities as well as threats to your career. It makes sense therefore to increase your chances of promotion by gathering the skills necessary to deal with uncertainty.

You will need to be capable of working above the ambiguity ceiling if you have any ambitions to join a high performance elite in business or politics or if you want to figure out how best to create a commercial advantage for your firm, develop true innovation or a powerful strategy.

you need to be capable of working above the ambiguity ceiling

Business management researchers have found that an ability to deal effectively with dilemma and ambiguity is an indicator of executive ability. Three internationally recognised business-school professors working with more than 30,000 managers from companies around the world discovered a pattern that shows a statistically significant correlation between higher profitable performance, executive level decision-making and the ability of senior managers to reconcile a dilemma. (See Chapter 10.)

Without such ability, you will struggle at the top AND be most uncomfortable. Ability in dealing effectively with ambiguities makes a substantial difference.

Organisational success

A recent IBM study[1] of a very large number of CEOs from around the world indicated that uncertainty and ambiguity are already major management issues.

What 1500 CEOs say about uncertainty and ambiguity

IBM thinks that skills of leading through complexity and uncertainty are really important. They conducted face-to-face interviews with more than 1500 CEOs from all around the globe.[2] To quote directly from the executive summary:

> Today's complexity is only expected to rise and more than half of CEOs doubt their ability to manage it. Seventy-nine percent of CEOs anticipate even greater complexity ahead. However, one set of organisations, we call them 'Standouts,' has turned increased complexity into financial advantage over the past five years.

According to IBM's interpretation, three major leadership patterns were seen more often in organisations that demonstrated 'standout performance', namely:

- creative leadership
- reinventing customer relationships
- building operating dexterity.

The first of three primary features of the skills detected in standout organisations, creative leadership, is described further as: 'Embracing ambiguity, taking risks that disrupt legacy business models and leapfrogging beyond 'tried-and-true' management style.'

IBM's 74-page report concludes with these two important questions:

> For CEOs and their organisations, avoiding complexity is not an option; the choice comes in how they respond to it. Will they allow complexity to become a stifling force that slows responsiveness, overwhelms employees and customers, or threatens profits? Or do they have the creative leadership, customer relationships and operating dexterity to turn it into a true advantage?

Their information suggests new ways of thinking, 'being', adapting and behaving are required to thrive in increasingly complex environments.

New thinking is required

Focus, logical deductive and reductive thinking will continue to make a valuable contribution. There are, however, other beneficial ways of thinking, living and being that apply especially when life gets foggy and uncertain.

Success requires a combination of thorough common AND uncommon sense. Avoiding ambiguity, uncertainty and complexity, in the hope that they will recede or diminish is not really a credible option.

success requires a combination of thorough common AND uncommon sense

Unnecessary delay in dealing with uncertainty can lead to increased fear or anxiety, loss of energy, hope and capability through reduced choice. Building resilience to deal effectively with a more challenging and uncertain future is not only about the quality of your material resources and systems. It also involves upgrades to your fundamental thinking patterns and beliefs.

Occasional 'change management' interventions are unlikely to build resilience to prolonged uncertainty. Instead, a sustainable way of 'being', thinking and behaving is required. Engaging ambiguity involves a step change in perception, beliefs, philosophy, reasoning and behaviour. Embracing ambiguity is a visceral experience and involves a revision to your habitual way of 'being'. IBM, for example, reinvented their business through a completely new way of thinking and behaving. It has become part of the 'organisation's DNA' and their success story. Their collective 'frame of reference' changed[3] and higher profits followed.

Executives at one of Dow Corning's innovation units discovered a variety of thinking patterns, contradictions and emotional states that define their success in graduating new businesses. (See Chapter 11, Section 4.) HSBC UK has adopted a particular way of thinking that they believe will not only guide their ethical decision-making but also lead to long-term sustainable success. (See Chapter 13.)

Each successful organisation discovered their particular truth. In each case, this involved new beliefs, new thinking, new values and new behaviours that would enable them to deal more effectively with uncertainty and ambiguity.

Some organisations that have held onto old habits or, in some cases, bad habits find their business beginning to take hefty hits to their ability to perform. Having the right thinking skills and the right working philosophies are not just nice-to-have bolt-on concepts, they are fast becoming crucial to survival.

Summary

The case for engaging ambiguity has upsides AND downsides. Energy can be given or drained away depending on how resilient you, your team or your organisation are. Overall, the benefit of reaching above the ambiguity ceiling is to live and experience life to the full and to maximise your personal and collective potential. Dealing effectively with ambiguity can improve overall performance and profitability. In the following chapters you will find many helpful tips and new models, plus a few quirky stories and valuable life skills that are rarely taught.

Chapter 2
Understanding the journey

We need to approach uncertainty from several directions at once, with an open and ready mind. There cannot be a simple formula or a right way to deal with uncertainty but there are things we can do to deal with it more effectively. Certainty and uncertainty are perceptions that can and often do influence your behaviour. So let's start there. In order to understand your perception you need to be aware on several levels at once.

Awareness

To gain personal mastery in anything, awareness and an ability to reflect are essential. Awareness needs to be outwardly as well as inwardly directed – i.e. context awareness AND self-awareness. Without such awareness, you will be driven by basic survival instincts and base desires. That would be 'lower you', the part of you that tempts you. 'Lower you' leaves you at the mercy of 'impulse' behaviour.

With heightened awareness you may be able to watch yourself and your inner workings in real time. With practice you can learn ways of overcoming your impulses. Higher levels of self-awareness present an opportunity to rise above a situation and, by living in the moment,[4] to exercise the direction of a higher sense. You might describe this as 'higher you, the watcher of you'. This is a form of 'engaged detachment' or watching yourself in real time AND remaining in touch with the higher good of a wider context other than pure self-interest. In my previous books, I described this as 'separation'.

Perceived uncertainty

Uncertainty is largely a **relative** perception. Our sense of uncertainty can be relative to a variety of **boundary relationships** to do with the context, our own and other people's behaviours or something named (or not) within our imagination.

Boundaries

Our perceptions operate within reference boundaries. Uncertainty can be perceived as acceptable and often enjoyable if we feel entirely safe. What I perceive to be uncertain you may not. A sense of safety that works for you may not work for someone else, no matter how well you believe you know them. The extent to which we feel safe AND confident with novel or unexpected situations is therefore very important.

What we believe to be true and the way we think lie at the heart of how we might improve the way we deal with uncertainty.

Our individual inner beliefs, emotions and capabilities collectively shape our focus of attention and therefore our outward-facing behaviours and therefore our relationships and subsequent viability.

Our attitudes and orientations are shaped by successive experiences and by personal, social and moral rewards or admonishments all compiled within our overall frame of reference about what we believe and how we feel.

If we appreciate what and where our reference boundaries are and how we tend to interact with them we can, given sufficient self-awareness, begin to master our uncertainties.

Macro model 1: Context awareness

The first mental model I'd like to employ is an 'onion map'. An onion map will not provide answers, only clues as to which contexts are involved. An overview of the layers of reality and perception that need to be considered could be represented by the simple illustration below. Following this overview section, the rest of the book falls into three unequal parts represented by this map.

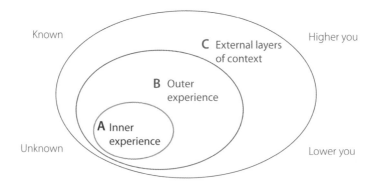

Inner AND outer journeys

Once you are aware and noticing both your inner and outer world there are multiple access points to improve your ability to deal with uncertainty. The journey I have mapped out around uncertainty starts with this brief overview and is followed by three parts:

(A) Your inner experience.

(B) Your outer experience of your reality; how your inner beliefs feelings and capabilities shape your outward decisions and behaviours.

(C) Wider contexts including how leaders, teams and organisations have wrestled with the ambiguity and complex uncertainty of innovation, leadership and strategy.

Macro model 2

This is an expansion of model 1. The inner (A) and outer (B) experiences are mapped out in more detail in the following macro model:

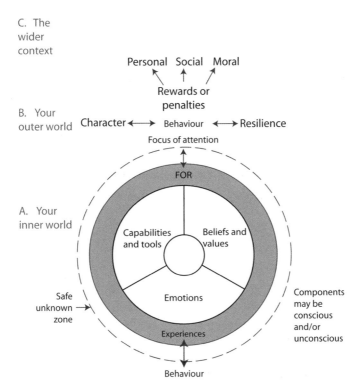

A – Your inner experience

This relatively simple model includes a personal safety zone, the size and scope of which will vary in general terms between different people according to their preferences for security/certainty vs novelty/uncertainty. Notice that the frame of reference here is shown as an outer circle. The core is intentionally left without a label.

In the illustrations of my earlier books I depicted a **frame of reference** as a conventional rectangular picture frame. The precise shape of a 'frame of reference' is not significant. That the frame envelops who we believe we are, our experiences, our capabilities and our emotions is what is important.

This model below allows me to illustrate how the rigidity or porosity of the boundaries of our frames of reference, our 'master program', may vary. For example, some people demonstrate an 'open-minded' orientation whilst other people may generally opt for a tightly fixed, rule-bound reality. It is important not to judge how other people construct their realities, especially when they differ significantly from the way you see the world. No matter how we build up our sense of perception, there will always be advantages and disadvantages.

All of the elements described above are dynamically cross-linked and inform each other. The model provides clues as to how we interact with 'reality' AND provides recognisable access points for continuous self-improvement. Each element is covered in detail in subsequent chapters.

Your frame of reference (FOR)

Just below the surface of your awareness of what you believe you need and want is your frame of reference. Your frame of reference FOR is a composite of your experiences, feelings and capabilities honed through the experiences you have encountered and been rewarded or sanctioned for.

Your FOR is unique to you and includes both positive and negative experiences. It is the story of your life. Your FOR shapes your current, future and past perception, your general orientation, your attitude and your expectations and norms. If you were a computer this would be your master file, your 'basic boot record'.

The foundation beliefs of your FOR hold the key to your behaviour. Your FOR is where your 'meaning or purpose' resides. Particular aspects of your FOR are hard wired to visceral feelings.

Your FOR is a wrapper for all that you see, sense and believe to be real, novel or uncertain. Your capabilities, beliefs and values and emotions are all experienced in relation to your overall frame of reference. (See Chapter 4.)

Capability tools models and maps

Within your frame of reference, you already have adaptive internal learning including an array of thinking tools, patterns and associations. For most people these are not necessarily explicit. Some people use only a few tools and patterns whilst others are capable of abstract synthesis and can literally 'pull new ideas out of the air'. Your or other people's thinking patterns may or may not access a variety of rational + creative + strategic mental models. The mental models and tools may be more extensive and better developed in some people than in others. For the most part, though, they can be acquired and learned.

The great thing about 'homo sapiens' is our ability to think, learn and originate new concepts and ideas. Most of all we have advanced by sharing and copying especially when it comes to ways of overcoming difficulties. I have included a variety of tips and tools that work in practice. (See Chapter 5.)

If you would like a wider array of tools, see my second book 'High Performance Thinking Skills'. It contains 82 easy-to-use thinking tools, each described in less than five pages. (Also available as an ebook.)

Emotional literacy/ability

Your emotions are an integral part of your frame of reference, but in some people the extent to which they are influenced by what they feel can be undeveloped or limited in some way.

The pressures to conform, to learn and behave in a prescribed way, to meet deadlines, to live to a schedule and to focus on the material tasks relentlessly drive us to focus. High focus on cold objective tasks and goals can denude us of our attention to feelings.

You are not a machine. What you feel is not always the same for other people since we each find our own meaning in different things at different times and to different extents. What is sometimes overlooked is that emotions do have a significant role in serious commercial decision-making. Individual ability in using feelings to make decisions varies considerably. Some of us are blind to aspects of our emotions whilst some have quite a refined repertoire.

Emotional literacy/ability involves an awareness of and an ability to differentiate between quite different feelings. Emotionally literate people may have a 'sensitivity' to different people, times, places and contexts, in addition to well -developed ways of expressing, venting and employing different feelings. Actors or politicians working a crowd, for example, can hold and project particular emotional states.

The people who love us, as well as our small children, can sometimes emotionally work around our resolve and completely upend our objective decisions. That much we may already know, but how would you employ your finer feelings in making decisions about something valuable, complex and uncertain? (See Chapter 6.)

Beliefs and values

(i) View of self, role and place
At a most intimate level within your frame of reference, your sense of identity, your essential 'being', is underpinned by your deeper values. These values are visceral and are the core of who you believe you are, and what you stand for. They are an important component of your resilience. (See Chapter 7.)

(ii) Working philosophies
As an outward expression of your values, your 'working philosophies' are the guidelines you turn to when things are uncertain. It is healthy to adopt a suspicion that your working philosophies may need to be upgraded or adjusted from time to time. They are your approximations, expectations, your 'rules of thumb', your heuristics or quick-fix principles. (See Chapter 7.)

Focus of attention
This is the inner element of your mind that is probably closest to the surface or at the surface of your consciousness. Our focus of attention has roots through

our frame of reference into our emotions and our beliefs and values. This is the bridge between thought and action. (See Chapter 8.)

B – Your outer experience of your reality

Your inner world of competing interests, desires, emotions and intentions shapes how you interact with the real world. I will focus briefly on just some aspects of your outward focus of attention that can have a bearing on your overall orientation to uncertainty.

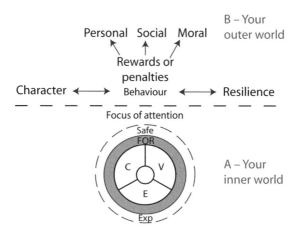

Behaviour, resilience and character

Resilience

Resilience is really important when it comes to dealing with uncertainty. Resilience can manifest itself internally AND externally.

Your 'resilience' is determined by your energy, tenacity and a sense that you have a solution or know the right way when perhaps others are floundering. A high level of active commitment to pursue something, despite the slings and arrows of misfortune, requires substantial willpower guided by strong feelings about what is 'right'. Almost anything you can do to build resilience individually and collectively is worthwhile. This is explored further in Chapter 8.

Resilience requires physical and mental fitness and toughness as well as access to resources in the form of meaningful supports and anchors. At the inner resilient core of your very being, there will be underpinnings, reason and clear purpose. Genuine resilience is not superficial.

Character

There is an internal and external reading of your character. How well you know and relate to your 'self' can contribute to your self-esteem and self-confidence. The way you behave illuminates many aspects of your character, your virtues, vices and abilities. Demonstrating resilience to those you connect with is an external aspect of your character, the 'brand' of you.

Groups, companies, products also behave in ways that develop an image. If they endure, they eventually develop 'character' in the eyes of the people who interact with them. Lasting impressions become 'brands' and therefore value.

The nature of our 'character' arising from our behaviour determines who includes or excludes us. We tend to choose the company of people we 'like', but is that the best policy during uncertain conditions? More on the virtues of 'character' in Chapter 8.

Chapters 9 to 13 deal with the practical aspects of implementation. In particular we will look at how teams might work under increasingly uncertain conditions.

Relationships

If the way you behave aligns well with other people then your ability to withstand uncertainty improves. Relationships are your bridge to success in the wider contexts. We gain strength when we work together; social interaction is arguably one of the most complex activities any human can engage in. Therefore team members must figure out the optimum way to work, despite these additional challenges. (See Chapter 9.)

Relationships operate internally AND externally. We have relationships with others, with causes, with a context and perhaps with a higher self or a higher principle. All are richly endowed with complex uncertainty. One relationship that can be overlooked is the relationship you have with your 'self'. It can be remarkably easy to cripple your chances of forming solid relationships if you don't have a good relationship with yourself. It needn't be perfect but it should be understood and accommodated if you want to appear authentic in the eyes of others.

When all our internal and external relationships work in harmony our confidence and performance find a higher level. It is therefore important to understand AND capitalise on our **useful differences**. Sometimes an adjustment of individual perception is required in order to see who or what is useful.

Uncertainty and difficulty rise considerably when we are obliged to collaborate to take important decisions, for example, to lead others, to innovate or to develop a strategic move. Uncertainty increases rapidly the more long-term responsibility you accept for leadership, innovation or strategy. See Chapters 10 to 13 for practitioner insights.

Summary

There is no precisely right or wrong way to deal with uncertainty. Any framework that attempts to deal with complex uncertainty must be viewed as fallible, temporary, likely to be incomplete and subject to substantial change. You therefore need to be alert on several fronts at once. Gather in as many tools as you can and, most of all, practise awareness 'in the moment'.

Chapter 3
Lighting the way

There are many **thinking tools, tips and ideas** that can help you. Below are some that get used a lot throughout the book. I encourage you to adopt or at least try many of them. Let's start with perceptions of meanings.

get into parallel thinking as opposed to serial thinking

AND

You will notice the word 'AND' emphasised. 'AND' is shorthand for **'and at the very same time'**. This is an important point. I want you to get into **parallel thinking** as opposed to serial thinking. I want you to practise holding at least two different ideas in mind **at the same time** until it becomes a habit of mind.

Few people consider, 'How am I thinking now?' as a matter of habit. If you repeatedly ask yourself this question, you may find that eventually the question is posed at the same time as you are thinking. Also get into the habit of detecting issues where AND would fit much better than the words 'either/or'. By adopting these simple patterns you will be better able to get into parallel, as opposed to serial, thinking. Getting into the habit of 'AND' thinking is a key skill and an important one to accommodate, especially if you are used to 'being' busy, focused or prescriptive.

The test of a first-rate intelligence is the ability to hold two opposing ideas in mind at the same time and still retain the ability to function.
F. Scott Fitzgerald

Use of one word for several

There isn't a single word that describes all of the messy, wicked and complex uncertainties. The word **'ambiguity'** is generally employed in this book to encompass a wide category of slippery issues such as dilemmas, contradictions and especially complex uncertainties.

Ambiguity vs simple uncertainty

There are characteristics that differentiate ambiguity from plain uncertainty. With simple uncertainty, resolution may be just a matter of finding the right information. With an ambiguity we often have competing options that may be equally valid or equally horrid. Ambiguity takes us closer to the possibility of decisions being made, but there is always an awkwardness or tension involved.

Ambiguity can arise as a consequence of:

- divergence (i.e. something being open-ended as opposed to convergent, focused).
- two or more different outcomes being possible or probable at the same time. These are accompanied by difficulty of choice, resolution or reconciliation.
- a tension between choices, where each may be plausible for different reasons at the same time, thus preventing a clear 'either/or' type decision. Each possibility need not exclude the other. They have the potential to coexist; however coexistence may present additional problems, dilemmas and tensions.
- the application of alternate valid reference points to the same situation producing contradictory, inconclusive or partial outcomes. For example, consider the multiple answers to the question, 'What is the best way to educate children?'
- changing, temporary or volatile rules, standards or reference points.
- insufficient or unpalatable information regarding different options.
- changed context or time. What may have been correct at a particular time and in a particular context may be incorrect or unsatisfactory at another time or in another context.

One or more of the above can be operative at the same time. Gathering more information does **not** change the character of an ambiguity to a simple uncertainty.

slippery problems yield slippery outcomes

Also, working harder to locate the 'right information' will not necessarily yield better results. Ambiguities are by nature incomplete, contentious, imperfect and out of balance. Slippery problems yield slippery outcomes. Pure, clean, concise answers are often therefore impossible.

Red indicators

Red indicators that scream out, 'This is complex!' may include:

- the problem/issue seems unique and we lack knowledge.
- it is creating tensions. Feelings are involved.
- more knowledge fails to resolve the problem/issue.
- despite previous best efforts, the problem/issue recurs again and again.
- outcomes are inconsistent.
- we suspect there are multiple, variable-value linkages that we do not entirely understand.
- we seem to only get things partially right. There's always something else that's wrong at the same time.
- whatever we do, we cannot get it absolutely right.

It 'feels' slippery and the relationship between cause and effect seems to have broken down.

Ambiguities come in a variety of shapes and sizes.

Dilemma, tri-lemma, polarity and multarity

These are truly complex. Clear unambiguous outcomes are not possible in any of them. A dilemma is a complex uncertainty where at first encounter, two potentially valid outcomes are apparent and each has a potentially serious downside along with a valuable benefit of some kind. A further level of complication would be a tri-lemma, being a step up from a two-sided dilemma ,involving three interacting elements where trade-offs or a balancing act may be required.

Polarities are situations in which 'conjoined' paired issues are mistaken for separate problems when in fact they are forever joined and cannot be realistically separated. Despite being fairly common, polarities are not widely understood. Consequently a lot of effort and passion gets wasted. The uncertainty as to what to do tends to get worse as the symptoms of a polarity recur relentlessly.

A 'multarity' is a complex combination of polarities working in concert. Polarities and multarities are covered in more detail in Chapter 5, Section 3.

Managing expectations of answers

Given the inherently messy, often irrational nature of ambiguity and complexity, there can be no particular magical formula or process to follow to get to the 'best solution'. Often, once above the ambiguity ceiling there is no best answer. Getting people to understand and accept this can be difficult.

slippery questions yield slippery answers

You will discover that when you deal with ambiguity, any answers, where they can be found, are often dynamic in nature. In short, slippery questions yield slippery answers. In that sense, you need to be able to think quickly and adapt. With this in mind, please pick out the ideas and suggestions that you believe can work for you. Experiment if you can. Find your own truth.

Absence of purity or simplicity

Learn to let go of the logic of pure, simple or absolute outcomes. Logic **is** valuable but of limited utility when things become uncertain. Relationships, friendships, work, teams, competition and economics are all dynamic living systems. They are not static nor are they fixed. In general 'purity' is avoided in biological systems simply because one (pure) evolutionary choice can be a fast track to extinction. When we look closely, variation appears to be the very essence of life. Most of life is quite naturally variable, uncertain and foggy. Our lives, like our biology, are not fixed, rigid nor absolute, thank goodness!

Not knowing engages all the senses

Uncertainty is not necessarily a bad thing. Much fun and joy in life is derived from what we **do not** know. Uncertainty is an emotion, a sense of unease, an agitation, a delicious mystery, a surprise or an enjoyable tickle. Uncertainties that are important to us can generate feelings. The higher the importance and the higher the uncertainty, the stronger the feeling will be. Get used to the different sorts of feelings that are generated by different types of uncertainty.

uncertainty can be fun, if we feel safe enough

Uncertainty tells you that you **are** alive. Uncertainty can be fun, if we feel safe enough. Confidence is an emotional sensation too. So by default the book will refer to how you might use different senses, including your feelings, to enjoy, embrace, accommodate and cope with uncertainty.

Scary philosophy

Some people recoil at the idea of getting philosophical, yet most of us have a collection of beliefs that we use to guide our way, especially when issues become complex or uncertain. A working set of beliefs that is open to question is all I intend to look for. And philosophers are not all boring, dry old academics who count angels on pinheads. For example, according to Bertrand Russell, Pythagoras believed that beans were evil![5] The 'working philosophy' I have in mind simply asks you to look out for ideas and beliefs that either help or hinder the way you think, feel and behave AND to then adjust your beliefs accordingly.

Some companies have performed well by developing their beliefs to a high standard. (See Chapter 13.)

Analogies and quirky stories

If you are faced with a quirky problem, you should not be entirely surprised if equally quirky solutions are suggested. Some readers may find my use of unusual analogies and peculiar stories a little odd at first.

If you are prone to resisting bizarre sources of inspiration, consider why. By resisting unusual sources you risk closing down an interesting array of possibilities. Thinking in terms of analogies, for example, encourages a fluidity of thought beyond the strictures of formal logic, and is probably one of the most powerful ways of thinking. Engaging with analogies will encourage you to learn to use parallel tracks of thought, an important aspect of higher performance. My analogies, images and stories are intended to be sticky and relevant. Please enjoy them and see where they lead your thoughts. Sometimes the answers analogies provoke arrive 'later', so please be patient.

Pictorial thinking

What helps me to 'see' sense and order in my occasionally disorganised mind is often a shape or a picture coupled to a feeling of rightness or awkwardness. If something 'feels wrong' or the picture I have in my mind is incomplete I'll wait and look for what is missing, even if I'm not sure what I'm looking for.

This particular characteristic of my thinking style is not something I would volunteer on any job application simply because many people would not understand the value of such a style; nevertheless, Pictures, for me, are a major part of, and not a minor adjunct to, my thinking. I recommend that if you do not currently employ pictorial thinking or 'visualisation' that you will ponder a little longer on the simple graphics and make a connection to something that 'feels' relevant to you. Make up some images of your own to help you work out what to do when you are uncertain.

When life becomes foggy and uncertain, use whatever tools and ideas you can to find your way! Mapping the issues you face together with the application of a variety of mental models may help.

Mapping the ambiguity ceiling

A central idea I have is that many people encounter a barrier to further thought once a situation becomes ambiguous. The ambiguity ceiling is a barrier that requires high intellectual dexterity and tolerance to uncertainty AND a willingness to appreciate impure or incomplete, temporary outcomes. In order to understand where or what the ceiling is, we need a map. The four-part crude map illustration (shown below) may help you understand the challenges and some of your headline options.

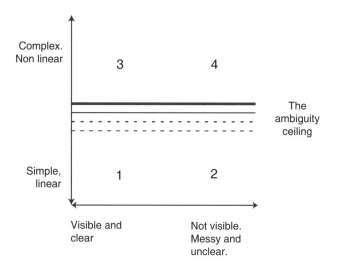

Know the different types of problems

1 The problem is clearly visible, simple and linear

Often this is the basis of 'sense' or binary logic, i.e. on or off. Right or wrong. Either/or. The answers derived here will tend to be reductive, short and linear. The answers are likely to be singular, being either 100 percent right or 100 percent wrong. The important operative phase that identifies the decisions and the thinking here is 'either/or'. You either have the answer or you do not. Pure, irreducible, timeless facts live here. This is where a lot of early formal 'education' sits.

2 The problem is messy, yet simple and linear when uncovered

This level of complexity is to do with the way information, people or resources are misaligned. Sometimes it's just wrong people, wrong information and wrong resources all muddled up, or a combination of these. A project management approach using rigour, discipline and logical procedure gets results. Increased effort in the right direction leads to progressively better results.

Type 2 issues, even though tangled or unclear, still have an outcome that can be maximised to tangible, absolute or almost 'pure' results. If you've got a 'black -belt' in systems and project planning – dive in, catalogue, sift, sort, schedule and process to your heart's content! You'll get there in the end and people will love you for it!

Type 1 and 2 difficulties are accessible to good, thorough, high-detail, high-rigour, high-precision, **disciplined** thinkers. A system of reduction and simplification to clear, concise, bounded rules and procedures works extremely well here. This is a sort of 'thinking on high-speed rails'; however, people who are highly efficient at this level can get into difficulty with type 3 and 4 problems. Eventually this performance barrier becomes a career ceiling if people fail to adopt quite different thinking styles, reference points and decision boundaries.

Working above the ambiguity ceiling

3 Visible but complex issues

To work effectively above the ambiguity ceiling different thinking patterns from those routinely used below it are required, along with access to a wider range of thinking tools. When my book titles were field tested with an executive MBA group, a newly appointed director said, 'Yes it's definitely there, but you don't appreciate that there is an ambiguity ceiling until you have actually gone through it.'

Robert Nuttall, VP Strategic Marketing at Rolls Royce said, 'What you describe as the ambiguity ceiling we call "working in the grey". A different way of thinking is required'

> **you don't appreciate that there is an ambiguity
> ceiling until you have actually gone through it**

Type 3 problems do not run along nice straight laid logical lines. For example, 'What is the best way to educate children?' There could be multiple answers in any multicultural neighbourhood. Another example could involve a dilemma where two quite clear but uncomfortable alternatives appear viable. Many people see a solution being an unfortunate matter of having to choose the lesser of two evils. Such a solution reflects an 'either/or' thinking pattern typically seen below the ceiling.

4 Unseen complex issues

An example of a type 4 issue might involve trying to predict something important about the future such as the development and implementation of long-term political and economic strategy, true innovation or the challenges of rising populations and resource depletion.

The future is inherently uncertain and unpredictable. You may develop a strategy or what you believe to be a genuine innovation but you cannot predict multiple other important variables. It is important therefore to recognise that any outcomes are likely to be volatile and temporary. Indeed, you may have to adapt or react and pursue a very different goal because events or competitors turn all your initial basic assumptions upside down. Solutions to type 4 issues are generally elusive.

One hidden aspect of a complex muddle of complex problems is the difficulties that arise from unseen or unrecognised linkages and dependencies that may exist between these issues, other people and/or other problems. In one small village I lived in during my early years they used to say, 'If you kick one person they all limp!' Please let me assure you that I don't go around kicking people, but my point is that we can sometimes quite easily overlook connections such as interpersonal loyalties and other important linkages at our peril. Genetically engineered foodstuffs initially fell down this particular hole. Assuming a hungry world would welcome yet another advance in food science, investors and scientists overlooked the possibility of fierce public opposition and government reactions to limited initial introduction of patented technologically advanced food.

The characteristics of ambiguous issues

- The first thing to appreciate with level 3 and 4 problems is that as the complexity of a problem increases the probability of **pure** outcomes diminishes rapidly. Absolutes cannot be relied upon here. Outcomes above the ambiguity ceiling can be multiple and cannot be relied upon to be simple.
- Importantly, the central foundation of logic based on **reproducibility over time does not** apply here.
- With ambiguous situations, decisions taken in one context cannot be considered as a useful pattern in a similar set of circumstances in another place or time. This sounds like 'madness' and for some of the time it may feel that way, particularly if you are forced to operate on best estimates and instinct to move forward.
- Outcomes above the ambiguity ceiling tend to be partial and time/context dependent. Outcomes of type 3 and 4 issues are likely to be partially positive AND at the same time partially negative to your interests.
- There may be a reduction in the extent or the duration to which something can be held to be true. In other words, truths become incomplete, temporary, expedient and context- and time-dependent.

- Sometimes different and quite contradictory options can exist side by side, for a time.

Given these basic observations **we can deduce that there probably is no best way and no neat formula to deal with the more exotic level 3 and 4 difficulties.**

Making tacit skills explicit

The skills used to deal with the more complex level 3 and 4 (above ceiling) problems tend to be tacit. Such skills are rarely made explicit or taught and consequently are generally not widely distributed. This is what this book is about. I want to share with you some of the ideas and concepts you will need in an uncertain future. In order to get above the ambiguity ceiling, you need a different way of thinking, which includes an appreciation and awareness of alternative plausible outcomes and likely pathways along with access to a wider range of intellectual tools.

Macro model 3: Reality funnel

One context, several perceptions

We all operate in some sort of context that we regard as reality, however, individual perceptions of uncertainty vary considerably, as do individual preferences and tolerances for novelty or security. If we lined up four quite different people and used the imagery previously employed to indicate frames of reference we might arrive at a representation like the one below.

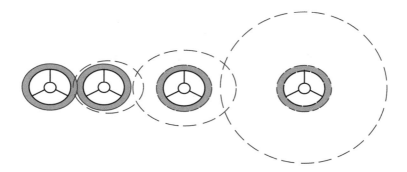

Notice how individual comfort zones differ with higher tolerance for uncertainty on the right compared to the left. Some would be comfortable, some less so. Each would bring a different perspective on what could and should be done. Also notice that the boundaries on the frame of reference circle (in grey) are closed in the two people on the left and are relatively porous in the two people indicated on the right. Also notice that a line of possible communication is indicated. An exchange of views is possible between adjacent perspectives but may prove problematic beyond this. Each individual's frame of reference employs the same elements of beliefs, capability and emotion, but the specifics will differ according to their preference for, and tolerance of, certainty/uncertainty.

Notice how the outer boundaries of the communication chain also suggest a funnel shape, the outer boundaries of which represent a perception of safety relative to uncertainty.

The funnel as a general guide

A standard tool employed frequently in this book is a simple funnel model (shown below) to indicate four quite different positions that can be adopted. This particular model has many uses. It can be used as a basis for further enquiry or to gain a better understanding of a person, issue, product, service, belief or situation. It is quite easy to grasp and has the same utility as a graph in demonstrating differences. Additional examples are provided in Section 2 of Chapter 5.

The funnel can be divided along its length into four approximate realms as numbered in the diagram. Notice the four rectangular zones overlap. The open end of the funnel shape (realm 4) represents either an unbound, low boundary or 'a lot' of whatever is being measured whilst the other narrow extreme of the spout (realm 1) represents a more bounded, tighter reality or 'very few'. There are two other zones in between. All four realms have merits and demerits and none of them represents perfection. In this particular illustration the funnel outline represents boundaries of certainty/uncertainty.

Reid's Reality Funnel
© 2001, 2006, 2011

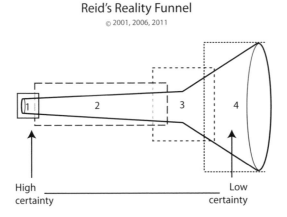

Your reality bias

We all differ in the tolerance we have for different levels of uncertainty. In that sense, we tend to gravitate to people, work, entertainments and situations that 'fit' our particular preferences for certainty and where we feel relatively safe. We are biased. In terms of your external behaviours, you will operate in a way that you regard as 'normal' for you. We are also biased in the way we perceive our own behaviour.

I would suggest you run the following exercise to plot how others perceive you in the environment you normally occupy, ideally before you read the rest of the book:

- Get a group of people together who know you and each other well.
- Paper a large wall and draw a large funnel with the four contexts.
- Describe the four contexts for certainty/uncertainty. Postulate likely behaviours therein.
- Each person then writes the initials of each of their colleagues on sticky notepaper and then places each initialled note onto the funnel map in positions representing the behaviours they most often experience in each of the colleagues they choose to map.
- Step back and compare who lives where on the map.
- Describe/discuss the merits of each group along with any perceived limitations.
- Some people will be perceived to span more than one realm. Very few span three. (No one in my experience spans all four.)

Starting with a clear honest self-perception of your 'native' inward AND outward orientation towards uncertainty is a very useful place to begin. You will be better able to appreciate where you may develop your orientation to different aspects of the certainty/uncertainty equation of life. Ask yourself:

- 'Which type of thinking or which type of people irritate me the most and why?'
- 'How could I locate value in the sort of people and patterns of thinking that I dislike?'
- 'If I cannot relate to particular types of thinking who could mediate for me so that I still benefit from the skills they are blessed with?'

Summary

You can upgrade your ability to deal with or master uncertainty by using a variety of access points. Assuming you cannot change the context, such access points might include the following:

Awareness of your inner and outer context and of the far wider contexts within which you operate creates opportunities to learn. Knowing the sort of issue you are dealing with from the outset conserves energy and resources and allows a proportional response. Understanding the ambiguity ceiling is therefore essential.

Being aware that your focus of attention and sense of meaning are derived and shaped by your inner perception allows you to understand your motivation and alignment with the reality that you perceive to be important.

Awareness of your feelings, beliefs and capabilities together with accumulated and reinforced experiences help you understand how your 'frame of reference' shapes what you are most likely to do.

Your frame of reference shapes your perception of what is safe or dangerous.

Your ability to deal with uncertainty can be improved if you gain an understanding of your own frame of reference and an appreciation of how other people may differ from you.

Part A: Inner uncertainties

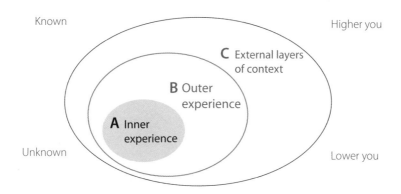

Known

Higher you

C External layers
of context

B Outer
experience

A Inner
experience

Unknown

Lower you

Chapter 4: Paper igloos

Chapter 5: Thinking skills

Section 1: The basics of thinking

Section 2: Symbolism

Section 3: Other thinking tactics and tools

Chapter 6: Emotional literacy

Section 1: Uncertainty and disruptive emotions

Section 2: Impulse control

Section 3: Intuition

Chapter 7: Beliefs and values

Section 1: Valuable values

Section 2: The darker side of values

Section 3: Working philosophy

Part A looks at your inner world using the model below to see where you might further develop additional skills in dealing with uncertainty.

A - Your inner world

Has conscious and unconscious elements

Focus of attention

FOR

Capabilities and tools

Beliefs and values

Emotions

Safe unknown zone

Experiences

Unsafe unknown

Behaviour

Each of us has a unique frame of reference. It is unique to you because no one else has experienced life in the way you have lived it. Chapter 4 takes an oblique look at how people choose patterns that are fundamentally different from the outset. Chapters 5 and 6 then offer access points to building your repertoire of capabilities, tools and skills, including using 'feeling' your way forward. In Chapter 7 we will look at how what you choose to believe and value makes a major contribution to how you behave and experience the world.

Chapter 4

Paper igloos

Who are you and what is it that makes you the person you believe you are? A large part of the uncertainty of life is shaped by perception, and I'd like to address this by encouraging you to visualise the ideas that follow as I paint a picture of our varied, individual **frames of reference**.

We are born naturally curious, open, somewhat self-centred and demanding. As babies, we are only partially aware of our selves, our relationships and our context. We are born with very few certainties, but an almost boundless resource of playful, growing energy and, importantly, a huge capacity for learning. It can be amusing watching a baby discovering itself. Oh look, there's that leg again!

The analogy I like to use to illustrate our individual evolution in an uncertain world is of a very young population walking across a wide vista littered with lots and lots of pieces of paper blowing in a gentle breeze. Most papers are initially dropped or handed out by other people. Each bit of paper holds a partial message or some information or perhaps a clue or even a memory of a feeling. Some of the papers blow our way and stick uninvited. Others we pick up, hold or throw away as we go. The papers we enjoy or believe we need, we keep and use to progressively build our own personal paper dwelling, our own little igloo.

The word 'Why?' is a very early pick-up that is kept and etched into memory by two-year-olds. As time passes, our collection of various bits of paper grows gradually. Our igloo becomes our safe, efficient, neat inner sanctum, and a personal comfy pod where we know things. Inside our igloos, we feel more secure and more certain than we do outside. The bits of information that we use to build up inside our igloo provide personal reference points to what we believe to be our real world.

Picture in your mind your igloo.

- Do you have an outer image of the igloo or an inner image?
- What size is it?
- Do you see a classic igloo with a completely sealed dome and a single entrance tunnel?

Our sense of certainty allows us to experience the world in terms that we have come to accept as normal or certain. Inside our igloo, the multiple reference points we have collected and embedded in the walls allow us to think and react very quickly. We tend to make friends with people who fit with our worldview and who seem to have acquired similar collections of ideas, reference points, beliefs and 'papers' fashioned into similar-sized igloos. Sometimes our friendships are formed with 'odd' people who complete a gap we know we need to fill.

We actively or passively respond to differences. We might knowingly or unconsciously stay away from people and structures that do not resemble our own reality. If we popped our head out of our igloo for long enough we might see different sorts of paper homes. Some are tightly comfortable and cosy. Some igloos are small and well rounded, almost hermetically sealed, whilst others may be very much larger and include more than one opening or even tiny windows.

There are inherent limitations to an igloo. For example, I can't see through snow, or paper. Can you? What we believe constitutes 'reality' is often the view from the inside of our own igloo through the script-covered walls. We imagine that our inside image is the same as the outside view.

Paper boats and balloons

Relatively fewer people decide they prefer an open vista and flip their paper igloo over and reshape it into something else. A small number take to flying in quite large baggy paper balloons, whilst others find ways of floating on ponds and puddles.

Once in a while, these adventurers have bumpy rides or get swamped – but oh, the wide open views! The extra experience was well worth the ride!

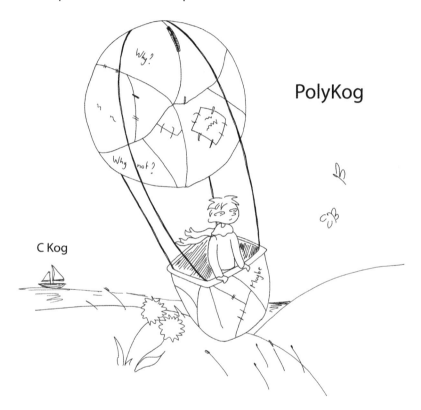

From time to time we may experience the need for a modest rearrangement of our personal pieces of paper that make up our dwelling to seal a leak or to plug a draughty cold corner. Just for 'away-day fun', we might poke a hole in our paper walls to peak outside. Some take just a peak, but no more, and their 'paper dwelling pod' is resealed. Clues with 'Why not?' written or spoken continue to turn up but don't get picked up any more. Provocations are avoided. Don't rock the boat! Careful with that match!

We all live inside some sort of paper pod. An easy life, staying voluntarily locked inside a cosy igloo, seems to be what many people want. 'Want' is very different from 'need'. Is the easy life what we really need?

'Want' is very different from 'need'. Is the easy life what we really need?

24 million extra igloo bricks

So how big can your paper pod be? Some fortunate infants get a head start AND also get a lot more exposure to bits of 'stuff', new words and ideas, but many miss out because of a lack of materials. Consequently, some igloos become temples whilst others can remain quite small, unfurnished dwelling units.

One much-cited academic study[6] in 1995 showed that preschool infants of relatively wealthier parents in America get exposed to 11 million words a year, whereas poor kids only got to hear 3 million words a year. The number of carer to infant interactions were the same, just that less was said. In three years, this amounted to a 24 million word input shortfall. Sadly, lower word exposure later correlated with relatively lower IQ scores.

Good input can help good outcomes. Words cost nothing. If you want your children to construct great lives, it won't cost you anything to stretch theirs AND your vocabulary in playful ways. Get a dictionary or some word games and play! Give them your attention. Put the phone away, especially when you are out and about. Mess about with words. Ask lots of questions. Young minds are open to be developed. Frequent positive playful interactions help us build their AND our world. A little more attention goes a long way for both of you.

Your inner dwelling

Each of us will face uncertainty in different ways. Your life is shaped by the unique choices, ideas and experiences that you interpret and post up on the inside of your own paper igloo, boat or balloon. Each of our lives is uniquely compiled from quite different ideas and distinct personal truths. You therefore cannot be certain that your particular worldview is held to be true by someone else. Perceptions of certainty and uncertainty, as we have seen, vary considerably.

So how is your personal world of ideas put together? Is your inner dwelling built like a paper:

- igloo?
- boat?
- balloon?

Have you ever made changes to 'the house of you' that were uncomfortable to begin with, but which, once completed, became heavenly? Think of a new brick extension to your home. It isn't satisfying until the very last thin veneer of paint and gloss is applied. Consider what you now enjoy is actually the thinnest part of the construction, the surface, just a few microns of paint or gloss. Reality or your particular truth can be just like that, microns deep. Prod the surface a little.

FOR – mindset choices

Your frame of reference gathers all sorts of inputs that you might call a 'mindset', an attitude or an orientation. Occasionally, your thinking can get stuck in a rut and you react out of habit rather than conscious choice. Adopt a 'win before you begin' attitude to your own frame of mind. As a routine, when faced with complex or uncertain alternatives, tune your mind to focus on the best outcome and work towards that rather than focusing on 'difficulties'. As an exercise in developing a winning attitude, look at the two columns below and consider which facets apply to you at work. What word or words would you put in the middle column? Which elements would you choose?

Success paradigm A		Success paradigm B
Embrace ambiguity and complexity		Focus on certainty
Risk taking		Risk reduction
Encouraging disruption		Enable compliance

Success paradigm A illustrates the three key headlines identified in IBM's definition of 'Creative Leadership',[7] whilst success paradigm B represents the conventional wisdom of many institutions. Notice that the attributes of each success paradigm contradict each other. When you filled in the middle column, were you thinking that the middle column was 'versus' or 'AND'?

The smart money is on 'AND', i.e. doing **both** at the same time in an organisation. Special thinking skills, especially those involving dilemmas and ambiguity, are likely to be very much in demand. Without these skills, you and your organisation will not get past the ambiguity ceiling and will be unable to foster **useful contradictions**.

Each of us has natural limits in terms of how far we are prepared to stretch the boundaries of our thinking or our behaviours and actions. Many of your major boundaries are predetermined by how much or how little certainty you believe you need to feel 'safe' AND content. Most of what you experience comes through your 'certainty/safety' lens.

Variable truth, uncertainty and renewal

If you are going to deal well with uncertainty you need to be sure of yourself first. It is important that you know where you fit in relation to the reality you believe you occupy.

The trouble is your frame of reference is underpinned not by 'solid' truth but mostly by your assumptions about what you believe to be true.

you can be wrong in your assumptions but fail to notice

Groups, companies and societies can create their own super-sized paper domes replete with 'certainties'. For example, if enough of us agree something is true, good or bad, then for some time, it becomes 'true' for a while in the minds of those that believe or fail to question. Fickle fashion follows the trend of temporary truth. Importantly, bigger forces follow this path too.

Our deeper unquestioned foundations of our frames of reference are assumptions of truth and this can prevent us enquiring a little deeper. At more than one point in history, brave people have faced a life and death judgement to argue that the Earth was not flat or that the Earth was not the epicentre of a particular deity's universe. Societies can decide to believe that one race or religion is universally good or bad. The tale of the good Samaritan, for example, implied he was 'good' as an exception. For 300 years, slavery was an accepted 'normal' truth by North Atlantic, European, Middle Eastern and African states. Thankfully, in most of the world now, slavery and indenture are not accepted. That does not mean slavery has gone away. It has not. The form has simply changed and there are still many forms of contemporary indenture at work. Far-too-easy credit traps the unwary, and the world's biggest commercial trade is in illicit drugs that enslave millions.

One useful part of our memory is the facility to forget, to paper over what we find distasteful and choose not to look at. When we paper over or fail to read historically valuable lessons, the past has a habit of repeating itself and biting us.

Your personal truth or a bigger society's truth may actually turn out to be temporary, uncertain, wrong or ambiguous. In present-day society, sometimes an everyday truth can be re-framed in a way that is as a little more flexible. Travel can open one's eyes if you go far enough and leave the cloned western places behind. For example, what is considered hygienic can vary considerably. In distant countries we may need to adjust our truths to fit the time and the place. All we need to do is become aware, to question and adjust what we may have regarded as our particular truth. Then we can renew.

Illusions and uncertainty

Another way of looking at reality is to employ a young child's perception that nothing is quite real or certain all of the time. From their perspective, ambiguities and contradictions are everywhere. A large empty box can become a rocket, a den, a shop, a boat, a castle or whatever the imagination allows. High uncertainty is 'normal' for a small child and they use it for playful experience. From a young person's perspective, life is experimental, fun, curious, magical – and, yes, alarming too – but rarely dull AND so full of energy!

As we grow, we lose that playful enquiry. Inside our uniquely personal internal worlds, we imagine who we are based on evidence we selectively collect or selectively ignore. We cease to see the rules of life as adjustable and possibilities as limitless.

order and reality are pleasant illusions that are easily pricked

Constancy and a sense of certainty are temporary phenomena. The '*Rubaiyat of Omar Khayyam*' tells us this much. We are all part of the natural, uncertain cycle of living things. To that extent, order and reality are pleasant illusions that are easily pricked. Only our virtues and values remain when all else is stripped away.

What we think is real or certain is influenced by the worlds we choose to immerse ourselves within. If you live in a bankers' culture or a gang culture or a village or a city culture, your reality shapes you and you contribute to your group frame of reference, simply by taking part. If you are seeking renewal, find some healthy younger people to spend time with and try to experience reality through their eyes for a while. You cannot take it in wholesale, as old Faust attempted to, but you might learn something useful.

Time changes truths

Another dangerous word in your frame of reference is 'always'. Much of your evidence for what you believe to be real will have come from the past. As time ticks by, the relevance and veracity of your older unchecked 'truths' can become overstretched. What was once certain becomes more uncertain as time passes.

If you haven't asked the right questions at the right times you may be shocked to discover your personal truths are significantly out of line with reality. You can get 'left behind' simply by not being aware of the shifts taking place around you.

Groups can suffer this particular fate too. 'Groupthink' is just a bigger paper igloo. Fortunately time dilutes or changes many truths as each new generation of vibrant questioning youth creates its own boundaries, beliefs and identities. They age, settle and become the old guard, and the cycle repeats. Frames of reference evolve.

Unwelcome change

Once in a while, someone drops a lit match and a whole section of your paper igloo goes up in smoke and all sorts of parts of your frame of reference get knocked out of shape. Occasionally, well-intentioned fire fighting does more damage than the fire did. Friends you used to be certain of can sometimes become a liability or simply leave.

When a portion of your igloo is wrecked or burnt open by major change, cold new air or an unknown darkness is exposed. Alternatively, previously unseen light or a better vista floods into your space.

- How will you react?
- Will you have the ability to choose how you will react at the time or will you let base impulse possess you?
- Will the curiosity of your youth be employed or forgotten?
- When you find your energy again as an individual, a family or a company, what will you do to rebuild?

Perhaps when you reread your charred bits of paper dislodged by the uncertainty of change you may find old certainties no longer fit or make any sense or they may fit better somewhere else in the messy jigsaw that is a life. Are gaps in the walls such a bad idea anyway? Some people call these windows and doors. Or are you better advised to seal all openings except one and rebuild another, perhaps much smaller, safer igloo, much like the one before? Alternatively, will you learn a substantial lesson and adapt? OK, it may be a little scary at first but you may be pleasantly surprised if you remain open for long enough to discover something new and beneficial.

Our worlds are as flimsy, transient and as flammable as the paper that our ideas and beliefs are written on. Let's remember, though, that we can as individuals, teams, organisations and even nation states almost always learn something new. We can rewrite and rescript our own pieces of paper! We can reshape our future. A willingness to be frequently surprised is an essential step to coping more effectively with ambiguity and uncertainty. Frames of reference evolve and can be rebuilt.

a willingness to be frequently surprised is an essential step to coping

Whether we like it or not substantial change is coming and many who are alive today will be required to adjust. In little more than just one lifetime, the population of our finite planet will have almost tripled to nine billion people by 2050. Perhaps with sufficient imagination and goodwill, nation states may decide they are going to embrace a very different way of looking at the world in order to prosper. Perhaps gross national happiness[8] instead of GNP might be the way forward. Bhutan has done this for several decades. If a country can adopt such a fundamental reorientation of perception, what might you decide to do?

Substantial change, whether good or bad, is invariably uncomfortable and involves further uncertainties. Change and challenge are, however, a matter of perception. How you deal with the ambiguity and personal challenges in your life are to some extent a matter of how you frame your present with your past and your future. You have a choice.

Everyone has the potential to be heroic and meet the challenges life presents and simply try to do better. One of the many keys required involves remaining open for long enough to be surprised and to learn new lessons. Dr Cherie Carter-Scott reckons we repeat our errors until we learn the lessons life presents us with, and then we get presented with a new lesson to learn.[9] For me this is a template for self-development AND for organisational insight. One of my friends, a former sheet-metal worker, often used to say, 'What's the point in getting any older if you don't get any wiser!'

In practical terms, the core of our frame of reference rests on 'truths'. Once a truth is established in our minds subsequent encounters do not require the effort of building a case to establish the same truth. We therefore operate far quicker when we encounter similar situations involving 'truths' we have encountered before. We operate so fast that we virtually automate what we do. It's what you are paid for in your job.

The key danger for anyone who engages ambiguity, change and uncertainty is that many of the truths built into your frame of reference are far from absolute. It is much safer to regard reality as being built on assumptions AND that many of your deepest assumptions of 'truth' are suspect. When faced with change assume that 'all bets are off!' Let me illustrate briefly with what happens when you change your job.

New job, new ways

Often when a middle manager gets a promotion and especially at a senior level, they make a number of fundamental mistakes. The first is assuming that prior rules and behaviours that led to their success still apply. Another relatively common error of assumptions is that prior 'friendships', loyalties or networks remain available. People **knew** you in a context. When you change your context, your colleagues don't **know** you in the same light. Your knowledge of them remains the same; however the relationship has moved. The meanings and focal points of attention have shifted.

another mistake is the idea that hard work wins out

Yet another mistake is the idea that hard work wins out. In simple situations it often does. Without a mentor to guide new thinking, energetic enthusiasm for a new, more complex role sometimes turns into haste and frustration. New ways of thinking and new philosophies are required if a burn-out, bail out or an 'early bath' are to be avoided.

Probably the very biggest challenge for a new leader is to acquire not just the ability to reconcile the more complex problems encompassed by uncertainty, dilemma and ambiguity but also the behaviours that go with this. It's a whole new frame of reference for some. This particular challenge is rarely made explicit nor can it be easily taught. It has to be experienced. Any new role requires new learning that rebases your assumptions. The remedies require new behaviours based upon explicit new beliefs and philosophies plus hard lessons of failure AND recovery. Another major adjustment to a frame of reference involves checking and adjusting your assumptions and truths in regard to the value of emotions as a basis for decisions and action. (See Chapter 6.)

Summary

We construct our reality based on the ideas we accumulate. Other people contribute, but essentially we have a choice in how we perceive reality. We can be brave and change the structure of how we create our sense of meaning and we can grow.

Some people are fortunate, some are not; nevertheless, all of us have choice. The way we construct our reality and exercise our choices determines the meaning of our existence. Lifelong learning creates the opportunity to provide additional building materials to build or repair our reality and helps us develop additional options from which we may choose.

Change and learning are particularly important when we feel comfortably numb. Step outside your igloo. Take a look around. It may be cold and breezy and perhaps challenging. You may feel exposed to the elements but once you understand, you will see that ambiguity and uncertainty are the essence of good fun, great literature and art. Ambiguity and uncertainty are at the core of great scientific discovery and can be a tremendous source of joy.

Take a look at yourself.

Here's an imaginary match … go light a candle.

Reflection

- How many words, ideas and experiences are you feeding your children and yourself?
- What does your world look like from the inside and the outside?
- What are the really big certainties in your life?
- Do you think in the round or in fairly straight lines?
- Can you switch the way you think about something?
- Can you switch the way you feel about something?
- When it comes to curiosity, do you enjoy or dislike being surprised?
- How often do you allow yourself to be surprised?
- How open are you to new, unusual experiences?
- How often do you seek out new, unusual words, ideas or experiences?

Chapter 5
Thinking skills

Section 1: The basics of thinking

Section 2: Symbolism

Section 3: Other thinking tactics and tools

Section 1

The basics of thinking

If we are to embrace uncertainty and we know the answer has something to do with the way we form our perception of reality, then perhaps it would be a great idea just to check in on the basics of how we tend to process our thoughts.

If you question people about how they think, most people just grin, shrug or say they don't know or that 'thinking is just something that happens'. Yes thinking 'just happens', but in different ways for different people at different times. How do you think? Your way, of course! But is your way of thinking the only way? If not, is the way you think the best way? Have you ever considered what is actually happening when you think?

Is the way you think the best way?

Appreciating how we process thoughts can help how we enter useful dialogue with our selves and with others. Dialogue differs markedly from discussion. A dialogue seeks to build a broad picture of understanding through open enquiry; in the West, we are prone to adversarial debate where we look for the 'winning argument'. A lot of uncertainty can arise if we fail to understand ourselves, the way we think and the way we communicate with other people.

Mind shapes

Some people have neat and tidy clear minds whilst some, like mine, can be incredibly messy, disjointed and full of shapes or rich pictures. Some people have minds with huge capacities for knowledge while others would rather play and 'just have some fun'. Some people are less able or less inclined to use their mental muscle and instead live life through more physical or emotional experiences. Some people have complex ways of thinking and being whilst others are refreshingly uncomplicated. Our thinking styles differ incredibly, but there are a few fundamental patterns that affect each and every one of us.

Direction

Our thinking can adopt one of three basic patterns. Two have a distinct direction whilst the third is characterised as having an unusual pattern and may at times be multidirectional.

1. Convergent
2. Divergent
3. Synthetic

Based on research from the 1950s and 1960s,[10] I described this simple pattern in 1995 in subsequent workshops and in a variety of publications.[11]

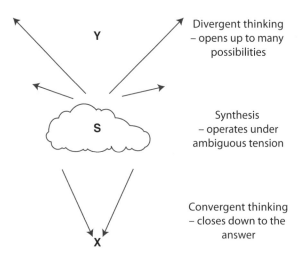

Divergent thinking
– opens up to many possibilities

Synthesis
– operates under ambiguous tension

Convergent thinking
– closes down to the answer

Convergent thinking

'X' marks the spot where the precise answer is. This focused thinking pattern involves taking information, reducing it to stable patterns and then coming to a once-and-for-all closed decision. This is the essence of rational logical deduction. People use this a lot at work. It is quick and runs along regular predetermined lines. Thinking this way is often characterised by either/or patterns. Thinking can be binary in nature. There is a mechanical efficiency to this way of thinking. Sometimes the most ruthless win at this particular game because emotion is not required to arrive at a logical endpoint. This is goal-driven thinking and popular with focused, 'kill to win', fired-up high achievers.

Divergent thinking

'Y' represents the eternal questions of why and why not? The direction of thought and the characteristics are the opposite of everything I've mentioned in convergent thinking. The fundamental characteristic is that of enquiry, looking around and curiosity. Closure actually spoils the experience. This thinking direction is all about opening up, not closing down. This particular thinking pathway can lead to multiple avenues of enquiry and does not run on predetermined lines or to time. Emotions **are** often involved because boundaries are crossed or emotional connections are made. People who are into detail and high focus can struggle with this direction and style of thinking because it is diametrically opposed to what they are used to doing and because the rules are so different.

Divergent and convergent thinking rules

Convergent and divergent pathways have markedly dissimilar rules. To be used to best effect each must be allowed to operate in the absence of the other. If you try to engage both sequentially you get a 'Christmas tree' thinking pattern. (See my first[12] and second books[13]). The two pathways simply don't mix.

Synthesis

This pathway combines the best aspects of the above. It is not a halfway house between the two other patterns. Synthesis involves multiple conscious and unconscious iterations of divergent exploration followed by conscious and/or subconscious synthesis, where original solutions are 'cooked up' over days, weeks or years or are seemingly 'plucked out of the air' sometimes with remarkable speed. Some people possess the ability to synthesise original solutions as a natural skill and others learn it later in life. Creative thinking training is merely an introduction to this particular thinking space. It is a mistake to assume that possession of creative ability implies other more dynamic skills. Inventive behaviour, the ability to innovate, think strategically or be an entrepreneur all involve many more skills, experiences and tolerances above and beyond simple 'creativity'.

A genius would be someone who has high capacity, speed and extensive experience as well as a fluidity of mind to be able to flex quickly between these three different thinking styles. People who have this level of fluidity of mind can be impatient of the inability of others to 'keep up'. Their ultimate success therefore depends on patience and an ability to influence other people to see what they see and to buy in and engage a new concept.

Spotting the two fundamental directions

The way I get people to appreciate the different ways we direct our thinking is by asking how men and women, in general, tend to shop for clothes or shoes. Whilst you may believe I am overgeneralising, large retailers cashed in on research that shows that generally women like to spend more time (divergently) looking around whereas men tend to be mission headed (convergent), focused and come away with an early result. Even if she spots the absolutely right pair of shoes in the very first shop, a woman will generally carry on looking because she enjoys the exploration of discovering what there is around the next corner. Stop her at your peril!

Notice that behaviour follows a particular thinking pathway. Conversations also mirror an open/divergent or closing/convergent pathway. Notice the direction different speakers adopt when faced with a novel issue. Some want more enquiry and dialogue, some want to focus and go with an adversarial debate. Occasionally some wish to reflect and have time to synthesise.

Too much of a good thing

One can sometimes overindulge a particular thinking pathway. Too much focus or convergent thinking and people will see you as possibly results orientated but narrow minded; dull once you get off your chosen subject. With too much divergent thinking, people may see you as creative and imaginative but lacking attention to detail or unable to complete tasks; an 'airhead'. Too much time spent in the middle ground of synthesis may create a profile where lots of embryonic and potentially useful ideas or projects are born but never get delivered or refined.

The trick, if there is one, is to be aware of which thinking and behavioural pathway is needed and to address your thinking accordingly. Ideally, you need access to all three patterns at different times. You are probably best at just one of these. When life gets complex or uncertain, team up with people who have the other skills, if you can stand each other's benefits and 'curses'!

Team up with people who have the other skills, if you can stand each other's benefits and 'curses'!

The influence of context

Circumstances – the context – can shape how we think. Unless you were raised in a war zone or a highly unstable environment, 'normal', calm, unemotional thinking is what you probably have done most of. Thinking when you are angry, conflicted or anxious and uncertain, when your brain is swimming in a chemical soup of survival hormones, is quite different from when you are calm and collected. You will think and react in different ways in different contexts. An important question for rising uncertainties, therefore, is how familiar are you with yourself under duress? To what extent do you retain self-control when things around you are 'out of control'? We will look in more detail at how you create a sense of confidence and how you can get ready to face the inevitable crisis later.

A sense of certainty

One very important survival boundary we all seem to share is a need for some degree of certainty. The basis of our sanity hinges upon what we can routinely predict to be certain or 'true'.

Our individual and collective needs, in regard to certainty, vary considerably. Some people need a little, some a lot. Some people prefer high uncertainty: the thrill and the novelty of change.

Tolerance for some uncertainty is really important because biologically we are inclined to 'act first, think later' when faced with what we perceive to be a genuine threat. When threatened we are less likely to think and more likely to be influenced by very basic survival instincts and impulses.

Some people use the rush they get from 'urgency' to routinely power their way forward, but the body chemicals induced by threat exact a heavy toll, simply because all the body repair mechanisms are delayed for fight or flight now. High anxiety, ill health and raised blood pressure are likely to be part of your life story if 'a crisis response' is your regular problem-solving pattern.

If your thinking is frequently hijacked by base impulse, how will you advance your higher abilities? Tolerance of uncertainty and impulse control are therefore essential. It is important to learn how to overcome base impulsiveness. We will look at impulse control in more detail in Section 2 of Chapter 6.

Summary

The capacity you are born with, the boundaries you acquire **or** the boundaries you create, together with your life experiences so far, shape the way you think.

You evolve. You are capable of learning and experiencing new ways of being. The direction you choose to think in shapes how you act. Context, whether stable or unstable, influences the way you think. Quite apart from the occasional acute crisis, we all have different comfort levels and show quite different tolerances for high and low certainty.

It can be beneficial to understand how and why you think and behave the way you do, in order to build up your ability to prosper in uncertain conditions, simply because the world is getting more complicated.

Reflection

- How do you think?
- Have you ever considered what is actually happening when you think?
- Who do you know who seems to think differently from you? What do they say and do that works well or fails?
- Is the way you think working most of the time? When do you struggle?
- In what ways does your thinking help or hinder you when uncertainty becomes uncomfortable?

Chapter 5 Section 2

Symbolism

Big, wealthy organisations such as banks seem to accumulate a surplus of seriously bright people, and I met one, let's call her Sarah, on a scenario-planning workshop in the mid-1990s. Sarah was a young, extremely quick-minded postgraduate who seemed to operate on several planes at once.

I asked Sarah how she dealt with something complex and uncertain. She replied, 'Before I do anything I go looking for a suitable model to process or frame the issues. If I cannot find a suitable model I will make one up, perhaps with some other people, test it and then run with it, if it works. I'd probably talk to other people too.'

Her revelation seemed so simple and pragmatic that I could not at the time understand why her decision pattern was not more widespread and explicit. After that meeting I resolved to see if Sarah's way of thinking was a consistent finding. I made a habit of asking a question about thinking strategies of anyone else who seemed clever. I've asked the question, 'How do you deal with something complex?' many times in order to understand how smart people operate.

When I asked what her future held, Sarah said, 'I'm not sure, but I've been invited to Harvard Business School for 18 months. They have given me a full bursary to travel, live and work there. They're covering all my expenses to spend my time with whoever I want there.'

The very best thinkers I have encountered often have remarkably fast, high-capacity minds and are skilled in reflection. People like Sarah tend to be self-aware, have a plan, a structure and lots and lots of models. (She's probably a PolyKog.)

Shape up

Hundreds of thousands of years ago, our species relied on visual cues before language cues, so it would make a lot of sense to employ visual imagery coupled with meaning as shorthand for potentially complex ideas. Symbols and images travel faster than a string of words can. A picture is worth much more than words. Some people think in pictures and some do not. Here are some of the tools I use during the course of my work on innovation, strategy, creativity and leadership.

I'm not intending these images to be locked-down, absolute structures with fixed meanings. Instead, I have flexibility in mind. Each of the following shapes has multiple uses. Simply change the labels to suit your thinking requirement.

First shape model: Funnels

Funnels are one of my favourite models and I have used them regularly since 1996. Think of the funnel shape as an alternative to the idea of a graph. As with graphs, funnel shapes can be employed to illustrate a variety of situations and people. With a funnel model, we use the concept of boundaries to create useful maps of four quite different situations. Funnel maps create headlines, approximations and rough estimates, rather than fine detail.

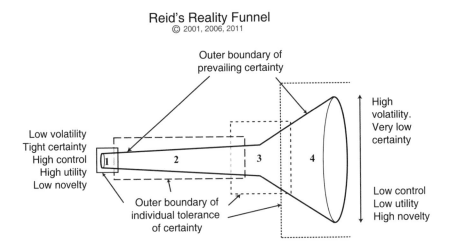

Reid's Reality Funnel
© 2001, 2006, 2011

Example 1: The certainty funnel

'Reid's Reality Funnel'[14] is used to help different people understand how individual comfort or tolerance levels with uncertainty significantly affect their thinking and their behaviour. Different people have different perceptions as to how much or how little certainty they need. 'Reality' is a variable perception.

reality is a variable perception

This particular funnel describes four different preferences for certainty alongside tolerance for uncertainty.

In 'Reid's Reality Funnel' the edges of the funnel shape represent boundaries in regard to uncertainty; being high on the right and low on the left. Overlaid on this particular funnel are four approximate realms and each overlaps its neighbour. You can populate these four regions of perceived certainty with people or issues and then think through likely behaviours, responses and possible outcomes. Each of the four realms will foster quite different boundaries, 'rules' and beliefs as to what constitutes reality, and therefore each produces quite different experiences and responses.

In this particular funnel model, there is progressively less certainty as the funnel opens up on the right. At '1' we see tight boundaries and therefore quite low levels of uncertainty and high levels of certainty. At '4' the opposite is true. With wide open boundaries, 'certainty' is in short supply. Please note that there is no such thing as 'the best or the worst place' on this map.

Tracking from left to right the value of logic progressively declines. A pure 100 percent yes or no answer is only available in one of the four territories where the boundaries of certainty are particularly well founded and very tight. In the other three territories, the outcome is going to be progressively less than 100 percent. You may notice that the four zones correlate with the map of uncertainties above and below the ambiguity ceiling mentioned earlier. The general characteristics of each realm are as follows:

Funnel realm 1

High certainty. In realm 1 we have irrefutable facts that will be true for time eternal. Here logic reigns supreme. The sums all add up. People who have a high preference for certainty and a low tolerance for uncertainty enjoy routine, predictability, repetition of favourite experiences, precision and thorough, exquisite, validated detail. Decisions may be based on instructions, rulebooks and lists. Variation or risk is not to be tolerated.

People upsides:

- Highly reliable.
- Thorough, precise.
- May have encyclopaedic knowledge of a particular area of interest.

People downsides:

- Can be pedantic, prescriptive or rule-bound. Change resistant.
- Check on assumptions at the foundation of what they believe to be true occasionally. From time to time the logic of something totally collapses because a fundamental assumption turns out to be wrong. Hey look! Our world is not flat and we are not the biblical centre of the physical universe! People here need a lot of time to readjust to change.
- Likely to clash with people from the opposite end of the scale.

Funnel realm 2

Moderate certainty. In realm 2, answers tend to be well-structured, almost perfect within acceptable, expected variances. Deductive, focused convergent logic still makes the major contribution here. Variation to a credible maximum is tolerated. Limited external input from strange sources might be tolerated occasionally – such as consumer feelings – but opinions need to be backed up by lots of rational, deductive, 'sensible' research. Decisions may be based on rules, protocols and procedures along with some rigorous risk-avoidance measures.

People upsides:

- Highly reliable, reasonably thorough and able to accept 'reasonable' variances.
- Wider perspective than '1'; will cover more territory but will remain grounded, thorough and relatively precise.

People downsides:

- May resist further changes when variance limits are exceeded. Can be relatively prescriptive or rule-bound. Occasionally assume possession of creative ability based on their 'wider structured perspective'.
- Associate their form of 'practical creativity' with more extensive or thorough deduction or grounded research. Regard genuine creativity as risky and may squash it as being 'out of control'.
- Moderately change resistant. They may need a lot of time to readjust to substantial change.

Funnel realm 3

This zone is high on ambiguity. It is above-ceiling territory because moderate certainty AND moderate uncertainty coexist. Here problems AND solutions become slippery or progressively more 'wicked' in nature. Answers to your questions become partly true AND partly untrue at the same time. The 'truth' may be context or time dependent . Often answers include the important phrase, 'it depends'.

What works: some logic + some 'rules of thumb' or heuristics AND other senses including instinct and intuition. Attending a meeting with an intriguing question and **not** having the answer **is** acceptable. Dialogue is expected. Decisions may be based on particular guiding beliefs and working principles, i.e. a working philosophy, feelings or partial information. Placing a bet is acceptable, expected.

The application of logic to increasingly open-ended questions can help you, but only to a limited extent. For example, logic is of limited practical use if you have to think about love, affection, strategy or genuine innovation. Open-ended slippery questions cannot be answered using the tools and rules of realm 1.

Paradoxically, 'life', living things and living systems abide here. The rules of hard science fail in the softer world of living beings in which fewer things are absolute. For example, I absolutely do need oxygen, but if supplied as 100 percent pure oxygen, it will kill me.

People upsides:

- Good with ambiguity. Often demonstrate a creative yet pragmatic perspective.
- Can act as mediators between visionary ideas people and the more grounded people of realm 2. Can quickly spot a tangible commercial or political opportunity or risk emerging.
- Able to take decisions with incomplete information. Welcome and expect change.

People downsides:

- Not necessarily 'completer-finishers'. Prone to distraction by the next novelty.
- Seek freedom to operate and therefore may be seen as rebels.
- Not always clearly aligned with patrons and protectors.
- Can derail unintentionally.

Funnel realm 4

Certainties are fleeting or rare. At the far right of our scale there is a fourth space where the neck of the funnel is open at its widest. Here the boundaries of reality are wide and relaxed. Uncertainty is normal here, and logic is therefore of fleeting value. Awareness is everything. The fourth space can be described with words (or more likely images) involving vision, faith, possibilities, hope and imagination.

Breakthrough creativity can be driven by 3s and particularly by 4s. Thinking here is more difficult to define, less amenable to rational explanation and is perhaps only understood and eventually accommodated after we have had time to adjust. For example, Van Gogh's work was only widely appreciated after he died. He only ever sold one painting. He never materially benefited; however, a huge market for his work lives on. Top-down originality can be highly productive. Einstein's ideas (realms 3 and 4) are still being worked on.

People upsides:

- Visionary. Find creativity and strategic thinking easy. Are strongly attracted to novelty. Can be good with ambiguity and politics.
- Can create a major long-term opportunity or can quickly detect substantial risk emerging.
- Able to take decisions with incomplete information.
- Welcome, expect and provoke change.

People downsides:

- Can seem vapid, ethereal to some. Often dislike detail. Can be highly disruptive.
- Can lose touch with the 'sharp end' of operations. Can lack pragmatic skills.

Individual preference for certainty

People will tend to orientate their lives to match their orientation towards their preferred level of certainty. In my first book, I identified three realms of certainty. Here I've identified four different realms to accommodate purists (1) and to help explain perceptions of two sorts of 'creativity'; namely, those below the ambiguity ceiling (2) and those who work above (3 and 4).

To be clear, both types of creativity are desirable and valuable. The first is suited to incremental developments, whereas above-ceiling creativity is associated with the higher risk of significantly bigger breakthroughs.

I have noticed that some people like to operate in just one realm whilst others seem capable of working across two. A chameleon-like ability to bridge three realms is uncommon. Bridging four just doesn't happen.

We each select our own particular 'worlds', perceptions, reasoning, friends, work and behaviours that fit well with our particular orientation to certainty. Understanding each of the different realities can enhance your ability on many levels; for example, in communication, relationship-building, negotiation, influence, leadership, team-forming and many other social and self-development realms. The shape has additional uses.

Example 2: Reliability and utility funnel

In case you have a perception that 'bigger is better' or 'the best place to be' is the creative end of the funnel as opposed to the 'narrow' end let me flip the same model through 180 degrees. We will change the funnel boundaries from high variation/high uncertainty to high utility. If you are more interested in implementation than creativity then this perspective may appeal to you. Reading from left to right, there is in realm 'A', a broad collection of high reliability, high predictability and therefore highly reproducible opportunities. A represents the cookie-cutter end of science and mass fault free production. Here many things are possible, whereas at the far right in realm D there is virtually no predictability and a lot less opportunity for realistic implementation. The likely number of realistic outcomes is therefore likely to be low in D.

An alternative perspective

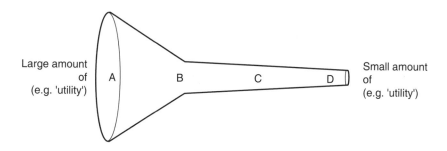

Large amount of (e.g. 'utility')   A   B   C   D   Small amount of (e.g. 'utility')

People who see the world in terms of high utility are great! If I'm visiting a surgeon or a cancer specialist, I need the therapy to be as precise as possible. If my aeroplane is due to land I want it landed by a precise, experienced, well-trained professional, by the book. If I see a lawyer, I want her to have all the details, laws, amendments, case studies, research and precedents at her fingertips. Person or situation A will offer good precision and efficient production. In contrast, person or situation D will offer novel ideas with high potential; however, most of these will have low initial utility because of substantial unknown or uncertain factors. If I'm looking for a clear result right now, D cannot help me.

no one individual has the capacity to formulate and then deliver unique solutions

Someone who has a high need for certainty is every bit as beneficial to society as someone who is high on novelty and low on need for certainty. The real skill is in getting these two very different types of personalities to work well together either directly or as part of a pragmatic intellectual 'food chain' or ecology. This is key to success since in an age of high complexity no one individual has the capacity to formulate and then deliver unique solutions. We need genuine teams and they need to be well understood, motivated and well orchestrated. Then, success involves a sort of ecology of abilities – an integrated 'food chain' of collaborating, well-led teams. Easily said but quite difficult to do, because we are all so different.

Direction of travel

Consider research in areas of high uncertainty such as in leading edge investigations into diseases and the discovery of new medicines. Initially the research yields very little (D) and there is high uncertainty as researchers screen thousands of compounds and situations. The process becomes increasingly expensive as the number is reduced via C and B and eventually to A to just a few viable, certain, relatively safe clinically active molecules. The direction of travel for pure leading-edge research on the certainty map would be 4,3,2,1.

Example 3: Long or short transition funnels

In strategic planning, a funnel that captures the shape of uncertainty and/or reliability can be used to envision changes that might occur progressively in the future. Stable periods for technology, for example, might involve long slender funnels with not so much major change in the short term. Water utilities fall into a long category: reservoirs last for a hundred years or so. Computer chips, software and high-street fashion, on the other hand, follow a very much shorter pattern of decline in value over a matter of months.

In volatile and uncertain times or with high-speed changes in technology, the funnel can be short and stubby. There is little respite between changes and an emphasis on imagination, ambiguity tolerance and risk taking if a market is to be captured and capitalised upon before it moves yet again.

The composition of an organisation working in a fast-change (short funnel) environment, we could predict, would be quite different from that of one operating in a slow, steady (long funnel) context.

Available certainty can change

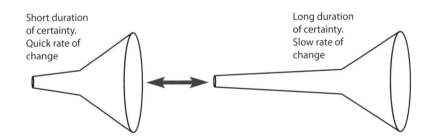

Short duration of certainty. Quick rate of change

Long duration of certainty. Slow rate of change

For example, a very large relatively successful UK conglomerate ran effectively for decades, making a wide variety of relatively mundane goods of reasonable, reliable quality. They had a multibillion cash pile to help ride through inevitable economic uncertainties and to keep on top of different business cycles. They operated within a long funnel and were very precisely run. Then the CEO changed. The new man wanted to spend the cash pile, restructure and move into faster moving, sexy, more profitable electronics and services. His proposition had a logic to it, but the new business plan now aimed itself at a relatively short-funnel market **even though** the people, traditions, habits and practices were 'long funnel' and steeped in slow, steady transitions. The managers and staff simply didn't keep up with a rapidly shifting market. They were not configured for fast thinking, fast decision-making and faster behaviours. The company tanked and thousands of good, bright people lost their jobs.

I lost out too. More fool me, I bought the hype and purchased shares, not once but twice, on the way down, believing they were cheap based on historical, i.e. long steady funnel, performance. I had failed to appreciate the dangers of transition and lost a lot of money. I missed a fundamental transition.

This simple shape is a general approximation tool that can help you better understand people, likely behaviours, industry change patterns, investments, outcomes, needs or contexts and lots of other issues too.

Funnel application and practitioner guidelines

The issue
Consider a problem you have. What are the issues that define the boundaries of a funnel that embraces your problem? How do the four realms then look? What are the most likely questions posed within each zone? What sort of answers can you expect to the same question posed in each realm?

The people
Then consider four different types of people involved and their preferences. Each will have quite different ways of interpreting reality and therefore different benefits, limitations and disadvantages. How are they most likely to behave and what will they tend to resist? How will the four different types respond to your issue? What can each of them offer from the best of their abilities whilst avoiding their worst fears? Is your own perception shaped or biased by your position in the funnel? Are you part of the problem?

Direction
Consider which way things or people are moving in respect of the issue. Is the direction of travel left to right or right to left? Alternatively, are things or people stuck at one particular point? Is the time line getting longer or shorter and

how does that affect the shape of the funnel? Who or what gets compressed or elongated?

Joined-up effort

A fish has, at best, only a fleeting experience of the air and unless specially adapted, it has far less experience of dry land than of its native environment. People who normally dwell in each realm are better positioned to answer each question. You need to collaborate if you wish to cover all four bases well.

The questions

Locate the general nature of the questions from each of the four types of people. Below is an example of four enquiries based on a boundary defined by the passage of time and uncertainty:

1. What is absolute, fixed, reproducible, timeless and incontrovertible?
2. What is mostly certain but has some understood degree of variation?
3. What is ambiguous, porous, variable, subject to temporary truths or subject to becoming untrue?
4. What is mysterious, novel, vapid, visionary, possible, magical, ethereal, -'right out-there'?

When formulating the right questions I find it a lot easier to remember the contexts suggested by the four-part funnel image and then to select the most appropriate interrogative of what, who, when, which, how and why. The funnel model is a simple, flexible but powerful tool that I have used since 1995. In 2001 I described how to use the tool in my first book *How To Think* (published in five languages). I also used a funnel model as the backbone concept of my second book *High Performance Thinking Skills* (2006).

Second model: Circles and contexts

Simple contexts

People sometimes talk about viewing things 'in the round'. It has no malice, kindness, consideration or intent. There are no agendas, no meanings. It simply 'is'. The image I have in mind is a circle.

Here there are no rights or wrongs.

Information is Judged

When we make a decision we parse information, situations and people into right and wrong. To do this we

The world simply 'is'

use reference points. In a simple world outcomes are pure and clear-cut. This involves 'either/or'

The information falls into clearly defined, absolute areas

logic. Issues such as this are amenable to computer management since the logic employed is neat and binary, on or off.

Split ying-yang model

This particular image sits at the core of an appreciation of ambiguity. Ying yang is **not** 'either/or'. Ying yang involves two dependent systems interlinked and revolving, with each forever seeking harmony with the other.

The two may be seen as opposites but this would be a misunderstanding, since they are not in opposition. They are instead two tied facets of the same reality. One cannot function or survive fully without the operation of the other. They coexist over time. Each has the seed of the other within it. Ying yang illustrates the eternal cycle of bound dependent pairs.

Ying and Yang

The energy and benefits of both aspects of ying and yang are available. Neither dimension is right or wrong. They just 'are' as they are. In the course of our life, work and business it is important that we experience the balancing influence of both, at appropriate times.

Meaning	Ying	Yang
Literally	The 'shady place' or 'north slope'	The 'sunny place' or 'south slope'
Is characterised	As slow, soft, yielding, diffuse, cold, wet and passive	As fast, hard, solid, focused, hot, dry and aggressive
Is associated with	Water, earth, the moon, night-time, femininity	Fire, sky, the sun, daytime, masculinity

I use a ying-yang symbol to guide thinking but most of all I use the imagery to illustrate the essence of ambiguity.

Remember that much of our decision-making process involves parsing information, situations and people into right and wrong. We 'cut' a decision by sorting relevance. Assuming all the information is presented within the circle and that the black section represents the 'right' data.

A ying-yang decision based on a 'cut' might look like this.

Be aware that the shape itself reflects reality in that the shape of the model is not static. It can wobble or rotate. Decisions are therefore unlikely to be reproducible. Over time black becomes white and visa versa. The lesson is **your decision will never offer a 100 percent pure outcome, so optimise, decide quickly and move on!**

What you have to look at and manage are multiple contingency decisions such as who will 'win' the least, who or what is left out, who will complain, who is damaged/benefited, etc, etc.

Optimise, but decide quickly

Nine ying yang

The symbol below arose as a direct consequence of a conversation in the summer of 2011 with John Kearon at BrainJuicer™. He said he found ying-yang symbolism just too simplistic. Within an hour, this particular image formed in my mind as a representation of complex uncertainty. Complex ambiguous problems often present as a 'nasty family group'. There is rarely just the one issue to deal with.

9 Ying Yang

Each shape has rotated to a different point. Some appear to be connected but are they? What if the picture was three dimensional? And what or where are the 'missing' three ying-yang shapes? Perhaps one is within you, another within the observed and another in the widest context. My interpretation is that you rarely, if ever, get to see the whole picture.

Third model: Onion maps

We tend to think within boundaries. Sometimes these boundaries are illusory or set too close to be useful. We can be at risk if we fail to see the whole picture. We may miss opportunities if we fail to spot how things, people, processes, situations, problems, relationships, etc, fit together.

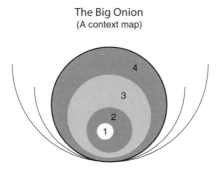

The Big Onion
(A context map)

The model shows interrelated territories, represented by a series of concentric circles that radiate outward from a starting point. Think of this as a Russian doll: one idea, relationship or thing fits inside another.

Practitioner guidelines

- Apply structure to the question first and then slot possible answers into its format. Look at contexts first then analyse what is happening in each context. Set up a series of concentric circles. Label them from a sensible starting point at the centre.
- Keep adding layers until you reach something ridiculous or funny. Why? Because when an emotion is registered this signals that you have probably hit the outer boundaries of agreed normal reason. You need to get to a point of unreasonable 'silliness' to ensure you have not set the boundaries too close to home. You can then work back a step or two to get within 'normal boundaries'.
- Populate each layer with comments about the problem, business, person, issue or whatever subject you choose. Look for what might have been missed.
- Often this tool serves simply to tell us where we have not been looking. When I have used this in practice, for example, during a strategic mapping process, I often find that several subsets (smaller related onion maps) can be created from any one layer. Each subset would have an independent series of important concentric contexts and relationships.

- The onion tool often provides clues and suggestions but rarely an answer. In my experience this particular tool is something to be employed 'along the way' to an outcome. Creation of such maps can throw up interesting leverage, enquiry or influence points.

Fourth model: Sedimentation

We go about our daily work and lives sometimes as if everything will **always** be the same. It is only when we face up to a major life change that we realise that life, relationships and business as well as career viability, are pretty fluid. They may begin with bright, new, bold, pioneering, fluffy realities that without attention can end up ossified and buried under many layers of other people's opinion and competitors' accretions.

This image is a prompt to thinking about the long term and the big picture of our lives, industries and, perhaps, countries. The analogy refers to the force of nature and applies especially when living beings compete. Whatever new entity is evolved, gravity and time will lead to tighter thresholds, sedimentation and, for the most part, lots of decay. Call it a system of a herd mentality, but people, processes and industries tend to move, in lock step, **downhill**. That makes evolutionary sense because people, novelty, innovation and therefore advantage 'wear out', creating space for new entities, new people and new ideas. Sedimentation happens gradually:

Sedimentation

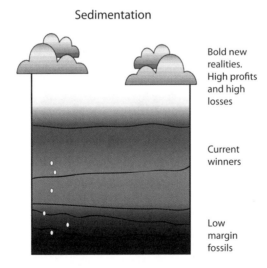

Bold new realities. High profits and high losses

Current winners

Low margin fossils

Bright new beginnings – the vision, the opportunity, the bright future of limitless wealth – enabled by a new rule set or a new technology. In 1987 the leading index of Japanese shares exceeded 25,000. In 1990 the same Japanese stock market index hit a high of 38,000 and stayed there for a while. With valuations vastly overpriced, journalists at the time said 'special rules' applied. More than 20 years later, market valuations are still nowhere near the earlier heights. The 'dot com' boom followed just before the turn of the century. Share-price valuations for loss-making start-ups seemed to stand on a cloudy self-validating logic as more and more people bought into the promise of future riches. A few people did become quite rich, which encouraged more people to join the 'game'.

- Following a natural selection or a battle for the best, the many bold new (fluffy) entrants get reduced to just a few current winners.
- Encrustation and hardening is slow to begin but starts to appear before the whole entity hits bottom and fossilises. The few remaining behemoths compete and repetitively slug things out until a relatively rigid, tight, highly refined, efficient but much less profitable order is established. Steel, cars and lots of basic industries follow this path. New entrants are discouraged from entering a 'spoiled' terrain where only large scale seems to work and the possibility of bankruptcy is quite real.
- Once institutionalised as 'normal' and therefore generic, profits get even thinner and progressively disappear. Things that are not special are not valued. Debt and entitlement to continue no matter what become an accepted feature. Reasons for remaining – heritage, obligation, sunk-costs and social welfare – are extolled. Without the lifeblood of spare cash = profit to finance inevitable human error, new product development or realistic dividends, fossilised entities are doomed to become someone else's bedrock to mine at a later date. Wealth remains embedded somewhere in these dinosaurs but only for the brave and the occasional original-thinking entrepreneur. A fossil with a few new whistles and bells is still a fossil.

Break-out growth

The only things capable of moving up in the opposite direction are entities, people and ideas that are lighter than their surroundings. By definition, these are likely to be simpler liquid or gaseous, possibly small, odd and seemingly irrelevant at first. Will you kill or culture them?

Stressed edges

My degree was in the biological sciences. When evolution or cancer growths were discussed, I noticed that edges and margins such as water to land/land to air – or at the cellular level, flat squamous cell to tall column cell – were very important. Boundaries are stress points where different rules and obligations collide. New life emerges there. Where are your personal or collective boundaries? Who is fighting the fight daily at your stressed edges?

When the balance at the border is disrupted, opportunities for good AND bad things can occur. New growth emerges either as a new viable species or as cancer. Therein lies a major uncertainty. When resources are very tight and liquidity is getting worse, what do you do about emerging new species or potential money-pit, cancer-like schemes? Allowing lighter transitioning elements to escape the confines of the current ecology can be important. Leaders, as well as strategists and innovators, need to accurately differentiate between good and bad new growths.

Summary

Our brains employed shape recognition long before we crafted the written word. Thinking using shapes is a legitimate way to sense your environment and to arrive at conclusions as to the relative place of people, ideas, issues, strategies and a whole host of other things over time. Shapes can be used to estimate a scale of possible viewpoints or probabilities. Shapes can also help us understand the relationships between people, situations and processes. I can commend my certainty funnel as a standard alongside ying-yang, as it has wide application in an uncertain world. Invent your own frameworks or image-based, sense-making system. For additional imagery see my second book *High Performance Thinking Skills*, which contains 82 thinking tools. Each tool is described briefly in just three or four pages.

Reflection

- Where are you, your team, your industry or your country on the sedimentation scale?
- Are lots of things bubbling up beneath you or has someone poisoned the wellspring, accusing every new growth of being bad or too risky?
- Any ecology ideally contains multiple niches. Where are the interesting niches and what is growing in there that matters to someone?
- How much pioneer, 'edge' exploration do you do? Who is listening or doing something with what you find? Forget the old track record. How adaptive are you today?
- Does large scale blind you to small cute opportunities? Bubbles burst. What is your strategy for when your bubble bursts, or when your whole ecology layer slides in deeper to tighter confines?
- Has anyone got a jackhammer and a hard hat?

Chapter 5 Section 3

Other thinking tactics and tools

The following subtle changes to perception and behaviour can make a large difference to your performance.

Step back to leap forward

'**Slow down**, step back and **reflect**, go and look for a model and some other people', is probably the most consistent feedback pattern I've had from the brightest people in the room.

They do **not** mean go looking for more data. Nor do they simply mean take a 'helicopter view of the situation'. They mean 'think', 'feel', sense and experience the issue.

the impulse to 'dive in' is resisted

Importantly, the impulse to 'dive in' is resisted. Generally, I've noticed that smart people possess a wide variety of experiences, but more importantly they also have a really wide repertoire of mental models AND often the ability to quickly synthesise alternatives. Above all, smart people retain a detached commitment to an eventual result yet are also able to remain open and flexible.

Muddy thinking and muddy problems

Problems do vary significantly, so apply a filter and think before you act. If the problem is simple and visible, be logical and, **if asked,** fix it. Don't over-complicate things. If your problem is complex, think it through, then act in a timely and proficient way – if you must. Remember, timely inaction can be a conscious and positive choice too. Procrastination, in contrast, is no decision at all.

timely inaction can be a conscious and positive choice too

The problem with problems

Problems come in all sorts of shapes, types and sizes.

- The first difficulty with complex problems is the nature of the problem itself. Not all difficulties can be solved. For example, it is difficult if not impossible to answer questions about 'the best ever tune' or 'the right way to lead people'.

- The second problem with problems is to do with people and the way their minds do or do not work. Sometimes someone will share a problem but will only want to talk about it and do nothing. Most people have quite different truths, opinions, preferred illusions, thinking patterns and sense of entitlement. Some believe logic reigns supreme and emotions play no real role whilst others have the opposite view.
- The third problem is one of interpretations such as wrong perception, wrong starting point or a poor understanding of the situation. Perceptions can vary considerably, so differences in opinion as to who is entitled to what and what is 'fair' can easily become serious points of contention.
- Then there's the problem of implementation of solutions. Even if people agree a decision, the question of how to put it into effect can be another contested debate. Here I will stick with the problem of dealing with complex and uncertain issues and leave aside implementation issues for another day.

Overrated common sense

Take a different track. Many people start by 'diving in' and attack a problem with good intent. Despite a lack of forethought, they hold a working assumption that prior experience, hard work and 'common sense' will see them through.

Common sense can be great with common problems. Common sense has merits but is overrated in some situations. When it comes to high-value interesting questions regarding uncertain futures, the difficulty with common sense is precisely that it is 'common'. Common sense is of limited value with slippery or wicked problems.

If everyone has 'common sense' where is your personal advantage?

Common sense does not necessarily presage novel or original approaches. Also, if your solution is indeed common, it will generally lack any kind of edge or advantage and probably cannot be easily patented. If everyone has 'common sense' where is your personal advantage? You'll need an uncommon sense for that.

Let us assume you have mapped a variety of possible outcomes. You have also thought through a variety of consequences of the events your likely course of action will set in motion. You have good intent and you still feel driven to act now. An internal conflict arises between an impulse to make a quick decisive move and your need to make wise choices. You feel awkward but your impulse to act is held in abeyance and this leaves you feeling frustrated. You accommodate these conflicting tensions and frustration, but now the question is, 'Have you got the right tool or model with which to make a wise and worthy decision?' Hopefully the previous models will help. Here are a few more guidelines.

Using negative space

As an artist, one of the tricks you get shown is to draw 'what is not there'. By drawing the spaces and objects surrounding the thing or person you are looking at, an interesting picture is created in which the object of your attention emerges – by not drawing it. It sounds peculiar but the technique works quite well in art as well as in business. Doing the opposite of what is expected can lead back to a more interesting aspect of 'the expected', an insight if you like. For example, consider an uncertain situation you are facing.

- What has **not** been said?
- What is happening around this sequence of events that creates the bigger picture and formed the event we initially focused on?
- What is missing from the picture?
- All of the available information says we should proceed in a particular way but what would be counter-intuitive? How might that look?
- How could a counter-intuitive choice be more fun, more productive or even better than what is on offer?
- Who will it surprise?

Dealing with dilemmas

Charles Hampden-Turner explains how we generally deal with dilemmas.[15] We can be influenced by our context, through a cultural imperative that shapes our choice. He plots the available options on a graph where each axis has a ten-point scale. The potential outcomes to dilemmas can be represented by five choices. Two of the five choices involve suboptimal solutions namely in the direction of 10/0 or 0/10, where one of the two horns of the dilemma is chosen at the expense of the other. A third option adopts a weak compromise position, e.g. 3/3.

Charles proposed that the better (but more demanding) approach covering the two remaining options involves an integrated approach and much higher scores. He proposes **two** alternative starting points followed by a non-linear route to reconciliation via a sequential, spiral, creative reconciliation to accommodate **both** horns of the dilemma. These are **not** simple, linear, either/ or choices between the lesser of two evils.

In order to progress, an extreme, but 'clear', position (10/0 or 0/10) first needs to be relinquished. For a while the perception of added value may seem elusive and even decline until a virtuous spiral takes hold.

Dealing with polarities

Perhaps one of the most common unseen and commercially costly complex types of difficulty is a 'polarity'. Barry Johnson has been delivering Polarity Management™ since the mid-1970s. He has unpicked the characteristics of a polarity and identified several archetypal patterns.[16]

What differentiates a dilemma from a polarity is that with a dilemma each horn of the dilemma has a potentially **independently** valid answer. A polarity involves two difficulties that are firmly connected in some form of dependency. They are NOT two separate problems to be solved. Also, they have a habit of recurring.

A very simple example of a polarity that Barry cites is breathing. Attempting to resolve a polarity using a lower level 'either/or' type mindset just doesn't work. If we treated a lack of oxygen or too much carbon dioxide in our blood as if they were two quite separate problems that would be plain dumb. Breathing in AND breathing out is a dependent paired process. Examples of other polarities include centralised AND decentralised, local AND global and on a social level, soft love AND tough love. In order to get a reasonable outcome with a polarity you need 'AND' type thinking that accommodates both aspects of the dependency to different extents. Because they have a habit of recurring, the two sides of a polarity are never 'solved' but managed in tandem.

A wise addition[17] to Barry Johnson's Polarity Management™ model was the addition of two important dimensions, namely a shared higher goal AND a shared deepest fear. Making a shared higher goal and shared deepest fear explicit helps describe the motivating forces that can help initially opposing parties or viewpoints to start to be reconciled.

Dealing with multarities

Once competent with polarities the next and probably the last step up is probably a 'multarity'. This is where life gets quite interesting or demanding depending on your curiosity and tolerance for multiple level systems thinking. A multarity, a term coined by Robert W. Jacobs, involves several interactive interdependent polarities operating at the same time in the same context. Solutions require a group approach because of the intricate complexity of balancing multiple dependencies.

Polarities and multarities are never 'solved' and come around repeatedly in different guises, so they require constant attention, often to faint signals.

Summary

The simplest advice for when things become complex is to slow down and find time to reflect. Unless your very life is on the line, resist your basic impulse to act. Instead, think, sense, feel and experience all of what is happening AND reflect as you do so.

Logic, common sense and project management skills are great for relatively simple situations below the ambiguity ceiling. Logic **is** of value above the ambiguity ceiling **but** that value is limited. When you are required to deal with higher value, more complex, above-ambiguity-ceiling issues you will need much more than sharp logic, discipline and hard work.

Anxiety and frustration will be created in people who lack the tools, experience or abilities to deal with elevated and prolonged levels of ambiguity and uncertainty. To illustrate my meaning, imagine living in a difficult, lawless neighbourhood and sleeping in a house where the doors are unlocked and accessible ground level windows are left open. Learning to rest easy, without fear or anxiety, despite the everyday difficulty, is part of the solution.

The most common obstacle to being able to step back and reflect on an uncertainty is haste to act born out of fear or anxiety. Most people feel a strong impulse to do something, anything, in an attempt to close down the discomfort of uncertainty.

I believe you can upgrade your thinking skills AND learn how to endure ambiguity and uncertainty. But in order to do this you need to look at overcoming fear and other obstacles as a precondition to defeating your own impulses to act before you think. Once these obstacles are out of the way, I'll attempt to provide some insight into how your feelings and intuition might work for you.

Reflection

- Are you aware of the types of problems you face?
- Do you classify the problems/issues you face?
- How many problem-fixing models or patterns do you possess?
- How do you most often deal with complex problems?
- How do you deal with the emotional turmoil that accompanies important, complex challenges?
- Who do you know that you respect who seems to manage these well and how do they do what they do?

Chapter 6
Emotional literacy

At the logical, cookie-cutter end of reality, emotions can be viewed as inconvenient, unnecessary and to be curtailed. As we are educated, we are progressively expected to suppress our passions and emotions to focus increasingly on cramming as many facts as we can into our heads only to regurgitate them in an orderly fashion to be graded right or wrong. Order and discipline are valued. 'Play' is progressively replaced by logical précis and rigour. Fun is proscribed as something to be removed from the classroom or workplace and placed in the context of 'free-time', often in a caged playground. Conformity and alignment are gradually impressed upon most of us.

With this as a context, emotions might be viewed as at best a distraction and at worst a hindrance to 'good' thinking'. As you encounter more ambiguity and uncertainty, this is a lesson that needs to be 'unlearned'. Emotional literacy/ability involves an awareness of and an ability to differentiate between quite different feelings. It is most important that you develop your ability to use your feelings as a guide to decision-making. The ancient advice to 'first know and conquer your self' applies. If you are uncertain about your inner self how will you be able to confidently cope with a volatile world? The subject of emotional ability is huge, so I will focus on just a few aspects that may contribute to your ability to deal with uncertainty, namely:

Section 1: Uncertainty and disruptive emotions

Section 2: Impulse control

Section 3: Intuition

Fear and anger are particularly disruptive and connect to our base instinct to survive. Base instincts override our higher, somewhat slower senses of reasoning and we become prone to impulsive reactions; we lose control. To overcome these stronger impulses we need to understand what motivates them in the first place. Patience is required. A habit of noticing feelings is important if you want to give them validity in your frame of reference. Building up evidence that your intuition and your instincts **are** a credible way of making a decision during times of uncertainty will help considerably.

Chapter 6 Section 1

Uncertainty and disruptive emotions

Uncertainty affects people in different ways. Some love uncertainty, whilst others simply detest it. High uncertainty provokes our emotions. Strong and unruly emotions can lead some people to behave like 'stunned bunnies' frozen in the headlights of an oncoming truck. Therefore, we will look first at a selection of practical emotional aspects of uncertainty to help you begin to reframe your existing pattern of responses, especially those to do with fear, blame and error.

An important question that follows after you have overcome fear is how much of the natural tension caused by ambiguity and uncertainty can you tolerate and how does this affect your **impulsiveness** and the feeling that you need to respond urgently? If you fail to master your impulses then uncertainty will master you.

Uncertainty and strong feelings

One of the strongest feelings we face during high uncertainty is fear. Powerful feelings can reduce your behaviour to base survival instincts that quickly bypass and overwhelm clear thought. Powerful fight or flight hormones are released when your brain is in survival mode. You lose control of your thoughts and react instinctively. Overcoming fear does not mean dismissing your feelings. In order to 'be' confident, fear needs to be put in its rightful place as a useful signal. Outcomes driven by fear or by impulsive decisions are less likely to be favourable, unless of course your very survival is at stake!

perhaps the strongest feeling we face during high uncertainty is fear

You will need awareness of your feelings to animate your instincts and intuition AND you will need sufficient clarity to think and react well when you are tasked to deal with complex uncertainty and ambiguity. Fear should not be a constant factor unless perhaps you live in a war zone. Do you live in a war zone? (Fear should not be a routine part of your daily life.)

One problem is that sometimes we mistake the natural feelings of tension created by uncertainty for fear.

Different types of tension

Recognise **what, where and how** you are feeling. Uncertainty and ambiguity can produce tensions of different sorts. Tension can be acute or persistent. Chronic lower levels of tension might be experienced, for example, by a project manager tasked with something fluid or by an artist building up an original painting. Persistent tension can balance finely between anxiety and joy.

Remaining 'open' definitely feels awkward; however, let me reassure you that such a feeling of tension **is** normal and you are not doing something wrong. Tension can inform us of an unexplored need, a gap or a blind spot that needs to be worked on, so use the tension to guide you. Hopefully the process of discovery will create enough positive feedback so that you start to enjoy the tension as part of your personal reward system.

develop your sense of humour if you want to hang on to sanity and a top job

Tensions can be interpreted as pleasant or uncomfortable. Some people enjoy the buzz they get from uncertainty, others do not. When emotional tension hits an acute peak, there are two major possibilities for the release of strong feelings, namely anger **or** laughter. Choose laughter if you can. A great antidote to fear is laughter, so develop your sense of humour if you want to hang on to sanity and a top job!

Uncertainty and emotional expression

As someone operating under tension, it is essential that you understand your energy flows including your highs and lows. Be careful how you use your personal energy. Make sure you do not burn too brightly, too often. Leadership is a very long game. It is important not to push yourself too far. Make sure you can listen to those that are close to you. For this, they and you need to be in range AND willing to listen.

Occasionally the tension can get to be too much. Avoid a burnout and make sure you find ways of venting your feelings safely and frequently. You may have noticed that many successful people balance their energy using some form of additional physical activity, which they regard as important. Proportionality and the balance of your activities, energies and attention form an important aspect of your character.

find ways of venting your feelings safely and frequently

How can you tap the energy of very different types of people you work with if you do not understand your own energy flow? When 'tension' is channelled it can propel but when frustrated will hold back individuals, teams and whole organisations.

Anger

Some people fear losing control of their feelings. (Then there is a fear of arousing fear!) Bottling up feelings may be judicious for a while, but can put your performance and future wellbeing at risk. Being 'in control' does not necessarily mean that your emotional or subconscious desires go away. A strategy of containment of strong feelings eventually leads to 'leakage' of pent-up emotions in unfortunate ways at inopportune times.

> *Anger makes dull men witty -- but it keeps them poor.* Francis Bacon

> *The more anger towards the past you carry in your heart, the less capable you are of loving in the present.* Barbara De Angelis

Our society places a great deal of emphasis on the need for anger management; however, there are times when spontaneous anger has a genuine role and you should vent what you feel.

> *The man who is angry at the right things and with the right people, and, further, as he ought, when he ought, and as long as he ought, is praised. This will be the good-tempered man.* Aristotle, *Nicomachean Ethics*

Anger can have beneficial shock value. Anger lets people know the extent of their errors and the magnitude of your feelings. Anger provides survival energy when threatened. Anger addressed directly at a bully at a critical juncture can shock them to reassess their behaviour towards you. Anger misdirected can also get you fired, so consider what is appropriate and how you will deal with the aftermath. There are ways of showing anger well.

If you are not practised in safely losing your temper, consider an acting class. Get an acting coach to walk you through the enactment of your fury, the face-off and the recovery. An excellent book to read is *Difficult Conversations: How To Discuss What Matters Most*.[18] If your world feels a little bland, take a look at the Jack Nicholson film *Anger Management*. Seek the guidance of a coach, mentor or friend if your feelings are becoming stronger or unruly or if you persistently use anger to drive yourself forward. Likewise, seek guidance if you feel absolutely nothing or if you feel dull or if you dread what you do.

Feelings of isolation

If you feel something strongly such as fear, stress, tension or doubt, then the odds are that you are not alone. People show their positive feelings but negative feelings tend to get hidden. Often at the top of a group or organisation you are surrounded by people but actually you can feel quite alone, for lots of different reasons. That is normal. Leaders frequently feel isolated AND unsure. Be assured, **it's not just you** feeling this way.

Aloneness is a matter of perception. It is not healthy to be completely alone in all dimensions of your life though. That really would be poverty. You can be alone in some aspects of your work whilst being fully embraced in other parts of your life. 'Aloneness' is a matter of adjusting perceptions. Life is, after all, a game. We can occasionally write new rules or play a completely new game.

Fear of failure

Another cause of fear, rooted in uncertainty, **is** a dread of 'failing'. All of us will fail at something substantial sooner or later because the future **is** uncertain. Get used to it. If you spend all your time avoiding failure you will probably not do anything memorable. Even with well-intentioned, professional, dedicated effort, failure should be regarded as normal.

- When you eventually fail, what mindset will you choose to adopt?
- What will be the philosophy you fall back on to reassure yourself when 'meaning' and 'purpose' seem pointless or when motivation, loyalty and commitment are all questioned and challenged?

When you do eventually face a crisis of your own:

- Use the experience well. Do not fear 'failure' or 'error'.
- Do not assume a victim status.
- Frame events as positive, valuable, learning opportunities.
- You will change and probably will be stronger and wiser after the challenge.
- In the long run you may benefit if you are wise and seek the right help.

Failure need not necessarily be a bad thing. In fact, failure can help you. It is expected of you.

Feeling success AND failure

Experiencing winning AND losing builds resilience and knowledge of how to motivate yourself and others when faced with the reality of setbacks.

John Chambers,[19] Director of Applications at a major UK company, says, 'It is important that someone has failed at something important. Failure teaches a lot. If you have never failed at something then you are not pushing yourself hard enough. How you deal with it says a lot about you and helps you succeed and others succeed in the future.'

Dr Narendra Laljani from Ashridge Business School conducted his PhD research into leadership and found that an important component of gaining executive leadership ability included harsh, difficult experiences.

Andrew McLaren, Head of Operational Risk and Internal Control at HSBC Bank Bermuda Limited, confirms this viewpoint. Andrew says, 'Some of my early work experiences were really tough, but in a sense I'm grateful because I have the confidence of getting through extreme difficulty and 'surviving'. Harsh life experiences change your outlook and the way you live your life. Seriously hard knocks in business will do that too. Hardship can be unpleasant but it is not necessarily a bad thing.'

How you frame a difficult experience is important. Businessman Niall Fitzgerald holds that, whilst pain is inevitable, misery is optional![20] Difficulty should not be regarded as a barrier but as an opportunity to learn.

pain is inevitable, misery is optional

The university of hard knocks

Psychologists say we have a bias of attention towards difficult, challenging or negative events. We are more likely to pay attention to and remember negative events than positive ones.[21]

It seems that negative lessons are cauterised deeply into memory: giving priority to negative events may be a fundamental survival instinct. We learn highly memorable guidelines from these experiences. How you deal with your 'failure' is important.

As a badge of membership above the ambiguity ceiling, most directors will tell how you they failed in a big way at least once. What they learned and how they recovered becomes an integral part of their sense of who and what they are today. Failure helps build character.

put the self-beating stick down

Failure as a beneficial tutor

Fear, blame and shame do not help. Get used to the probability of failure. As a leader you **will** fail sooner or later. Learn, put the self-beating stick down, then get over yourself and get on with the rest of your life. Hey, you might even get promoted for trying!

Overcoming fear

Some jobs involve a lot of natural uncertainty. Independent consultants, actors, musicians, project team members, leaders, politicians, artists and those in executive roles are expected to turn uncertainties into certainties. People in these roles can feel isolated and stretched. Ideally, such demanding jobs, especially during the early years, should be externally mentored, irrespective of age. Who mentors you? If you do not have an explicit mentor, go and get one. The best people get the best help they can find. Look around. Who could help you? Who do you mentor and what can the person you are helping offer you?

Deal with it

What you fear is perhaps unfounded, is a false projection or the consequences of what you dread are going to turn out better than what you anticipate. Often a simple conversation can help unpick the uncertainty or at least validate what you feel. The energy of 'worrying about worrying' can be better invested! Strike an emotional bargain (i.e. it costs you less) and deal with or share what is bugging you rather than suffer it. This can be very difficult to initiate if you are someone who is 'self-reliant'. Do it though.

Often we carry a whole list of uncertainties, most of which we can either do nothing about or aren't worth the worry. List what you fear or are anxious about and dump the ones of no consequence. Get some coaching and face up to, dump or reframe what you believe you fear.

blame and shame should be reserved for moral crimes

Imparting negative feelings of fear, blame and shame should be reserved for moral crimes or where people are at risk of actual harm. If you are not literally at war and you **do** use fear to rule and direct people, ask yourself why. There are much more fruitful sources of energy and more wholesome ways of 'being'.

Grace

If you and your colleagues want to face the long-term prospects of running an operation without buckling under the inevitable pressures that come with uncertain times or a top job, a personal sense of balance and harmony is essential.

a personal sense of balance and harmony is essential

Balance and harmony

Balance is difficult to achieve if you are mentally constipated and bottling up suppressed fears and doubts. You risk an unsympathetic colleague providing a mental laxative at a most inopportune moment! What you need may not coincide with what you want.

To locate a sense of balance, review the validity of your personal anchors. Hold on to your positive beliefs AND be selective about what you 'show others'. You need to know that part of yourself remains consistently you. Boundaries are important, so keep some of your behaviours and your private life private. Channel your energy constructively.

Useful dissent

Keeping harmony **with yourself** does not mean avoiding dissent with others. Dissent in the face of uncertainty is not necessarily destructive and can lead to better outcomes if it finds appropriate and timely avenues of expression. If you fear 'speaking the truth', overcome the fear of what you might do or say – talk to someone; rehearse it. Be sure to emphasise your basic intention behind your dissent. Senior managers who are often on the lookout for alternative perspectives sometimes welcome well-intended expressions of differences of opinion.

Mindfulness and proportionality

Mindfulness can help you find grace.[22] Mindfulness requires your active yet detached full engagement with life. This may sound like a contradiction, but the truth is you as an individual and as a team player need both energy AND calmness, passion AND patience. (See Dow Corning example in Chapter 11.) Full-on energy may appear manic, whilst total calmness may look like lethargy. The strength of your character is shaped by your ability to demonstrate a proportionate response in difficult and uncertain times.

rising above uncertainty is essential

Grace under pressure

People judge you based on what they see and experience. Balance is required at great heights and, in this case, at great depths. One of the selection criteria for choosing the captain of a nuclear-armed submarine from a small number of exceptional Royal Navy individuals was once neatly described as 'grace under pressure'. The higher you go in any organisation the greater the expectation for you to demonstrate 'grace under pressure' – a quality of comfortable, reassured charm and confidence, no matter what.

Andrew McLaren at HSBC Bermuda puts it this way. 'It's about a sense of serenity. It is not about simply being laid back.' I asked, 'Can serenity be developed?' He replied, 'You can't put an old head on young shoulders. Experience of going through hard experiences and the confidence gathered over the years can allow one to show "grace under pressure", most of the time. Showing restraint and keeping some of the feelings to yourself, especially when you have responsibility for others, is most important. Staff expect you to set an example. With persistent ambiguity, rising above the uncertainty is essential.'

Grace under pressure does **not** mean you are indifferent or that you do not care. On the contrary, caring is important if you wish to take people with you through extreme difficulties.

Feeling confident

Confidence is an emotion too. Confidence is a state of 'being' that can be undermined by fear and impulsiveness. Confidence is a matter of feeling genuinely safe, despite the prevailing uncertainty. Consistency is a central tenet of sanity. It is important, therefore, to create several consistent anchor points that you can rely upon. These will differ from person to person. You will need to locate your own. What or where are your anchors and how do you nurture them?

Key anchors

No matter what happens in a crazy mixed-up world you need to be sure of some things, processes and people. Perhaps most of all you need to be sure and confident of yourself and what you believe in. Having some idea about where the shipwrecker reefs and sirens are in an uncertain choppy sea can help you too. Here are a few of the safe ports and some pitfalls.

Core being

'Being' comes into question when you examine your life in depth. Your sense of meaning and purpose, as well as your philosophy or beliefs that drive you and keep you on the rails when the going gets tough, all get questioned. Take care of what you 'do' most often and of which emotions and behaviours you most frequently engage. Aristotle, the Greek warrior-philosopher, suggests that **you become that which you do most often:**

> It is right then to say that a person comes to be just from doing just actions and temperate from doing temperate actions.

Aristotle continues:

*… the many however do **not do these actions**. They take refuge in arguments thinking that they are doing philosophy and that this is the way to become excellent people. They are like a sick person who listens attentively to a doctor, but acts on none of his instructions.* Aristotle, *Nicomachean Ethics, Book II*, 4; 1105b lines 10 to 16

In other words, if you want to **be** confident then be prepared to think very deeply about your real self and particularly about what you spend most of your time doing. Consider the things you do most often and the emotions you engage most often and then behave consistently with what you believe. 'Walk your own talk'. Make your beliefs a habit of mind AND a habit of behaviour. Then you will be '**sure**' of your self. You will not let yourself down.

'Being' confident

Developing an inner and outer consistency when faced with high uncertainty is a really deep thing. Stability can emerge from a sense of 'being', as opposed to 'having'. You are a human 'being' not a human 'having'! The things you 'have' can be lost or taken away; your 'being' cannot. In other words, the character of self-confidence needs to become embedded, a natural part of you. Confidence is not simply an act or an add-on. Gaining a state of 'being' self-confident, involves:

- reaffirmed positive experiences gained through a few harsh lessons and recovery
- fear being kept in the right place as a useful signal
- a number of secure anchor points
- available alternative choices, supports, routes and options sustained by an ability to improvise and adapt to what you are presented with
- ever-present mindfulness of the moment – openness. A willingness to risk, explore, learn and accept error as normal.

Backed up by:

- well-thought-through personal values
- modesty, genuine humility and, importantly, an ability to laugh
- concern and care for others
- an ability to forgive yourself and others and move forward.

In short, **be** the honourable man or woman and you will find natural confidence. Confidence comes as a consequence of 'being' centred, despite the turmoil, and not because you are working at it.

Uncertainty AND 'can do' cultures

Some companies and some leaders foster group and individual confidence as a natural activity, despite the risk of failing from time to time. Building resilience is key.

John Chambers is Director of Applications at a FTSE 100 company. He is an experienced leader of fast-start, scalable, IT business operations. He says, 'My company is a great enterprise in which to build a business at speed. The culture is very "can-do"/entrepreneurial AND at the same time has tight controls. We remain very focused on cost control AND at the same time spend the money saved on smart investments.'

'Sometimes you have to take substantial decisions with incomplete information. You call on your own and other people's experience AND their intuition to take the decision. You have to have the confidence to sail away from a shore to a point where you can neither see the shore you left nor the shore, if there is one, ahead of you. Decisions require an act of faith AND intuition. Then we get on with it.'

'Once in a while, if it goes wrong, we analyse it and move on. There is no victimisation. Attempts to apportion blame would be dumb. If everyone acted in good faith going in, you sort it out and move on. It isn't personal. Blaming people just stops them making good judgement calls later on and that kills a "can-do", entrepreneurial culture. If you go down the blame route, you end up with an average performance culture, at best. I don't want that. We don't want that. The way we work pays off. Most of the time we do get it right and our company continues to grow and deliver great results.'[23]

Fear – in summary

Work can be difficult enough without having fear suck the life out of you too. If you can rise above 'the game', play your role and find pleasure from what you do, so much the better. Perhaps this may mean changing your individual or collective working philosophy, or moving to where the current working beliefs suit you better. Fear has a place but not a day-to-day role, so accommodate fear properly. Don't allow it free rein.

If we collectively accept that failure and occasional error are normal parts of human 'being' then the work environment should be safe and blame free. Fear of error or fear of failure blocks learning. Don't let it. Weed out leaders who lay blame or who rule by fear.

Ideally, managers need success AND failure to hone their intuition as they grow. Past wins AND losses can inform future intuitions. Such collective experience takes time to build.

Confidence is not a 'bolt on' or an act. Confidence is a consequence of your way of 'being' you.

Reflection

- How do you and your colleagues deal with your passions – or lack of them?
- What is your individual, or the collective, safety net for strong emotions? What do you do and what does 'recovery' look like?
- Are you aware of alternative forms of emotional expression?
- How often do you worry? What do you fear most often?
- Who do you share your concerns with? If you answer 'no one', why is that and what are you afraid will happen if you do?
- Who is safe to talk to? Do people respect or fear you?
- Are people who work around you inspired by what you say and do?
- Do you lead by diktat – by assertive command and control?
- Who are you at your very core and do you like yourself?
- Have you made your beliefs explicit and tested them?

Chapter 6 Section 2

Impulse control

Impulsiveness can undermine our idea of self-control and therefore our sense of personal safety. We all have feelings of major and minor impulses. The question is, do you engage them and present yourself to the world as being spontaneous or as a victim of uncontrollable urges? The emotional tipping point is about your self-regulation of genuine **need** versus **want**. Self-control is about being able to withstand temptation.

self-control is about being able to withstand temptation

Forty years ago, an experiment was conducted with preschool children involving temptation and a delay. Children aged about four years old were presented with a plate of marshmallows and given a choice: take just one marshmallow now or wait a while (15 minutes – an eternity) to get three. They could ring a bell at any time before the researcher returned and take just one marshmallow if the tension got too much. It was subsequently found that impulse control skills learned by children **before** school correlated statistically significantly with better cognitive ability, self-regulation, coping competence and SAT scores obtained years later.[24] Self-control or self-modification of feelings when faced with a tempting impulse is clearly a very important skill. Deferred gratification is a skill that can be learned.

Uncertainty, fear and impulse

When many of us face raised uncertainty we can experience an impulse, an anxiety to do something – anything – soon, just to relieve an unruly feeling of tension. The 'act now think later' impulse helps us survive through our inbuilt adrenalin-fired fight and flight response, however, this is not a sustainable day-to-day learning pattern. It is highly reactive and this gets in the way of higher thought processes and better performance.

Personal mastery of uncertainty as an adult involves understanding and then accommodating or modifying our own emotional trip switches including our various impulses.

- If you don't control your impulses and filter what you say and do, you may lose out over the long term.

- Too much self-control on the other hand, and you may end up lacking spontaneity, becoming predictable and perhaps a bore!
- Strike a balance and choose when to rein in your urge to decide or to act.

Withholding skills

With more than 15 years of running a variety of thinking-skills workshops, I have noticed that seriously bright thinkers appear to be good at 'withholding' on several different levels at the same time.

- Judgement is temporarily suspended, and importantly, they demonstrate 'impulse control' over the urge to close down an uncertainty. They resist the imperative to come to a quick decision, just to relieve the immediate tension.
- They don't let pure emotion become the sole purpose of a process. They accept the feelings but hold out for better solutions.
- They refuse to accept the impulse to choose a simple one-sided answer to a dilemma until they have had the opportunity to reflect, reconsider or synthesise a more integrated solution.

Resisting our impulse to act and setting up deferred gratification is perhaps more difficult to accomplish than we might expect. The research shows that many of us are prone to choose quick fixes ahead of better long-term prospects.

Impulse and temptation

Professor George Ainslie demonstrated that people really do prefer a 'bird in the hand now to two in the bush later'. For more than 40 years he and others researched how most people deal with a simple dilemma of, 'Do I take the small sooner reward (SS) or do I select to wait for a larger later (LL) reward?' Their results indicate a consistent tendency by many of us to strongly favour SS rewards.[25][26]

The way our minds discount future value compared to sooner value is even faster than exponential, it's 'hyperbolic'. In other words, many of us are significantly more motivated by what is in front of us here and now. The closer, physically and in time, to the SS reward we are, the higher the temptation to take a quick early win and to forgo the alternative LL reward.

One practical insight in regard to immediate consumer temptation is that if left to their own choices, research indicates that substantial numbers of people would **not** put money or assets aside for their pension provision. Also, on a personal level, the smaller sooner reward might be a sweet fatty snack – or spending more on credit for something. The philosophy of free consumerism can fuel AND undermine the interests of an individual, as well as a nation state.

Temptation and resilience

Ironically, other research shows that our resolve to 'resist a temptation' can be undone simply by exercising self-control. They found that people who had been asked to exercise self-control in some way tended to make more impulse purchases and spent more money than people who were not asked to impose self-control. Their findings suggest that we have a reservoir of 'resistance' that can be quickly depleted, leaving us prone to be more easily tempted shortly afterwards.[27] If we possess such a reservoir we could learn to bolster and stock it higher.

Impulse control and internal negotiation

Professor Ainslie proposes that we arrive at our actions or decisions through a 'free internal marketplace of motivation'.[28] Negotiation takes place between different options, with each component acting as a free agent and taking a value that is weighted or discounted as a function of its availability over time. The winner gets acted upon. From my point of view, Professor Ainslie's idea would explain a lot of our behaviours, especially if **subconsciously** we are playing games with what we **really** want!

Self-aware and in control

Early work with children suggests there is a connection between an ability to counteract or manage our impulses and higher order thinking ability. Impulse control seems to involve a **conscious** negotiation between thoughts and prevailing emotions. In order to do this you would first of all need to be aware of your inner world as well as the source of the temptation to act AND multiple consequences.

Research suggests that some animals and some humans can develop strategies for resisting quite compelling impulses to accept smaller sooner rewards. Example strategies include the following:

- Sabotaging personal access to accepting the small sooner reward whilst leaving the larger later reward option intact.
- Bundling up the value of larger later rewards so they become overwhelmingly compelling and 'swamp out' short-term impulses.
- Knowing and moderating the cascade sequence before your particular emotional rollercoaster starts may be one route to gaining control of your impulse patterns.
- Having coping strategies in place could be another.

- Perhaps the most powerful control is actually not to need control because the importance of the issue has been diminished substantially by personally detaching from it at the deepest level.

Once we have removed irrational fear and anxiety from the equation we can begin to consciously influence our internal marketplace of negotiations for priority of attention.

we can influence our internal marketplace

As far as I can see, a number of preconditions exist to getting control of our impulses so that we can withstand uncertainty and better manage our choices and behaviours. These include:

- Personal accountability; no one else is going to do it for you so it is up to you. A willingness to make sacrifices, to change mindset and behaviour.
- Honesty to oneself, no self-deceptions, no denials, no cheating. Planning and preparation to reduce the opportunity for spontaneous temptation. Out of sight, out of mind. Set up useful boundaries, routines, rituals and helpful constraints.
- Goal clarity and total goal commitment. (Your goal is visceral, vital, deeply sensed.)
- Self-awareness and time for reflection on what your body and mind tell you. Meditation can help.
- Discipline; not slipping back to old unhelpful habits can lead to increased self-trust. (Cheating seriously undermines personal resolve by creating undeniable evidence for exceptions that will be used within your unconscious internal negotiations to adversely reset your priorities.)
- An optimistic outlook. Forgiveness.
- Continuous support from people who clearly understand their new roles. Surrounding oneself with the right people and things. Stay away from toxic associations and prompts to deviate.

Impulse control – summary

Most of us are easily tempted by visible short-term smaller rewards. Forty years of research indicates that many of us choose lesser short-term rewards over larger later rewards. There may be problems to do with a lack of patience or a lack of impulse control or perhaps a shortage of trust and faith in the long term because choosing larger later rewards is more than exponentially difficult.

Exercises where we are required to exercise self-control seem to weaken our resistance to temptations that are offered soon afterwards. A lack of general experience of self-control may indicate that we simply have not built up sufficient beneficial reserves to enable a repetitious easy habit of deferred gratification. As in many things, impulse control requires frequent practice to maintain 'mental muscle tone'.

Recognising our personal impulse patterns and adopting the habit of internally renegotiating problematic impulses early on can help us build resilience, a sense of determination and self-esteem.

Learning 'withholding' techniques can help. The deeper answer to the problem of impulses may not be about 'control' over something we feel attached to but instead may involve genuine detachment and 'letting go'. We can, quite literally, change our minds.

Reflection

- If doting parents pandered to the every whim of a child or a young adult, how would a need or the skill to reconcile conflicting interests emerge? How would deferred gratification skills be built up?
- As soon as possible, we need to get used to reconciling conflicting issues particularly with needs vs wants.
- We risk overindulgence, loss of self-control, sense of safety and therefore self-esteem if we lack the ability to selectively manage our impulses.
- When do you most often feel an impulse that you later regret? What is it connected to and what long-term rewards does it undermine?

Chapter 6 Section 3

Intuition

What is intuition?

One common association we have about dealing with ambiguous situations and uncertainty is that some people are able to usefully employ their instincts and intuition as part of a natural value-adding decision process.

As a boy I lived in a poor 'mill town'. Left-wing local politicians arranged for compulsory purchase and demolition of large parts of the town and mass construction of replacement 'housing units'. Consequently, large numbers of local people were obliged to move house as old houses were demolished.

From that time, I recall a powerful story of instinct. One day, two men parked their large furniture van outside a house located on one of the steep hills of my home town. Their job was to help a family move to another house across town. When the van was almost full of furniture, the braking system failed and several tons of a heavy truck along with a house-load of family possessions set off downhill, picking up momentum and striking several other vehicles on the way down. Unfortunately this particular road ended at the bottom of the hill in a T-junction facing a row of terraced houses. Inside the front room of one of these houses was a baby sleeping in a pram near the window.

Moments away, the heavily laden, out-of control truck was headed for the house. The baby's mother suddenly dropped what she was doing at the back of the house and ran to the front room. She did not hesitate or stop to think or enquire about what was happening. Her instincts had kicked in. She grabbed her baby, turned and immediately ran to the back of the house, followed by the truck crashing into her front room. Thankfully the mother and child survived unhurt, but the front of the house was demolished. Her instinct saved her baby's life.

There was a court case and facts were heard and lessons learned. After events, it is easier to reconcile what may have happened in a logical way. The mother's hearing may have picked up the approaching sequence of uncharacteristic bangs from the street on the hill in front of her house. Perhaps in her subconscious mind she might have wondered about such an event being possible, given the unfavourable location of the house. We cannot definitively 'know' how her instinct really worked, as it was drawn from her unique life experiences. Just because instinct cannot be logically explained does not lessen the fact that instinctive reactions saved a child's life.

Insights

Logic travels consistently and in reproducible ways, whereas feelings and individual interpretations do not. Explaining an intuition or an instinct to someone else is difficult, if not impossible, because both are largely faculties of feelings. Feelings and 'sensation' generally cannot be deconstructed or logically explained.

feelings and 'sensation' generally cannot be deconstructed or logically explained

Anatomy of instinct and intuition

One case comes to mind, in which a front line fireman suddenly ordered his team to get out of a burning building, just minutes before it turned into a complete fireball. He was right, but he couldn't explain why at the time. 'The fire was "wrong", Something wasn't right,' he said. Later research explained just how dangerous the fire had become. Investigations of video footage detected some new useful indicators. His extensive experience helped inform his instinct that the burn was not following one of the many 'usual' patterns.

With instinct, the feelings are unmistakable, powerful and acute. It may feel belligerent or awkward. Deep visceral sensations are triggered. Our whole body is made aware that our situation is not normal AND that a particular path of urgent action is required. The feelings are strong enough to totally override our higher cognitive senses and controls. When it comes to survival, adrenalin fired-instinct is far quicker than reason. The overriding characteristic with **instinctive** reactions is that we are impelled to act **before** we think.

Instinct and intuition share similar characteristics. Both are crude feelings. One is urgent, while the other 'nags'. **Instinct is an acute experience** whilst **intuition has a more chronic pattern**. With intuition the drive to 'do something' is there but nags at us for longer at a much lower level of urgency. Both motivate us towards a particular direction or decision. Instinct and intuition differ from base impulsivity, where any reaction will do to relieve a state of tension.

In both cases we do not rely on having a full set of logical information. Accessing your intuition therefore involves learning to trust your self with a course of action without a full data set. An element of risk is to be expected. Some people squash or ignore these weak nagging intuitive signals whilst others are tuned in.

Eve is always going to be successful according to her peers. She has boundless energy, is very intelligent, positively orientated, curious and, most of all, she has learned to trust her intuition. Eve says, 'Lots of big decisions involve uncertainty.

If I have to put my energy behind something uncertain I know that there is much more energy available if my own feelings are behind my belief in what I'm trying to do. If I'm following someone else's belief and I don't feel the same then the required energy just won't be there for me. Intuition is vital. I've learned to trust the feelings I get. More often than not they turn out to be right.' Intuition relies on a series of subtle signals. How in touch are you with what 'nags'?

Reconciling instincts and intuition to memory

People who fail to use their fast survival reactions tend to get Darwin awards and leave this mortal coil early. Those of us that do employ our instincts to survive a crisis may not reflect or reconcile our experiences accurately.

In the moment, an instinct has a sense all of its own, which subsequently can be difficult to articulate in a form that other people will understand. Different people reacting to the same event may recall different experiences and stories. Sometimes logic is retrofitted so that we can explain and frame the experience in a way that works for us and other people.

in the moment an instinct has a sense all of its own

You and I might take different instinctive courses of action in the same circumstances and yet we both might succeed. Unlike linear logical issues, ambiguous situations often permit alternatives to be right at the same time.

Counter-intuitive

Dealing with ambiguity is about balancing multiple issues and impulses at the same time. The difficulty is about knowing what to pay attention to and what to reject. Notice the possibility that your mind may offer up a 'go signal' AND a 'do not go' signal at the same time.

Instincts and intuitions are not foolproof and can fail just as badly as when logic fails. As I write this, many unfortunate souls today perished on a bridge in Cambodia at a festival of light because of a panic reaction to 'leave'. Each individual survival reaction in isolation may have been correct but the unintended consequence of mass panic crushed 350 people.

Occasionally a counter-intuitive course of action – doing the opposite of what your intuition tells you – is actually exactly the right way to proceed and can be advantageous. Sometimes the countervailing impulse will be an imperative of self-restraint, i.e. NOT to act, despite other compelling desires. Intuition is a visceral sense that we 'know the right thing to do'. Balancing multiple feelings is not easy. Fighting our deeper desires and going against instinct takes great courage and strength of mind. There are no guarantees.

Where does your intuition live?

Quick answer: not always in your head. If you wish to access your intuition more often, what might you do? First, you need to be aware of the presence of your own internal signals, where in your body feelings first manifest themselves and how they build up, often as quite subtle but uncomfortable feelings.

Locations and degree of impact may differ for your instinct or your intuition. For example, on those occasions where you experienced an instinct or an intuition:

- did you feel slightly sick or giddy?
- perhaps you felt something within your throat or neck?
- was there a twist in your stomach?
- did the hairs on the back of your hands, neck or arms stand erect?
- did you engage in an odd ritual?

Identifying where, how and when your body tries to get your conscious attention is really important if you want to access these signals.

Getting in touch

In order to engage instinct and intuition, you have to be bodily, holistically aware of yourself and what you are in 'touch' with. Sometimes a hectic life whitewashes out the finer details of experiences that deserve your attention. Your experiences will differ when you are totally 'still' and relaxed enough to sense what is actually happening.

An activity that sits well with several religions and is non-religious in nature is silent meditation.[29] For many people quiet meditation is difficult to accomplish, so as a precursor I would strongly recommend yoga as a way of gradually locating inner calm. Both benefit body and mind, particularly if your body is no longer willing or able to exercise vigorously.

As an amusing reminder for the need to find inner calm, you might find this useful:

> If you don't like being in a quiet room all on your own, you're in the wrong company!

It is worth accepting that living **with** your own feelings is not necessarily always a comfortable experience, nor should it be. Life is a wave of ups and downs. Meditation can allow you to leave the wave for a while.

Nagging niggles

If you want to increase your intuitive ability, you need to develop your sensitivity towards the feelings it arouses. In the north of England we call the feeling I'm trying to describe as a 'niggle'. 'What's niggling you then?' a friend may ask when they can see you've got something small or undefined on your mind.

With intuition, these are feelings that simmer as opposed to boil. There may be a nagging feeling going on in your head, a sense of irritation and unmet expectation or a feeling that something is not quite right. A niggle is a minor but lasting annoyance, a feeling that one's sense of the world is incomplete, unrequited or as yet unfulfilled. All of these intuitions hinge on what might otherwise look like an inconsequential detail and subtle feelings. There is often a current of underlying awkwardness.

The feeling and the obligation to follow it through are slightly obsessive. If you want to master uncertainty, don't drop the niggle! It's working hard subconsciously for you!

Don't drop the niggle!

A niggle or any enduring awkwardness is a clue to be heeded if you want to access your intuition. If you want to keep an intuition alive and benefit from its fruition you need to learn to tolerate the discomfort of the open, unmet need an intuition brings with it. These feelings crystallise as intuition when you believe you have an answer or a course of action and do not yet know why. You just 'know'. When you get the answer the emotional payback is a great big 'AHA! moment'.

Unfortunately, just how an intuitive person arrives at 'an answer' or a clue is not accessible to linear logic. Intuition is by nature slightly mad because by definition we seek as yet unframed answers compiled from fragments beyond the usual boundaries of perception, beyond logic. Keep the niggle!

Have faith in that awkward feeling

Encouraging the use of intuition requires a general act of faith. Staying open takes energy. A tension is set up because an important question remains unanswered. It is important not to let go of these feelings.

intuition requires a general act of faith

Deciding with feeling

For many people, using intuition is not a natural exercise. Intuition feels awkward. Well, that's how it should feel! The important thing to remember is the awkward feeling does not suggest you are doing something wrong.

One way to engage the faculties of intuition and instinct is to decide to allow them in as part of your decision process and to feel and acknowledge the experience of them, when an appropriate opportunity arises. Experiment. Try writing a note to yourself with an intuitive or instinctive decision early on in a process AND as you write your note jot down the feelings you had. Is there a way to amplify the feelings you detected? See if your later decision or observation changes. After several dry-run experiments, try something relatively safe. Remember you are changing your behaviour. You AND other people may feel initially uncomfortable. Try to learn as you go from both good and less beneficial outcomes. Nothing of value or character is achieved without some difficulty and hardship. All outcomes, whether pleasing or difficult, provide lessons.

Acknowledging instincts and intuition

Upgrading your ability is going to be a bit like learning to ride a bike! A guiding hand on a safe road is a good place to start. You won't learn to be proficient until you've scuffed your knees a few times and found your own balance; therefore, do not be too ambitious and accept that time and experience will improve your ability.

The key to developing a skill with intuition is to experience many things and to develop a virtuous habit of paying attention to what your feelings tell you. Remember the signals may be subtle, faint or uncomfortable. Sooner or later when your job gets tougher, a bet has to be placed under time pressure and will most likely be based on incomplete information. Give it your 'best shot' using what you do know and adding your best intuitive guess as to the right decision. That is all even the best of us will do.

Fallible logic

Review your rational outcomes alongside your first intuitive insights in order to help you sustain your intuition. Ideally, you need sufficient positive feedback to motivate further use. Get your rational decision process into perspective first. Is it as good as you think it is? Make an honest assessment of how often you believe your logical decisions turned out exactly as you expected. Then validate your findings with people affected by your decisions. When you review your prior logical decisions you may find success was perhaps not so universally successful as you previously believed.

In uncertain situations, you may need to redefine good and bad. Remember that ambiguous questions often involve multiple, often **partial** outcomes, some of which will be in your favour whilst others will not. What you need to seek out is is the **beneficial balance** as opposed to a pure outcome. If you can beat the odds used in flipping a coin then your intuition and instincts will have paid off. There is no requirement to be 100 percent right.

Resistances

Perfection barrier

Perfection can get in the way of listening to intuitive and instinctive impulses. If you firmly believe it is important to 'be perfect' all the time then you aren't cutting yourself enough slack to cope in an ambiguous world. Here, few, if any, outcomes are absolute so put the perfection stick down and stop beating your self up with it! In an ambiguous situation the trick is to get things mostly right at the time, and then fairly quickly, move on. Indulgence rarely improves an ambiguity. Your personal positive benefit of managing an ambiguity is that you get to decide quickly at a time when speed is of the essence.

indulgence rarely improves an ambiguity

Getting it 'right'

Consider how you frame an unsuccessful outcome. Is error perceived as a 'disaster' or another opportunity to learn something you didn't know before? The way you regard error or 'failure' will influence your ability to perform in uncertain or ambiguous conditions. Comfort with and tolerance of uncertainties and ambiguity are a matter of familiarity. The more you get used to dealing with alternatives and multiple options AND the intuitive or instinctive feelings that go with them, the easier it gets to see and experience their imperfect outcomes.

Social resistance to intuition and instinct

Even though there is general agreement that instincts are necessary for survival, the ability to employ instinct and intuition is not so well articulated nor widely recognised by the population at large as a valid management skill. The greater emphasis in business education is often placed on logic. However, a complex world demands both rational AND non-rational skills. Regrettably, our exam-passing education system, followed by task-focused career progression lead many people to assume that:

- logic, scientific deduction and reason rule supreme
- having all the facts and as much authority as possible allow control and efficiency so that the best job of work can be delivered and the highest profits realised.

The 'efficient logic' philosophy only applies to simple realities. These beliefs become a severe limitation when complexity increases. Additional above ceiling 'AND' style thinking along with the best that logic has to offer, as well as access to other skills such as instinct and intuition, are required to create the next raft of high-value products and services.

Caution required

Until perceptions about intuition become more widely accepted it is wiser to be discreet about your real decision process when dealing with highly uncertain or ambiguous decisions.

Intuition – summary

We should not live by reason alone, nor should we rely entirely on instinct or intuition. We need to employ both. They are essential above-ceiling skills. When times are uncertain, complete data sets or precedents are rarely available. If a decision is forced then it will be a matter of placing a bet or a 'judgement call'. In these conditions, any extra subtle input that may give you an edge becomes valuable. Ambiguities often permit multiple outcomes that can be partially right AND partially wrong at the same time. Detecting the subtle balance point requires the use of some rational AND non-rational senses. Like many outcomes in life, you as a person are neither 'fixed' nor absolute. You can learn and adapt as you evolve.

Reflection

- Identify examples of when you made a major decision 'on the fly'.
- What feelings did you sense within yourself prior to such a decision?
- Where do you feel your 'niggle'; is it alive or did you kill it off?
- Who or what do you still have faith in?
- How will you learn to trust yourself (and others) during uncertainty?
- How will you cope better with the idea of error?

Chapter 7
Beliefs and values

Your sense of identity, your essential 'being' is underpinned by your deeper beliefs, values and experiences. Your deeper values that form your foundations on which your sense of personal identity and meaning rest are very important to you. They are hard-wired to powerful emotions. If someone steps on one of your values, you are likely to feel incensed. Conversely, if they support your value you may feel affirmed. Your sense of meaning, purpose and personal identity are an important component of your resilience.

This aspect is covered within three sections:

Section 1: Valuable values

Section 2: The darker side of values

Section 3: Working philosophy

The penultimate chapter of the book is entitled 'Business philosophy'. It encompasses not only fundamental beliefs but also how they are exercised through the application of shared values. I placed this particular chapter at the end of the book, in the section dealing with the widest context because the outward behaviours of many people are involved as part of a deliberate strategy to create a sense of meaning and a shared/collective focus of attention.

Chapter 7 Section 1

Valuable values

The moment is replete with uncertainty. My four-year-old daughter is giving me hell. She wants the sweets. She is trying every trick in the book to get me to buy them. 'No dear, I don't have enough money' failed last time. She immediately exhorted me to, 'Just go to the hole in the wall and get some more money then!' She doesn't **need** the sweets but she **wants** them anyway. When she sets her mind on something she wants, she will manipulate and negotiate the back leg off a donkey! The real challenge is not just about these particular toffees. If I lose this tussle, a precedent will be set and I'll probably keep on giving in, so we set a trend where she eventually becomes unable to control her impulses and appetites. How do I get her to make her own mind up in a better way?

How do any of us make our minds up when it gets messy, complicated and confusing? Dilemmas can emerge from some of our smallest, 'considerate' decisions. I've got a couple of people in my project team who are just as narrowly obsessed. Perhaps we need to agree some guidelines that we can all live with. Dealing with a particular difficulty then is no longer about my decision; instead it becomes our decision, based on our guidelines.

Ground rules

How do any of us make wise decisions when faced with so many choices? You could set up some common sense rules for yourself and try to stick to them. If you get that far, the next hurdle is reconciling your rules with other people's self-imposed rules and protocols. As a starting point, organising people around 'rules' is not such a bad first idea, but this strategy quickly bumps up against more problems.

the problem with rules is that they tend to grow in number

The problem with rules is that they tend to grow in number, in layers and complexity simply because real life is so full of exceptions, 'grey edges' and ambiguous situations. Rules are poor performers at the grey margins. After a while people, become deluged and immobilised by rules. In the UK the guidelines to teachers taking children on a school trip runs to 150 pages.[30] In 2011 the government attempted to reduce it to eight pages using 'common sense'. Rule clean-ups don't get done too often, so the burden imposed by a surplus of rules gets progressively worse until a crisis forces a major overhaul.

Values

Sound values, general principles and acknowledged virtues can provide a more sustainable stronger basis for reasoning and behaviour. As yardsticks, values work at the individual level, and at the team and organisational levels too. Sorting out just which set of principles or values to follow, however, can be problematic at a personal level and even more so when many people are involved. As I have suggested earlier, finding and defining your personal truths is paramount.

Humankind has struggled with this complexity for millennia and has gone to war over who has 'a particular god or righteousness' on their side. Some companies get the values and vision thing right, along with lots of other important factors, and outperform as a consequence of higher resilience and better communication, so the investment is worth a try.

Locating group values

If you haven't got a meaningful vision or sense of collective purpose, then go back to the original basic questions about why you exist at all AND start to explore or create your options. Good values will deselect certain choices. Get your front-line people and customers to figure out when and why you need values and then negotiate for all round added-value in terms of simplicity of expression AND validity of meaning. Sometimes the job is done for you. Great values are occasionally handed down by someone wise.

Well-produced values can help guide right behaviours, good commitment, fair leadership and, most importantly, better decisions right across a business. This creates positive attitude. Well-thought-through values and beliefs can contribute to the 'tone' of the workplace. These benefits can be had at home too, if you agree as a family to adopt a particular set of values.

One way to figure out what might work for you is to use an artist's trick of looking obliquely at both negative and positive spaces. Ask what looks and feels right and define who is doing a dreadful job. Then consider, 'What do we need to do for the best and what do we need to avoid?'

Robotic clones

Let's look first at what might be missing through the lens of a negative example. At the beginning of 2009, just after the North Atlantic banking crash, I spent a few months studying vision and values statements posted onto websites by large financial and other companies. I located both good and bad examples of what companies declared they valued and the extent to which this harmonised or contradicted with other things they said or seemed to be doing.

One of the worst examples of an organisation's portrayal of what they claimed to value showed up in a cartoon animation on a graduate recruitment site at a major British bank. It showed a batch of robotic, grey-suited, briefcase-holding human clones being chuffed out in clouds of steam from a large machine onto a conveyer belt. This raised, in my mind, questions about their focus of attention, frames of reference, values and beliefs, capabilities in terms of controls, emotional sensitivities and therefore the character and resilience of the institution concerned.

Who was watching their shop window to the world?

Who in the bank's senior management was watching their shop window to the world? Who allowed this to happen AND to persist? This particular bank failed and was absorbed by another major bank. Despite this, the new management failed to notice the offending robot cartoons and the graphics remained in place for many months. Again, we need to ask, 'Who was watching the shop window they acquired and where was the employee imperative and empowerment to act?'

Success and values

Remember the added benefit of working with agreed values is the added resilience of an emotional credit reservoir of commitment, loyalty and cohesion that you can call upon during challenging and uncertain times. In general, I have noticed that the companies that did a good consistent job of expressing their values with clarity and honesty seemed to correlate with sustained profitable performance. Successful companies were genuinely in touch. They walked their talk too. The dilemma for an organisation is one of how to provide what can otherwise be a faceless institution with a 'human' character of both reason AND heartfelt meaning.

Parts of the added benefits of values are non-rational. Values and vision are worthwhile when they honestly connect with the right places in people's hearts AND minds of employees, customers and the whole web of suppliers. For example, one global French bank espoused the idea of a commitment to stay at the front in terms of innovative ideas and backed promising young artists, as well as entrepreneurs. Their website was lively, imaginative and displayed a consistent track record for style and élan validated by tangible evidence. They affirmed their beliefs in the form of multiple awards over many years. They made good money AND were clearly **not** just about the money. Profits were a consequence of several levels of committed behaviour as opposed to a simplistic mechanical goal.

The positive side of values

A sense of fulfilment is rarely just a matter of money. Work can be enjoyable because it can fulfil important human needs including the opportunity to grow and develop, to be included and to have a genuine sense of purpose, and to be involved in praiseworthy endeavours. Pride counts.

There are upsides to an investment in upholding values:

- An organisation that consistently upholds shared beliefs through good AND bad times is likely to build employee resilience.
- If these values are evidenced and maintained through senior management behaviours, such an organisation improves long-term prospects for outperforming less well-integrated companies.
- The acid test comes when times get tough and genuine values are upheld. The contrast between the labour relations at Virgin Atlantic and British Airways, for example, has for some years been noteworthy. One seems to have fostered a huge reservoir of social credit with their employees, whilst the other, as evidenced by industrial unrest, has not.
- Where minimal groups stay integrated and loyal, the company stands a far higher chance of survival during uncertain times simply because everyone pulls together for common interests.

Leaders AND teams for uncertain times

Nature is volatile, uncertain AND loves biological variation. Economies (and some companies) that are **not** complex often end up being run by the most effective, and often the most ruthless, dictator. Paradoxically, building resilience may involve allowing things to become more complicated and more uncertain. With increasing uncertainty, the potential for dilemma, ambiguity, opportunity AND risk increase. Enter new leaders and new team players for uncertain times.

Higher order individuals, Titans of men and women, build not just a strategy of things and processes but also develop people, character and sufficient resilience to withstand the inevitability of uncertain times. Finding ways to knit together basic human instincts to strongly bond within minimal groups strengthens collective long-term prospects. Preparation to withstand the inevitable crisis also involves building up the way individuals and teams think and react to uncertainty, ambiguity and dilemma. Underpinning their actions are clear values and beliefs.

Chapter 7 Section 2

The darker side of values

As the demand for 'service' accelerates, some organisations will progressively develop more Orwellian interests and demand your total commitment. Your individual beliefs will soon be of corporate and organisational interest. The next big challenge to leaders and staff will involve their beliefs, because what you fundamentally believe shapes important social and financially valuable authentic team behaviours and ultimately profitability. Attitude, mindset and individual philosophy will come under increasing scrutiny.

Intrusion or inclusion

As far as customers are concerned, the very first level, often 'low-cost' front-line employee **is the business.** Getting this primary interaction with customers right is vital in those businesses that need to score highly on customer care.

If the attitude or mindset of just some front line employees is wrong, then the whole business reputation and performance becomes uncertain. Individual beliefs will therefore be increasingly of corporate and organisational concern.

Unintelligent attempts to gain compliance through pressure or fear can lead to reprisal, involving withdrawal of discretionary effort, and at the extreme, sabotage behaviour.

right behaviours and right decisions have to be visibly modelled to high standards

Costly uncertainty and employee-led disruption are predictable when there are regular major inconsistencies in terms of what an organisation asks for and offers in return. Genuine high-quality employee engagement and the contribution of discretionary extra effort will only emerge in the right conditions. These would include a harmony of the beliefs of the organisation and the beliefs of individuals from the very top to the bottom.

Doing the right thing

In the USA in late 1982, someone laced the leading pain relief product Tylenol® with deadly poison. Tylenol® had a 37 percent market share and was marketed by McNeil, a division of Johnson and Johnson. Several people in the USA lost their lives as a consequence of taking the tampered product. Johnson and Johnson's quick response, urgent product recalls and product redevelopment and replacement cost hundreds of millions of dollars but because the executive leadership focused on doing the right thing and putting customers absolutely first and foremost, no more lives were lost.

Sales of Tylenol®* did crash and at the time some believed the brand would never recover; however, it is noteworthy that it took the company just a few years to regain their brand leadership position and market share of this highly profitable brand. Johnson and Johnson's executive leadership also gained widespread applause from customers and the business community. Trust was established and confirmed. Their exemplary leadership behaviour became a representative case study of how to 'do the right thing'. Regrettably, the criminal case remains unsolved.

Several long-established companies, including Johnson and Johnson, operate according to explicit principles and declare that they aim to 'do the right thing'. The Johnson and Johnson Credo,[31] for example, pre-dates the Tylenol® scares. It is a worthy document.

Words only have power when people genuinely believe and then follow through their beliefs **in the spirit** of the original meaning. In the light of the Johnson and Johnson decisions to 'do the right thing' 30 years ago, how would you view the more recent behaviours at McNeil,[32] (a pharmaceutical division of Johnson and Johnson), involving a 'phantom product recall' of a medication? Look up phantom recall and Oregon Sues JandJ on the web.[33,34]

How would you expect the curious behaviour of one major division to affect the reputation of other distinct Johnson and Johnson business units on a global basis? Would the whole company lose out on their reputation? Perhaps. In one year alone, some estimates put the cost of this most unusual recall at hundreds of millions of dollars in lost sales. But do lost sales in the short term really go to the heart of the issue? Possibly, a better line of enquiry is why the very top leadership at Johnson and Johnson didn't take the same level of control of this recall as they had done so clearly and deliberately in the 1980s. Alternatively, was everyone at Johnson and Johnson's McNeil business dumbstruck and impotent to step up and ask the right questions before they stepped onto a slippery slope? The right to a Credo challenge about a 'phantom recall' seems to me to have failed here.

In all fairness, no lives were ever at stake, but some may argue that an important principle was.

---

* Tylenol® is a registered trademark ultimately owned by Johnson and Johnson, New Brunswick, USA

Scale and values

Perhaps, given its huge size and very deep pockets, Johnson and Johnson will ride out this and a variety of other challenges, and possibly most customers will forget or forgive. So is scale a values issue? An interesting question is, 'Can **any** really large organisation employing hundreds of thousands of diverse employees really maintain and hold true to a set of values?'

Can any really large organisation really maintain and hold true to a set of values?

If you are part of a vast organisation, eventually someone will break generally accepted rules in pursuit of a material or personal gain, and behave badly. If the problem occurs low down in a large organisation it is bad enough, but it can often be patched and managed. The higher up the rot though, the greater the damage. Employees, customers and society at large tend to trust people in responsible positions based on what we witness them do on principle and in practice. If the failure to adhere to shared values is systemic or if there is a fundamental failure at the very top to 'do the right thing' for the long term, then decline is inevitable. In both cases the operating philosophy of the whole AND any established brand promise will have been undermined.

In the 1980s, Johnson and Johnson showed how damage could be repaired if the challenge was seen by staff and customers to have originated outside the covenant between customer and supplier. When covenants with employees and customers are broken, what next in a globally wired world? Indeed as this text is being redrafted one of the planets' biggest circulation newspapers, the 168-year-old 'News of the World' was summarily closed because of widespread public disgust following a scandal involving the illegal phone hacking of a murdered schoolgirl and others.

not doing the right thing costs and then costs even more in the long term

Not doing the right thing costs and then costs even more in the long term. Billions can be lost and reputations tarnished. It is better to live up to your values and to take tough costly decisions on the chin, than to create a rolling debacle of customer suspicion and gradual erosion of reputation. Deeply held organisational values and virtues recognised by employees and customers have an extremely high commercial and loyalty value. They take decades to build yet are the most ethereal of assets that can be negated in minutes. Leaders need to be vigilant.

Bad apple management

Every once in a while the original deep-seated values that your organisation fought so hard to establish need to be revisited to ensure the beliefs and behaviours remain valid AND to prevent or flush out wrong behaviour. This is best done when you are individually and collectively 'in credit' and before it is too late.

Felps, Mitchell and Byington published a paper in 2006 entitled, 'How, when, and why bad apples spoil the barrel'.[35-37] One particular study they cite proposes that we humans need **five positive experiences** to outweigh the influence of one bad experience. The authors also note that an organisation's success depends on **all** players fulfilling their roles. Whilst one employee cannot direct the outcome of the whole, he or she can disrupt or confound the efficient working of the whole by subversive, sometimes contagious, 'bad apple' behaviour. Negative individual behaviour is potentially infectious and undermines whole team behaviours. Getting attitudes and behaviours right and screening out bad apples is important at all levels, but especially so at the very top.

Walking the talk

My observation is that, when it comes to good intentions, people adapt their behaviour in response to what is actually done more than what is said. Top people set the tone by action more than by words. Therefore right behaviours and right decisions have to be visibly modelled to high standards from the very top AND witnessed as consistent daily practice. This is especially true when the work becomes complicated, challenging or uncertain.

Not walking the talk

Construction company X was a business that had annual revenues of more than a billion dollars a year. They invested several million dollars with a top-class, best-selling author and enthusiastic advocate of empowerment to motivate a company-wide empowerment programme. Managers were told to, 'Take the initiative!'

A matter of weeks after the programme concluded, one enthusiastic junior manager adopted a low-cost, high-return initiative but was promptly fired by a 'job's-worth' middle manager for overstepping a defined authority to act. In less than a day the company grapevine completely unzipped almost all of the staff goodwill of the empowerment programme. Almost all discretionary effort was withdrawn. Senior management seemingly had little or no credit in the hearts and minds of many of their middle managers. A few years later company

X was broken up and sold off in parts. When profit margins are very thin, fear and overwork tend to increase. Simplistic, logical but quite mean behaviour can then replace imagination. Hard cold reason often sees no place for sentiment or anything intangible or 'fluffy' such as values.

Cold reason vs warm hearts

In highly uncertain situations, collaboration between individuals and teams can be difficult to sustain. Several contradictions need to be engaged, one being the need to reconcile harmony AND necessary creative conflict. One particular conflict involves the reconciliation of task-minded individuals who focus intensely on cold reason and getting 'results' with people who have more concern for other people and their feelings. Both types of people are needed.

Aligned mostly towards warm issues

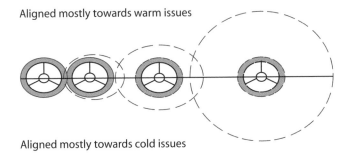

Aligned mostly towards cold issues

Any sense of harmony would not be the absence of tension but one of balanced tensions. Often the mission to 'survive' takes precedence and 'cold people' prevail. A brief increase in efficiency follows involving the dismissal of people who 'no longer fit'. In a world of finite physical resources, my fear is that ruthless machine-minds will prevail. History provides ample evidence of despots reducing people to objects.

The only way to prevent this is to make sure that purely machine-minded individuals never hold absolute power. Unfortunately, being more ruthless they **do** tend to get power. The ancient Greeks had the right idea. Power should **not** go to those who crave it. History shows us that absolute power corrupts absolutely. Given that ruthless people often do prevail, it is wise to ensure real power is divided across several counter-balanced institutions.

Summary

Values, like good intentions, can be difficult to sustain. As situations become increasingly complex, ensuring that different types of people can engage open and honest challenge and dialogue is essential. The ability to reconcile differences constructively requires experience, confidence, resources and creative conflict skills.

Reflection

- What do you and your colleagues use as agreed guidelines when things get 'foggy, ambiguous, demanding and uncertain'?
- Have you made your values explicit?
- Do your values often get used positively in conversation?
- Does most of the organisation know what the values and vision words are actually there for?
- Is there independent supporting evidence that words translate into action?

Chapter 7 Section 3

Working philosophy

This is an outer layer of your belief system where you've turned particularly memorable experiences into your personal principles or virtues for getting things done your way. Because the process of developing a personal working philosophy has to be derived from your experience, I should not write too much here. Remember that 'rules' can unintentionally lock you down and leave you inflexible. Therefore choose concepts that will help AND remain sufficiently flexible to respond in proportion, and in a good way, to what life presents you with.

With awareness and reflection you can begin to create an adaptable set of principles or virtues that help you lead a 'good' life. Make your list explicit, as did Benjamin Franklin.

His list of 13 virtues was kept in a diary and he monitored how well he lived up to each one. In brief, these were: temperance, silence, order, resolution, frugality, industry, sincerity, justice, moderation, cleanliness, tranquillity, chastity and humility. Each word is expanded upon in his notes.[38] Your working philosophies can form a useful part of your adaptive learning.

Four examples of my working philosophies are: the 'truth' can be a variable; 'find your own truth'; 'anything done in a hurry is likely to turn out flawed' and 'win before you begin'. The first two I've covered extensively so far, the third is self-explanatory. The fourth example is a philosophy that guides my behaviour. This is what it means to me:

Win before you begin

One of the best ways to begin to deal with highly complex ambiguous or uncertain issues is **not** to jump straight in to say or do something but instead to first appreciate the sort of issues you face.

Ask yourself, 'Why should I even consider or engage this? Is this solvable? Is it likely to have single or multiple outcomes?' Then consider various possible outcomes of different actions. 'Are the outcomes resulting from a "solution" likely to be better or worse than the current problem? How long am I likely to be involved with this? Where is the exit point?'

'Win before you begin' prompts me to think and enquire **before** I act so that subsequent actions have more impact. It also reminds me to reflect on what constitutes 'winning'.

The bridge to wider contexts

Your working philosophy can become a daily part of your focus of attention and your motivations that influence your everyday behaviour.

If your working philosophies produce good results then other people may adopt and follow them too. A deeply shared collective sense of meaning can then be developed. Allegiance need not be dependent on individuals but can be aligned to a 'good' cause and a sense of 'worthy' purpose.

Summary

A working philosophy is something **you** locate and engage in order to judge and improve your life and the way you conduct yourself daily. I would encourage you to take a look at almost any source of inspiration including philosophy, fiction, autobiographies and religious texts to try to find useful guidelines for living, even if you choose not to buy into any particular system of belief or lifestyle. Then write down your beliefs as 'works in progress'!

Collectively, a sound philosophy is absolutely critical to leadership, developing innovation and for creating strategic purpose and intent. Good values, principles and philosophies form an essential part of the guidelines that help with creative conflict and the productive forward movement in the reconciliation of useful differences. Commercial examples are provided in Chapter 13.

Part B: Your outer experience

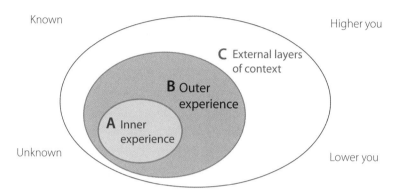

This is a relatively short section that deals with the bridge between your inner and outer experience of yourself. This is an important place to dispassionately observe how experiences in A, B and C play out.

If you have achieved a raised level of self AND context awareness you may be able to watch AND engage with the whole story of you, in real time. This sounds like a contradiction, particularly if the way you are engaged is emotional, however it is still possible to maintain two states of mind at the same time. When I see, I can at the same time experience touch and smell. When feelings are engaged I can remain thoughtful, reflective and aware, unless of course I am blinded by rage or primal instincts.

Chapter 8 is divided into four sections:

Section 1: Your focus of attention and sense of meaning

Section 2: The importance of character

Section 3: Personal resilience

Section 4: Rewards on a personal, social and moral basis

Chapter 8
Bridging meanings and actions

Each of these will influence your behaviour and the successes and failures that you experience. Your experiences then feedback to your frame of reference. Other people may judge you and your behaviours and then decide on the extent to which they will or will not support or collaborate with you. In an uncertain world, your ability to work with others is vital.

Section 1

Your focus of attention and sense of meaning

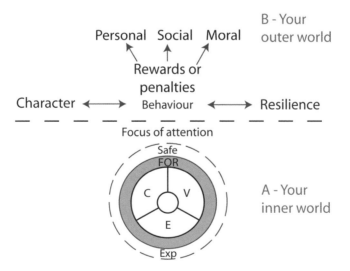

Your focus of attention is the bridge between your inner and outer worlds. The way you behave stems from your focus of attention which is rewarded and motivated by something that has valued meaning. The extent to which you are successful in varied conditions and the way you deal with failure creates character and resilience to future difficulties.

You pay attention to what you believe you need or want the most. Your focus of attention is driven either consciously or unconsciously, by reason or by feeling. Your behaviour is shaped by your immediate sense of 'meaning' that in turn is shaped by a variety of rewards, constraints, and negative factors. Your individual goal achievements and trade-offs (that you are aware of) are reaffirmed by evidence that feeds into your frame of reference for future use.

Your focus of attention is the bridge between thinking, deciding and acting on what you believe you need to do. What you 'do' most often can shape who you are. It is worth thinking about doing and having as these are elements of 'attachment'.[39] In other words, when you are denied something you are deeply attached to your world will be rocked. You will become uncertain and emotionally engaged. Learning how to manage or relinquish your attachments is an important step to enlightenment.[40]

Doing

'Doing' what you expect, hope or wish to do informs your inner sense of meaning, purpose and identity. When people meet you for the first time, one of their early questions is often, 'What do you do?' Your answer allows other people to position their sense of who you are relative to others they know. It is more polite than asking how much money you have or earn! How attached are you to what you 'do'?

Having

A feeling of 'having' what you expect, hope or wish to have can also inform your sense of meaning, purpose and identity, particularly in a materialistic setting. 'Doing' can be mentally much more active than passive 'having', particularly if novelty or pleasure is involved. The pleasure of 'having' can fade after a relatively short burst of pleasure. 'Doing' (what is important) AND 'having' (what is important) can contribute in different ways to our sense of meaning. 'Having' something symbolic that confers a meaning such as 'freedom, belonging, status or security can create a sustained level of attachment. For example, having the explicit approval or recognition of others is most important to many people. Understanding these differences has relevance in brand development, consumer acceptance and learning situations.

Being

A sense of 'being' is by far the deepest sensation of who you are. 'Being' is deeper than any sense of meaning created by 'doing' or 'having' and is much more difficult to access or modify. For most of us, our focus of attention rarely goes that deep. Instead, most of the time, our focus of attention faces outwards towards meeting perceived immediate wants and needs.

Your focus of attention is constantly modified or reaffirmed. Your **perceived** track record informs your frame of reference about your personal capability and sense of who you are relative to what you and others expect.

There are two occasions when our sense of 'being' is thrust to the fore. One involves a life crisis, the other, pure harmony with all that we are and do. When we face the deepest uncertainty of a major life crisis, our sense of who we are can be seriously questioned. 'Doing' and 'having' can lose their 'meaning' or may conflict with our deeper sense of '**being**'. A life crisis at this far deeper level of uncertainty can be particularly difficult for self-reliant individuals. Consider who might need coaching on how to deal more effectively with uncertainty with a view to preventing them from burning out.

In direct contrast, when someone feels very well aligned in all elements of who they are, what they truly need and are capable of, then their whole being moves in unison and harmony with their goal AND the wider contexts. They 'fit' perfectly and perform elegantly, smoothly and almost effortlessly. Golfers, athletes, artists and actors call it 'being in the zone'. Performance soars. These are two sides of the same coin.

Without a clear focus of attention and a sense of meaning the intention to act lies dormant. Leadership involves not only an individual's arousal to act but also his or her influence over other people's focus of attention. A good leader will be capable of creating meaning for others even during uncertain times.

Personal, social and moral rewards and penalties
Your focus of attention, whether vague or clearly directed, whether conscious or not, eventually results in some sort of behaviour. At some level you will pay conscious or unconscious attention to feedback that supports your frame of reference and therefore your various perceptions. Remember, each person sees the world through a very different lens. We are all selective in what we choose to see and experience. What actually rewards you? Will this be the same in ten or twenty years time? Do you seek rewards at all three levels and if not, why not? Constructive personal, social or moral activities that bolster you will build resilience.

Miscreants
Negative activity, as far as your peer group are concerned, will undermine you in some way and leave you more exposed to future uncertainties. These don't

always appear logical; rewards often have a sense of their own. A gangster, for example, may do terrible things, but if these serve his interests and perhaps those of a few associates, he will feel rewarded from **his** point of perception. A military commander or a businessman may exercise questionable enthusiasm that enormously benefits a few but hurts many more. Again, they will feel justified **from their perspective**, as long as they are not penalised in respect of something that i**s highly significant** to them. If there is a neutral response (they get away with it) or best of all, if they can find a way to be rewarded in a manner that fits their perceptions they will repeat their patterns.

The same principles apply on a wider scale. Where enormous wealth and power are concentrated in the hands of just one or a few people, the last line of sanction is that of a moral compass in the individual and failing that the risk of widespread public vilification that undermines not only the individual, but importantly, takes away something important to them. This sort of sanction should impact the institutions involved AND also have a wider, ripple effect on other players.

For example, fining or suing a large corporation several hundred million or even billions of dollars may not actually register as a personal penalty in the minds of those who are accountable, particularly if financial penalties are rolled into a regular cost of running a highly profitable business.

For some people the 'buck' passes them by and is handled by accountants, lawyers and media advisors. Since no shock to the system is experienced there is no change in perception or subsequent behaviour. Jail is perhaps the ultimate penalty, but there are other meaningful sanctions against organisations that do wrong. For example, one way would be to **fine every employee,** without exception, in proportion to their annual salary plus all benefits with an additional multiplier based on seniority so that those closest to real power feel the harshest penalties. If decisions are collective everyone should gain or feel the pain. This sort of risk should not be insurable.

Chapter 8 Section 2

The importance of character

During times of great uncertainty, the impulse to put personal interests ahead of group needs increases. Friends in need get left behind and true friends step up. When the ground beneath your feet is shifting reliable relationships become especially important.

Over time other people read the behaviours you exhibit as 'character' and will offer or deny support accordingly. The length of time may vary considerably. As character is conferred or assigned, it can also be removed. A badly behaved character can be 'cast out' or ostracised. Characters that you can count on, no matter what, will be increasingly valued.

Predictability, trust, accountability and reliability are important social glues that allow great works to be engaged. The west was built on, 'My word is my deed'. In an uncertain world, I believe that 'character' will again become a valuable reference point for individuals, companies and brands.

Assigned character

A quite subtle success factor is the 'character' that other people 'see' or have assigned to you; the 'brand of you'. Have you thought through the expression of your true character as opposed to the character other people ascribe to you? Are they the same or not? Think of the sudden contrasts of perception and relative sense of meaning and purpose in a young musician suddenly catapulted from poverty into the limelight. The scale of experience may be different but the pattern is the same. Is there alignment or dissonance?

The way you understand and reconcile yourself with other people's opinion about you can to some extent influence your fundamental orientation and your subsequent behaviour. For example, how would you conduct yourself and live your life if your feckless parent christened you at birth with the name of Winner or, alternatively Loser? One parent did just that to two of their boys.[41] Winner acquired a criminal record whilst Loser became a successful detective in the NYPD. A daughter in another not-so-smart family was named Temptress. She did have problems. The authors of 'Freakonomics' located a daughter from yet another family who had been named Marijuana Pepsi who did make something of her life, earning a master's degree in education.[42]

Building character and 'virtue'

Character has status value. The 'brand of you' is how other people 'know' you. Consistency is important, but just a few remarkable moments, whether good or bad, can define your character in the eyes of others. This affects the extent to which other people will offer or deny support and therefore affects resilience to uncertainty. Status matters.

In regard to your character or the virtues conferred on you, the messages you allow into your mind can influence your behaviour for better or worse. Choosing the people you will spend time with and the conversations you engage will influence your evolution.

hold your virtues in mind in the past tense

And I'm not thinking just about young adults. A leader of an organisation who believes his or her own press regarding how successful or innovative they **are** as opposed to **used to be**, is an example of dangerous thinking and isolation that can lead to hubris. (See the Marks & Spencer and Ratner examples in the next chapter.) It is safer to hold your virtues in mind in the past tense just to keep yourself alert to the possibility of slippage.

A collection of capability, emotions, beliefs and working philosophies contribute to your behaviours that underpin what others experience as your character.

Character, rewards and penalties

To be positively and easily remembered as a deep habit of mind by many people as their most acceptable, first-choice character or brand is a commercial and political 'sweet spot'. That level of trust takes a long time to establish but is very quickly dashed. With a great deal of our economics tied up in 'brands' which themselves have a 'reliable character', the prospect of a 'brand strike' or a 'brand backlash' against perceived wrongdoers is increasingly likely in a web -enabled society. The trend already exists. Examples would include the 'New Coke' consumer backlash in 1985, and a European consumer backlash in June 1995 to Shell's plans for Brent Spar, and more recently in web-enabled people networks that include UK and US Uncut.

Summary

Building character AND resilience at several levels is important. Be careful what you believe about yourself. Character is earned or assigned. It can be shaped by what you do or do not do and by the way you evolve amongst your chosen peer group.

Reflection

- How are you dealing with the hand that others have dealt you?
- What could you do to change or adjust your own and other people's perceptions?
- Are you engaging the right sort of conversations with the right sort of people?
- Who or what could you change for the better?

Chapter 8 Section 3

Personal resilience

It is difficult, if not impossible, to develop a sustainable sense of resilience if you are not inwardly and outwardly 'aware' because without such awareness reflection and deeper adaptive learning are not possible. Personal resilience is increased once you have overcome the primary dilemma in the relationship between what you believe you need and the needs of others.

Personal resilience

At the core of a resilient strength will be some sort of underpinning, reason and a clear purpose driven by energy, determination, tenacity, a firm ego and substantial willpower. Resilience is not just about fitness and toughness but also includes access to important resources in the form of various supports and anchor beliefs. Someone who possesses such determination and clarity as to what they are aiming at can often act as a guiding light when others are floundering in darkness.

Like any good work-out habit, the more practice and varied learning experiences that are encountered by a healthy mind and body the better. Your learning events need to include both **good and bad** experiences if resilience is to be fully developed. These principles apply to groups too.

Bad experiences

The bad experience element really does count. Any senior executive will relate how major difficulties contributed to their eventual success pattern.

John Chambers,[43] Director of Applications at a major UK company, says, 'It is important that someone has failed at something important. Failure teaches a lot. If you have never failed at something then you are not pushing yourself hard enough. How you deal with it says a lot about you and helps you and others succeed in the future.'

It is important for you to embrace the concept of useful hardship and failure within your working philosophy if you have not done so already.

embrace the concept of useful hardship and failure

Resilience is not just a matter of resisting and surviving the tough difficult times but importantly resilience also includes a resistance to the sycophancy of success. Remaining human and in touch with everyday reality at the height of your material wealth and power can be just as difficult as staving off bankruptcy during difficult times. Spiritual, social and moral bankruptcy are far worse than the loss of material wealth. In the tale of the sword of Damocles, King Dionysus resisted the false notion of giving in to 'success'. He remained alert and sensitive **especially at the top of the game**.

resilience also includes a resistance to the sycophancy of success

In February 1997 the Deputy Chairman of Marks & Spencer presented a United Kingdom countrywide government-sponsored annual lecture on innovation.[44] He explained how innovative the company was particularly in its relationships with suppliers. One example highlighted how they had extended the season for raspberries. Not so long after the talk, Marks & Spencer's pattern of success seemed to evaporate. What had contributed to past success suddenly didn't seem to fit the market and the company experienced difficulties on several fronts. It took Marks & Spencer another decade to regain the traction they had lost in their home market.[45]

When drunk on success, foolish decisions are more likely. For example, Barclays sensibly walked away but the Royal Bank of Scotland pursued and acquired ABN Amro in 2007, at far too high a price AND at the wrong place in an economic cycle.[46] Resilience requires a consistent level of inner AND outer awareness coupled with optimism AND healthy cynicism.

Wider resilience
Resilience can be built into systems and processes too.

The characteristics that enable resilience are similar within individuals, groups, teams and organisations and include features such as trust, loyalty, faith, reliability, consistency, commitment, inclusion, sharing, steadfastness, adaptability, accountability, depth, resourcefulness and, of course, fitness and energy.

Overall strength is based on the support of more than one pillar of belief or asset. Another important feature of resilience is the integration of several different resources so that the sum of the parts working together is significantly stronger than any individual component. Resilience involves redundancy. When one support is not available, another seamlessly delivers the required support. A resilient person, group or system is therefore more effective than it is 'efficient'. In a sense, they are more expensive but perform better.

Tenacity

Not giving in. Sticking at what you are doing is perhaps the most obvious characteristic of resilience. Sometimes leaders speak of antidotes to fear using a few simple ideas. In talking to people who seem to win I hear phrases like, 'Push through and keep pushing'. Another really good example cited by Randy White, co-author of *Relax It's Only Uncertainty*, from a senior executive he works with was, 'I don't care if you fail, but I want you to fail forward and fail fast!' Therein lies another clue about confidence and success, namely a level of tenacity that borders on wilful stubbornness!

'I want you to fail forward and fail fast!'

Think about where a few adjustments in how you think and behave might make substantial differences to your performance. Reshaping your own thoughts and feelings when faced with chronic uncertainty to focus on what can be done, helps. Then push more than you normally would and see what happens. Very often quite large differences in performance are down to quite small differences between people and what they deliberately do.

In order to stay at something longer than seems reasonable requires not only willpower but also an inventive, adaptive mind to roll with the difficulties. This particular array of characteristics is important to anyone who wants to truly innovate. For example, it took James Dyson well over a decade of frustration, perseverance and over 5,000 prototypes to finally launch the Dyson DC01 vacuum cleaner under his own name.[47] 'One of the things I did when I was young was long distance running. I was quite good at it, not because I was physically good, but because I had more determination. I learned determination from it. A lot of people give up when the world seems to be against them, but that's the point when you should push a little harder … you just get through the pain barrier … Often, just around the corner is where the solution will happen.'

Enduring strengths and the need to yield

If you are largely self-reliant then it is important that your foundations are valid, reliable and secured. As a self-reliant person, if you lose your self-belief then your world will become very difficult until you have had time to heal or change. Adjustment at this level is only likely to be possible when some form of personal crisis or significant hardship exposes the foundations. At that point you will need to allow someone to help you if you wish to make progress.

Summary

Resilience is an outward expression of an inner state of mind in a healthy, fit body. It is an outcome of beliefs and behaviours. Resilience can be created and developed within you and, in organisations, within people, systems and processes.

Reflection

As the world becomes increasingly complex, consideration of resilience at all levels of ability will become paramount simply because the rate of challenge and dramatic change are unlikely to slow down.

Part C: The wider contexts

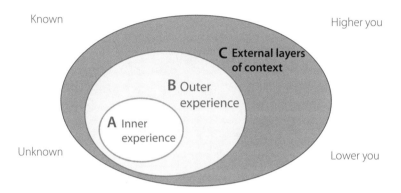

Beyond the immediate 'world of you' lies the far wider context of other people and situations over which you have significantly less influence. Here there is enormous day-to-day uncertainty even within 'organised systems'. The remainder of the book considers selected uncertainties.

Chapter 9: Uncertainty and resilient teams

Chapter 10: Leadership

Chapter 11: The uncertainty of innovation

Chapter 12: The ambiguity of strategy

Chapter 13: Business philosophy

Chapter 14: Legacy

There are many aspects to each subject and several books could be written on the ambiguities of each one. Therefore, I've chosen a selection of important uncertainties and where possible provided commercial examples and tools that may help you work your way through the ambiguity ceiling.

Chapter 9
Uncertainty and resilient teams

In relatively simple environments a hierarchy of command and control will suffice for most of the decision-making. When life gets really uncertain simple command and control systems reach a limit beyond which they cease to add value. As complexity or volatility increases, the pressure to change becomes significant.

Resilient interaction and the execution of decisions are fundamentally important to families, gangs, tribes, teams, networks and large conglomerates alike. How decision patterns are enacted and formalised during uncertain times determine resilience, performance and survival.

Work on building resilience during the easy times is a good investment. It's best to 'fix the roof when the sun shines', however we miss a trick if we fail to build resilience during the hardship experience of a crisis. Building resilience should be an ongoing job of work for you, your teams and your systems. The following chapters consider how teams' decisions-making structures can build resilience.

Section 1: Uncertainty, loyalty and minimal groups

Section 2: How teams can handle uncertainty

Section 3: Resilient organisation

Chapter 9 Section 1

Uncertainty, loyalty and minimal groups

A workplace presents a variety of uncertainties including the intentions, perceptions, priorities, loyalties and motivations of other people inside and outside of a team. Each of us has an aspect of our reality about which we can get quite prickly when we are uncertain. Teams of any size can grow prickly aspects of their character too.

The hedgehog dilemma

Schopenhauer's hedgehog dilemma[48] is an analogy about the challenges of relating fully to other people. A hedgehog's spines provide defence AND create a barrier to closeness. Schopenhauer's analogy implies that intimacy with another person is limited by the reality of spines, yours and theirs. The potential for hurting someone close to you is greater than is the case with people you do not know. Group problems are proportionately more difficult. Even if closeness is achieved within a group, it is difficult for injury to be avoided even with some form of synchronicity of movement.

uncertainty leads to cautious behaviours

The implication is that when 'spines' are a part of the ecology of any close relationship – in a team or family – intimacy is likely to involve discomfort and potentially mutual harm, despite good intentions. Consequently, this leads to cautious behaviours that by necessity combine self-interest and maintenance of distance from others in order to be able to demonstrate careful consideration. The inherent uncertainty produced by the presence of so many spines can result in weaker relationships than what is desired.

Resilience within groups therefore involves an acceptance that from time to time a relationship will hurt in some way. Collaborations are rarely pain free but benefit from the potential to create far more rewarding outcomes than mere cooperation. Despite the bleakness of Schopenhauer's analogy, neither hedgehogs nor porcupines seem to be at risk of extinction. They find a way to gain intimacy.

One of many resilient ways to deal with prickly, uncertain situations and people is to employ AND-type thinking. Remaining open to non-prescriptive outcomes can facilitate better leadership and good team contributions.

In contrast, if team members adopt a more rigid 'either/or' thinking pattern flexibility is substantially reduced. 'Management by objectives' doesn't work well in uncertain situations. Reduced choice can lead to a negative spiral where some people simply withdraw and become progressively more prickly. Room for manoeuvre diminishes in proportion to how defensive people become.

it is wise to be judicious about when and to whom you commit your energies

Employing 'AND' thinking generally involves a lot more energy plus imagination by all concerned. This level of emotional commitment is biologically expensive, so it is wise to be judicious about when and to whom you commit your energies. There is a limit to how much warmth an individual can or will share. Employing 'AND' thinking requires consistent collaboration, trust and faith **even though** you may get a little hurt along the way. Who or what do you trust?

Loyalty and cohesion

Many teams I have encountered are not real teams at all. More often than not these collections of people are better described as 'co-located groups'. They happen to share an office or a boss or a project but as for teamwork, no, that hasn't happened. If you want resilience, it pays to build genuine teamwork on several levels.

We are more likely to offer our energies and form the deepest bonds with those we feel strongest about. Our deepest commitments are generally invested with immediate blood relatives, then to current lovers and then to what I call a 'minimal group', where an emotional connection exists based upon fundamental experiences and shared beliefs.

A minimal group

I have several friends who served in the military in the ranks and as senior officers. Over the years, I have explored with them the way soldiers form teams and the way they are led. This, taken together with my experience of working inside companies that are going through a crisis, has helped me to witness a pattern of behaviour that I call the 'minimal group'. You've heard the expression 'brothers in arms', well, that would be a minimal group. These are exceptional, highly resilient interpersonal relationships that have an especially high value in times of great uncertainty.

minimal groups can begin to look, sound and feel like 'family'

A well-adjusted family group is where the self/other relationship is at a biological acme and where human commitment is at its highest. Love is the common thread. A minimal group comes in at a close second with extremely strong bonds between each member. Minimal groups can begin to look, sound and feel like 'family'.

Minimal groups are often formed socially outside of a formal management organisation system. Alternatively, some minimal groups can be the whole or part of a well-established team. For example, there may have been four founder members of a company who were joined later by three non-executives. The four think and behave as if they possess one common mind and one shared purpose. They are very quick and more powerful as a result. The three non-execs find it difficult to be included or to match the level of rapport enjoyed by the four.

A minimal group cannot be mandated. The conditions for its creation can, however, be fostered over time. Minimal groups need to create and maintain a history of evidence of reciprocal goodwill to confirm values and commitments. This allows teams to remain cohesive and cooperative, despite lay-offs, setbacks and huge uncertainties.

Acknowledged values and virtues, as well as stories and legends, are vital elements of the resilience pattern because they knit groups and individuals together within a shared identity. Consistency and adherence to agreed philosophies allow members to trust each other's commitment. Organisations can adopt the same patterns to gain an advantage, but the lead has to come from the very top.

A 'higher cause' or 'a calling' can also develop into a powerful, intimate, committed connection. Connections to other people who share the same passion for a particular idea, ideology or philosophy are then facilitated. The core affiliation, though, is with the central cause or concept. Strong bonding to a particular set of beliefs can build resilience through improved 'self-belief'.

A true sense of meaning

The mighty bonds and high resilience value of a minimal group show up best in a harsh crisis. A mother will lift a truck to save her child, a man will dare the odds to break through ice or swim a raging river to rescue his brother. True friends step up to help you when fair-weather friends melt away. Soldiers do not die for king and country but instead step up to help the men and women with whom deep visceral bonds of friendship AND purpose have been formed during harsh training or battle experiences. These relationships are replete with meaning that perhaps explains why life after being in the services, for some veterans, seems less engaging, less 'vital', once the intimacy of their former group has been lost. Most of us enjoy a sense of 'belonging'.

In the long-gone age of a 'job for life' people would 'belong' to an organisation. People would commit, work longer hours and put in some extra effort to pursue a better career and shared gain. Is it wise to commit so wholeheartedly with far fewer guarantees?

Organisations want the extra

Organisations want higher levels of energised deep commitment, **if** they can get it, because they get a whole host of benefits over, above and beyond normal service, often at no extra cost. The question during times of prolonged uncertainty is, 'On what basis will people commit to an organisation or an ideal when conditions are highly uncertain?'

GE had an interesting concept that worked for a while in volatile conditions – employability. All employees were highly trained and those that left or were let go remained highly desirable to other employers.

High commitment to a genuine team, organisation or a purpose is **never** free. It's earned, banked up over time. Resilience and higher levels of commitment can be developed gradually and are either galvanised or undermined during a crisis. Therefore don't waste the potential positive gains of a good crisis!

The power and danger of uncertain times

The problem with a crisis, though, is that when a working environment becomes highly uncertain, cohesive behaviour within ordinary teams breaks down. Committed connections that people imagine exist simply evaporate when redundancy or major change programmes are announced.

When the going gets really rough subgroups become self-interest, survival groups. Individuals are then more likely to place their personal and minimal group interests above those of the organisation. Gossip proliferates as uncertainty increases. Subgroups hunker down deeper into defensive silos. 'Hedgehog' behaviour proliferates. Working through a crisis requires confidence, energy, imagination and foresight AND solid relationships.

Resilience and a loyalty audit

In life we encounter all sorts of relationships. Friendships, loyalties and commitments can ebb and flow like the tides, yet our perception can sometimes be wrongly fixed at an earlier value. Any relationships below the primary level of intimate friends, a minimal group or immediate family can be suspect. Many of the relationships that we imagine we have may in fact be weak or offer little or no actual reciprocation.

Preparation counts. Build resilience in advance of a crisis by considering who would really step up and stand by you when you need them. On closer inspection, some will be revealed as worn out or imagined and non-existent. What could you reasonably do to test who will and will not help you?

Also consider the dilemma you may face when people with whom you are not that intimate expect undue commitment from you.

Under pressure, it is not unusual for ambitious people to overstep reasonable boundaries and ask or expect too much of others. Also be mindful that by offering **too little commitment,** you can damage existing relationships. Your resilience can be reduced if you accidentally or subconsciously vote yourself out of a group. Loyalty should be considered, timely and proportionate.

As an organisation, if you expect a high level of commitment:

- what is it that you undeniably offer in return, no matter what?
- what would corrupt this offer/promise?
- in terms of gaining commitment, are you using fear to get what you want?

Genuine commitment pays off

'Pink and fluffy' socially orientated ideas are very difficult to put a value on. It's far easier to put a price tag on them when things go wrong though. Only a fool believes that consumer or employee loyalty can be purchased at the last minute when the chips are down. Nor can you buy loyalty back after you've 'blown it'.

In a company that has **not** built up genuine loyalty during the good times employee cohesion is easily disrupted when the going gets rough just when you need the extra effort. Putting this right costs at least twice for the repair AND the catch up. With sufficient forethought and preparation this high-cost uncertainty can be mitigated.

Who's really on your side?

In the USA government agencies using 'qui tam' whistle-blower legislation have reaped billions of dollars through fines collected from pharmaceutical and other companies. Former employees who 'blow the whistle' on their firms' behaviour get a substantial share of the multi-million dollar fines levied by government. When an employee can legally access a windfall share of millions of dollars from a higher moral standpoint, behaviours **will** change and not to an employer's advantage.

Building up genuine loyalty based on a long-term investment and authentic commitment to people AND to shared beliefs as well as an agreed common working philosophy pays off.

Such a commitment need not tie the hands of management if loyalty also fosters collaboration between teams for the good of the whole over the long term. Auto workers in Germany and Japan have outperformed for a variety of social reasons, one being the quality of management and staff relationships. The sustained loyalty and somewhat easier employee relations history of staff at Richard Branson's Virgin airline contrasts with some perceptions of the relationship between the staff, unions and management at British Airways under various regimes.[49] Less-than-optimum staff relationships in a high customer service industry reduces competitive performance. Good loyal relationships contribute towards commercial resilience and profitability.

Reflection

The adult questions you should ask yourself in regard to your important relationships are the following:

- Are they (the company, the team, the organisation and sometimes my friends or my family) worthy of receiving my continued **total** commitment or not?
- Who is 'prickly', sensitive and needs careful handling?
- How and when and why might each individual or system let me down?
- Where and when might my expectations and sense of entitlements need readjusting?

Consider the commitments you give:

- As a peer group member, what is involved in your own minimal group, if you have one?
- What do you hold in common with the rest of your group and why?
- What do you do to sustain your minimal groups?
- What do you do to foster or undermine the creation of other minimal groups?

Chapter 9 Section 2

How teams can handle uncertainty

It is easy to assume that the way you experience uncertainty is similar to what other people feel; however, different people experience uncertainty in remarkably different ways. Some people love the challenge and stress of uncertainty whilst others loathe it. For example, it can be a mistake to assume that high levels of stress are unwanted. One business development group I worked with said they explicitly needed the adrenalin rush of raised stress levels to propel them forward. Just how do you get teams to build resilience towards uncertainty when we differ so much?

Team training for uncertainty

Andrew Griffiths, a former Royal Naval officer, believes that skills in dealing with persistent uncertainty and ambiguity are an essential top-level leadership requirement.

Andrew is a big confident chap, tasked for many years to train real fighting men and women to deal with life and death crises. More recently, he has led business leaders through the art of managing uncertainty and crisis in the commercial world. He uses a redesigned version of a high impact, naval training experience alongside a combination of grounded commercial leadership theory.

The core of Andrew's model, the Coral Curve™, was developed in conjunction with the Ministry of Defence and is used to demonstrate how freedom of choice rises and falls before and after the uncertainty of a crisis.

The Coral Curve model has been used successfully to pinpoint where high and low-cost interventions can be made. Costs tend to escalate as options to act decline. The price of putting things right is highest during and after a crisis. The lowest cost, greatest choice leadership interventions involve prior preparation and, importantly, mental readiness for both the fact of a crisis AND the emotional turmoil of the attendant calamity.

At the core of Andrew's skill development is the Coral Curve and 3Cs.[50]

- Commitment
- Capacity
- Capability

Andrew says, '*HMS Endurance* was saved from sinking in the Magellan Straits in 2008 by prior training and readiness. There is no doubt the ship would have sunk with loss of life if the crew's crisis and uncertainty skills were absent. Preparation makes a huge difference.'

Andrew says, 'In order to develop all of the necessary skills in dealing with uncertainty, you really have to feel it deep inside. Theory alone cannot accomplish this. You need to really know "yourself" and how you and others cope with a real crisis. Such experience builds genuine long-lasting confidence.'

The Coral Curve ™ - Crisis and Freedom of Choice

Reproduced with the permission of Andrew Griffiths

Andrew says that the only way to embed deep visceral learning is to literally get wet and get immersed in a real, hands-on crisis, and then do the theory. Being inside a sinking vessel, filling rapidly with cold water, qualifies! Andrew's sinking ship provides a genuinely beneficial, unforgettable, visceral experience.

Andrew says, 'There are lots of lessons to be had from this crisis experience. It is a total mind AND body learning event for individuals. It works best with a whole team.'

Virtual storming

In the last century an age-old formula for team-building involved, 'forming, storming, norming, performing' (FSNP). The storming part is essential and involves necessary conflict to test boundaries and to evoke discomfort, and subsequent readjustments of authority or permission to act. Distance between individual team members or separation by time, language, culture or technological experience can foster uncertainty.

With reductions in travel budgets and increased use of virtual teams operating over long distances, the basic FSNP team-forming process is likely to be denied.

In particular the 'storming' part is likely to be compromised. Hidden tensions can build up, eventually leading to a substantial drop in performance. Without the proper FSNP process, relationships risk being purely transactional, lacking passion, interpersonal commitment or loyalty.

Ideally, people need to meet face to face at work AND socially with collaborators. At some early juncture, they need to engage in solving shared difficulties in a way that engages their true feelings so that deeper commitments can be formed. With this in mind, it is my firm belief that teams are best trained, developed, challenged and stretched **as a whole team**, for some of the time, even if for most of the time they live on different continents.

Individuals need to be prepared to do some 'storming' once in a while because once the dust settles, rules and roles tend to solidify. Creative, productive conflict can be both healthy and refreshing.

Creative conflict or fudge

Creative conflict is a very necessary skill in high uncertainty environments. People need to be capable of having 'difficult conversations' as required. Passions need to be aired during high uncertainty so that others understand differences of emotional commitment. When emotions are engaged, people's boundaries of perception become more pliable, allowing new ideas in and old frustrations out.

Buttress your resilience:

- Get a Thomas Kilmann conflict mode profile[51]
- Take advice on psychometric measures that will create helpful insight

Attend:

- a negotiating skills workshop.
- a creative / alternative thinking skills workshop.
- a practical influencing skills workshop.
- an acting class.

Read: *Difficult Conversations: How to Discuss What Matters Most*,[52] and Fischer and Ury books, particularly, *Getting to Yes*.

Are you trained and ready for productive creative conflict and difficult conversations? Was the last conflict papered over or 'fudged'? What uncertainties remain?

In uncertain times, conflict has to be constructive but this does not mean conflict is devoid of emotion. As a team member, if your emotions start to override your ability to be constructive, take time out.

Jonathan, a director of a large bank, says, 'I occasionally do the 30-minute unscheduled walk. I know three other execs that step out and take a long walk too. Their PAs know the routine and cover for them while they are out.' Jonathan continues, 'Occasionally when it gets too intense I simply take off and take a brisk 30-minute walk away from the office. It's a lot better that way. It is like the email you shouldn't send. A brisk walk helps reset the perspectives.'

Invest sufficient time in team formation

Complex teams work on complex subjects. By definition, their working environment will encompass more uncertainties, ambiguities and dilemmas, not to mention different time zones, distance and most likely varying degrees of under-resourcing. Anecdotal experience of several team builders at Ashridge Business School suggests that it takes a lot longer to get a complex team to real team performance compared to a simple team.[53]

In 2001 Mike Brent, Mary Kennedy and Karen Ward identified five factors of complexity that influence real teams. Top of their list of five factors was: 'The increased need for solutions to multifaceted, **ambiguous dilemmas**, not binary problems. The cost of developing high-performance teams can be high, yet such teams engage high-impact, high-value decisions.[54]

How much of an investment do you have in high-performance teams? In particular how much time do you collectively invest in developing skills for dealing effectively with ambiguity, dilemmas or a major crisis?

Building cohesive group behaviour

When faced with a crisis, overall performance in a team or an organisation can get worse in the absence of team cohesion leading to increased vulnerability. Collaboration needs to become an everyday, expected habit especially during uncertain times. Groups need to locate ways of helping individuals avoid their survival instinct to pursue self-interest. Ambition needs to be collective, adaptive and intelligently responsive. To sustain an organisation over the long term, intelligent decisions need to be 'shared' and not hierarchical and not just for the benefit of a few at the very top.

You don't need to be the boss to lead or facilitate beneficial change. You can find ways to educate your peer group or 'manage upwards' to demonstrate a better way of collaborating so that you and your team excel during a crisis and outperform during uncertain times.

Reflection

- How often do you engage in a creative conflict or 'difficult conversation'?
- If rarely, why is that? Is there a risk of raised heartbeats?
- Are you too tired or too scared to bother with the fuss? Is someone not playing by fair rules?
- Would you or the team benefit from a few more surprise tussles?
- Are team or board meetings an endless bout of histrionics?
- Consider an outside view, independent facilitation or a referee.
- Have you considered different decision-making structures and systems?

In order to gain outstanding performance you may have to fundamentally revise the way you work. The examples that follow are systems that are already in use. None of them is perfect.

Chapter 9 Section 3

Resilient organisation

In competitive and uncertain environments, organisations need to adapt their structures and processes if they wish to be resilient. Hierarchies may offer clarity and simplicity but they cannot always embrace fast, fluid, complex change. Alternative decision-making structures are possible. To illustrate these I will use the certainty funnel and then a couple of conventional graphs.

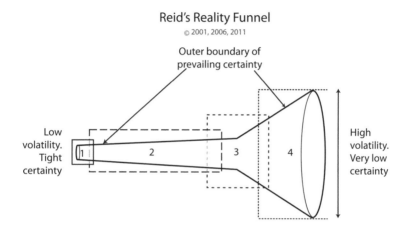

Reid's Reality Funnel
© 2001, 2006, 2011

Organisations structured for uncertainty

Using the Reality Funnel as an alternative to the graphs we can visualise how increasing complexity and volatility lead to increasingly open systems of collaboration between people. Each of the four contexts demands a different pattern of behaviour and different approaches to decision-making.

Level of personal/ group certainty	Group forms	Primary behaviours
1 High	Hierarchy	Command and control
2 Moderate	Consensus and/or matrixes	Negotiation
3 Ambiguous	Networks	Influence, connection
4 Low, speculative at best	Volunteers Ad hoc arrangements around a common purpose	Spontaneous effort Temporary activities Alignment to a belief or a 'truth'

Transition uncertainties

In the last 20 years, many Western companies and organisations have removed layers of management and 'non-essential' staff together with attendant bureaucracies. They took a strategic decision to strip down to their core staff and core activities with a view to reducing cost and gaining increased agility AND to be as responsive as possible.

The problem that follows this desire for 'simplicity' is a significant increase in the complexity of relationships and required behaviours. Any move away from clear command and control requires people who are capable of dealing with ambiguity. In order for different reporting structures to work personal accountability and responsibility need to increase in line with increasing complexity and uncertainty. The formation of strong, socially interconnected, informal shared interest groups is also essential.

Failure to understand the new behaviours can seriously undermine the aims of a reorganisation. Like it or not, as the volatility or complexity of the environment increases, organisations are forced to adapt or fail. One likely evolutionary sequence is mapped out below.

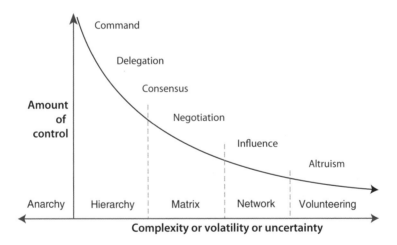

This model is an extension and variation of an original model by Stephen Carter.
See page 234 of 'Renaissance Management'
by Stephen Carter. Kogan Page, 1999

Hierarchy

A command and control ideology has been the most common organising system over the last several hundred years. Hierarchy involves high procedural structure, tight controls and people who are rule compliant. Management by (highly defined) objectives is a feature of this world. Another maxim is 'if you can't measure it, you cannot manage it'.

The challenge of managing people becomes progressively more demanding as volatility or environmental complexity increase. Bureaucracy tends to increase in response to difficulties. More rules and contingencies are prepared and documented. New ways of managing people and opportunities are only sought when the need for agility and flexibility becomes critically important. Major changes made under duress produce even higher levels of challenge and anxiety.

In complex and uncertain environments subordination is not desirable. The collective intelligence of unhindered minds is required.

The matrix

A matrix management system holds the attraction of working across 'silos', but can also be a nightmare, especially if someone forgets to tell the staff how to operate in an optimal, new way. Anyone who brings a hierarchical leader or a 'follower mindset' into the matrix space will struggle at several levels.

In a matrix, there are many more variables and allegiances to juggle with. People have more than one boss, each of whom expects 80 percent of their time and effort. Other people get confused about who will give permission, instruction, measurement and the provision of direction. Negotiation, relationship management and conflict management are essential skills, as is the ability to restate expectations and to say 'no' to someone in authority. Generally accepted boundaries, working principles and shared beliefs and goals are very necessary.

The networked organisation

A networked organisation can arise in several ways; for example, when staff are either outsourced or retained as a variable cost as associates within a 'collegiate' network. This is a diffuse management model where people are expected to locate and work with other people both inside and outside the organisation. Social self-starters are needed. In the network space, 'authority' or 'status' is all about influencing skills, networking, making connections and the ability to access immediately useful resources.

Networks often involve multiple, small, potentially interconnected tribes. Alex describes her large successful academic institution as a cohesive collection of villages. Ten years ago half the teaching staff were full time and half were associates. Now more than 70 percent are retained as associates. Many have now relocated to different parts of Europe and work virtually with their offices.

The benefits

People operating within a matrix or a flat, networked environment are expected to challenge and rebuff others as well as regularly influence and socially engage people, as a natural course of their work. You might call this sort of habitual positive challenge 'useful volatility'. When these habits are positively engaged, the energy of differences can be put to good work. People can align and feel motivated despite the higher potential for conflicting views, given the right climate and development work.

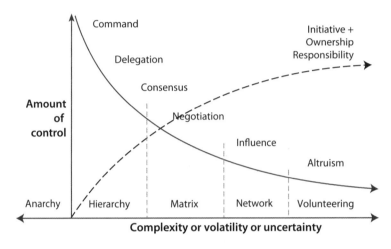

This model is an extension and variation of an original model by Stephen Carter.
See page 234 of 'Renaissance Management'
by Stephen Carter. Kogan Page, 1999

The risks are that a matrix work environment can become increasingly political and fail in the absence of a cohesive sense of higher purpose and motivated leadership. A matrix is not at all easy to lead. Occasionally a desire for even greater simplicity sometimes leads to a lurch back in the direction of hierarchical control.

newer management arrangements do not necessarily reduce ambiguity

These newer management arrangements do not necessarily reduce ambiguity. Ambiguity is more likely to increase with increased interaction, **but** a matrix and a network should help provoke more original, cost-effective, adaptive results once people become familiar with the new rules of how things get done.

Transition requirements

One of several key success factors involved in increasingly complex working environments is an adult transition to increasing self-reliance and personal accountability, together with the social and politically astute skills required to remain connected within a disparate group of powerfully minded and somewhat independent people. (Have you ever tried herding cats? It's not easy!)

New environments and new behaviours

The essential 21st-century skill set

As new ways of managing become more widespread, businesses and educators need to look increasingly frequently at the new skills required. These are likely to include:

- ambiguity/uncertainty enabled skills and experience.
- prior hardship experiences with evidence of resilience to failure and error.
- the right level of decision-making ability.
- sufficient imagination to 'flex, adapt and synthesise' new options.
- faith, trust, humour and optimism.
- speed and confidence to quickly choose a viable option.
- a sufficiently flexible mindset, attitude and good influencing skills.
- the right character, virtues, values and philosophy.

Truth, discretion and alignment

As reporting lines become diffused in uncertain work environments, trust is absolutely essential. The dilemma is that we are all inclined to stretch the rules and make exceptions. When we think about cheating we may assume the conversation is in regard to someone else.

'When I drive my car just one mile per hour faster than the law prescribes for a particular street I am bending the rules. OK, I'm actually breaking the law, just a little bit – but surely I'm allowed because everyone else is doing it.' As you can see, I'm rationalising away a misdemeanour, even though I believe I'm a good citizen. Working in virtual, flat or networked arrangements has its risks when it comes to 'trust' and allowing discretionary behaviour.

Professor Dan Ariely from Duke University has researched how individual subconscious bias sways our behaviour more than rational processes. He found that many people do cheat. He also found that reminding them of their ethics or getting them to recite the Ten Commandments reduced cheating. In a more recent article on behavioural economics, Professor Ariely discusses his findings regarding cheating and raises the concern about how individual and team cheating: 'Could have serious implications for unsupervised collaborative work in organizations.'[55,56]

Allowing discretionary behaviour AND ensuring compliance is yet another team leadership dilemma for those of you who are working across distances and across silos. This particular dilemma requires reconciliation, not micro management of each horn of the dilemma; in other words AND-type thinking.

Uncertainty, high performance and speaking up

During volatile times, organisations need to remain productive despite the uncertainties. This means striking the right balance between harmony (or respect) AND people having the confidence to step up to someone senior to point out something that is substantially wrong.

When the lowest operator has the right, the authority AND the responsibility to stop the shop when something important is wrong, honest, open, threat-free communication is required. Several Japanese manufacturers introduced this policy decades ago. Johnson and Johnson, in the past, allowed any employee the right to exercise a 'Credo challenge' at any level.

Karl E. Weick and Kathleen M. Sutcliffe's book,[57] *Managing The Unexpected*, offers a great repository of examples of why, how, when and where this has been vital. They illustrate life aboard an aircraft carrier where deference to expertise (not rank) in mission-critical situations is an embedded behaviour that builds system-wide resilience. **Any** rank has the right to call for direct attention to a detail. The consequences of an onboard accident in dense concentrations of men, fuel and munitions requires all eyes and ears to be present, alert and responsive.

Weick and Sutcliffe make a strong case for adopting a Buddhist practice of 'working mindfully'. This involves remaining alert, observant in the moment without getting distracted or bogged down by detail AND at the same time being flexible and sufficiently resourced to respond.

Weick and Sutcliffe highlight five key messages in regard to managing the unexpected:

1. Track small failures.
2. Resist oversimplification.
3. Remain sensitive to operations.
4. Maintain capabilities for resilience.
5. Take advantage of shifting locations of expertise.

Oversimplification can kill

I particularly like point 2 above. One of the downsides of efficient logic is a powerful tendency toward reduction to a simple, easy answer. Oversimplification switches conscious, aware thinking off. A really big risk in teams that simplify events and experiences is a pervasive assumption that 'someone else is taking care of it' and that something simple is 'dealt with'.

Also the shortened language used such as, 'Job done!', indicates an attitude of simplification. 'Moved the empty fuel barrels, job done!' Conscious 'presence of mind' and active thinking about something important is terminated at that point. A potentially explosive situation can remain out of conscious awareness.

Oversimplification stops awareness of ambiguity and washes out interesting faint signals that a disaster is looming.

Oversimplification can also devalue an opportunity. Simple closed-down conversations can stop people experimenting or 'keeping their options open'. Simplistic assumptions such as, 'The boss knows best' or 'that valve will hold' can cost lives if someone lower down the ranking knows better but is too fearful to speak up. (See the NASA studies of pilots and crews cited in Chapter 10, Section 1.)

Uncertainty and negative beliefs

When things get stressful and ambiguous, some leaders attempt to gain control over uncertainty by exercising their willpower over events and people. Some confuse the boundary between assertiveness and aggression and bullying behaviour emerges. If people are fearful, they will simply do their required work and foster their higher energies, hopes and aspirations elsewhere. With fear, hearts and minds are absent; you only buy hands and presence. Value-adding discretionary effort evaporates. Cohesion falls, blame rises. Communication fails. This is not a recipe for success. A leader who routinely tries to use fear to overcome uncertainty has failed, is in need of retraining or is not well.

Summary

Life is not simple. It is fabulously complex. Embrace, rather than fight, the complexity and uncertainty of things and people. Your deeply held values and your feelings can act to guide the best interests.

In networked groups, honesty, trust, integrity and reputation are vital. For groups to remain successful teams AND remain aligned, a deeply shared and respected higher philosophy tied into worthy aspirations or values is absolutely essential.

Consider and reflect on some of the uncertainties, ambiguities and dilemmas you are likely to face as a team member.

- **Intimacy, commitment and motivation.** What we believe shapes our behaviours. Are you included or not? We are a tribal species and some of us form small minimal groups involving intense loyalty and commitment bonds between members. Organisations will progressively seek higher commitment AND belief in order to outperform despite complex and uncertain environments.
- **Reporting structures and systems have a big influence.** Quite different rules apply within a hierarchy, a matrix and a network. Do you know what the rules are in your particular 'game' at work or at home?
- **Conflict AND collaboration.** The more we grow, the further apart from each other we can get. We differ hugely, but we still need others. We have to work harder as we age to stay widely connected.
- **Shared values matter** because they offer the opportunity to create common reference points across multiple boundaries.
- **Faith, trust and optimism matter.** It is almost impossible to embrace uncertainty without these attributes, and is almost impossible to convey 'hope' in the absence of these three essential behaviours.
- **Resilience at many levels** is crucial because teams and organisations eventually face a make or break crisis. Crisis testing ahead of time is highly recommended. The army says: 'Train hard, fight easy'.

Reflection

Assuming your beliefs, values and philosophies are explicit:

- how much do people trust each other in your organisation and in the supply chain you occupy?
- are you and your people and decision systems arranged in the best possible way to respond to uncertainty now and in the future?
- what new skills do you and your colleagues need to invest in to increase your adaptive abilities?

Chapter 10
Leadership

Section 1

Leadership uncertainties

Leadership is by nature uncertain.

The sword of Damocles

In the fourth century BC, King Dionysius ruled Syracuse. It was the richest city in what we now call Sicily. One day, Damocles complimented the king on his wealth and power and reminded him how lucky he was. King Dionysius turned to Damocles and said, 'If you believe me to be so lucky, try my life and change places with me for a day.'

The following day, Damocles was dressed fêted and entertained all day, as if he really were the king. Damocles found the role to be everything he imagined. Everyone did as he directed. In the afternoon he enjoyed a feast and reflected how good life could be and how lucky he was. Taking a huge sip of wine Damocles rocked his head back and in so doing saw for the first time the horror that had been with him since he sat down. Damocles had been blissfully happy until he noticed directly above his head, a huge sharp sword, suspended by just one thread of horsehair.

For fear that any sudden movement might cause the thread to break and the sword to fall into him, Damocles froze. He could not imagine a moment when he might rest knowing the heavy scabbard hung by a gossamer thread immediately above his head.

The joy of power, exquisite food, fine garments and the pandering courtiers evaporated. 'What is this my King? Why do you do this to me?' Damocles cried out. King Dionysius replied, 'I do not do this especially for you, Damocles. The same great sword is there for me every single day. A great, sharp sword always hangs above me. It never leaves me. Wherever I go, wherever I sleep, it hangs over me. I could take this particular blade away but there would always be another in the form of a whim of fortune, an unwise decision, a war-like neighbour or even a jealous courtier. Anyone of them could end my life in an instant.'

Damocles begged King Dionysius to take back his throne early. The King obliged and Damocles refrained from commenting on luck, wealth or power.

This legend concerning the sword and Damocles is one that young leaders often find helpful. The moral of the story is that leadership almost always involves sustained uncertainty, ambiguity and contradictions. Damocles ran away from the ultimate uncertainty (an untimely death); however, it is worth recalling that Dionysius remained very well rewarded. We all die eventually. Why not live boldly whilst we do?

There was a sword hanging from this particular ambiguity ceiling and Damocles failed to get past it. Any leader who looks up will see such a sword. It comes with the job but it's not in the job description or the health and safety manual!

There is a huge difference between someone who merely administers and someone who leads. The former tends to stick to rules and the security of established guidelines whereas a leader will adapt and take people into account as dynamic, flexible and adaptable feeling beings as opposed to cogs in a cold machine. A leader will discard rules that don't work and create new, sometimes temporary, expedient guidelines to lead people out of the fog of uncertainty. Leaders need to deal with **multiple ambiguities**, but his or her followers are more likely to expect **comfortable certainties**. That particular dynamic may need to change if a collective intelligence is to be fully engaged.

Rewarding ambiguity ability

Our individual and collective focus of attention is maintained by evidence that motivates or constrains us. King Dionysius kept his throne. He passed the ambiguity test long ago. He knew he couldn't hold on to the role for ever and that one day one of several heavy swords would drop and kill or harm him. However, that did not stop the king doing his job AND enjoying his role to the full, in the moment. People who take accountable roles in financially important and powerful situations involving uncertainty, ambiguity and dilemma are, more often than not, very well rewarded.

Philosophically, money is a means to an end, not an end in and of itself. High rewards at a personal or a collective level are justified, to a point. Beyond such a point, natural biological balancing forces should kick in. Pent-up pressure to correct unnatural imbalances can build progressively till harm is done somewhere.

At the executive level of life, decisions tend to be more complex and involve incomplete or conflicting signals. Dealing with ambiguity and knowing what to pay attention to, what to balance, what has true meaning and what to ignore is not easy. Such skills are relatively rare, so people who demonstrate abilities above the ambiguity ceiling eventually command higher status and pay.

An IBM study of 1500 CEOs indicated that uncertainty and ambiguity are already major management issues.[58] They say that, '… *complexity is only expected to rise and more than half of CEOs doubt their ability to manage it. Seventy-nine percent of CEOs anticipate even greater complexity ahead.*' IBM's report concludes, '*avoiding complexity is not an option; the choice comes in how to respond to it.*'

Clearly there is a market for leaders who can respond robustly to the challenge of uncertainty.

Academic views on leadership and ambiguity

Geert and GertJan Hofstede

Geert Hofstede's work with IBM demonstrated that tolerance of uncertainty was an important factor 40 years ago. Geert Hofstede researched a huge IBM database of employee values' scores from 40 countries collected between 1967 and 1973. This internationally recognised work identifies dimensions that differentiate different cultural characteristics.[59-61] Geert Hofstede originally identified four axes of behaviour on a high-low scale in the 1970s, namely:

Low		High
Power distance		Power distance
Uncertainty avoidance		Uncertainty avoidance
Individualism		Individualism
Masculinity (competitiveness)		Masculinity (competitiveness)

An alternative expression of these four dimensions might also be described as:

High		High
Consensus		Hierarchy
Tolerance of uncertainty		Uncertainty avoidance
Group orientation		Individualism
Cooperation / inclusion (femininity), sustaining		Competitiveness (masculinity), winning

(As an exercise in perception, do you regard the paired dimensions described above as conflicting or complementary? Do you see 'either/or' in the centre column or 'AND'?)

Different patterns of bias behaviours can be consistent to the extent that representative patterns of typical responses become part of a marriage, a team, a company and a nation's culture. Hofstede's work provides a map of macro-level cultural orientation.

One important aspect of this work is that the dilemmas Geert and his son identified are encountered frequently enough to study. You therefore need to be conscious of the role these common dilemmas play in your decision-making **as well as** how different nationalities **tend** to respond to particular dilemmas.

A collective sense of meaning and focus of attention can be shaped by a collective bias. The focus of attention and sense of meaning between different races faced with the same dilemma can be substantially different. The different patterns of response to these ambiguities have particular salience in international leadership, supply-chain relationships, international negotiations and global marketing efforts.

Geert Hofstede later added a fifth dimension, 'long-term orientation', based on Confucian dynamism. Geert Hofstede's son, GertJan, advises that a sixth dimension was added in 2010, namely, indulgence vs restraint.

Hofstede's partner consulting group offers a free online map of individual country measures for these markers.[62]

Trompenaars, Hampden-Turner and Woolliams

In the mid-1980s,[63] Fons Trompenaars embarked upon research for his PhD thesis at Wharton to identify and study six dilemmas commonly encountered by leaders, but used different measures than those employed by Hofstede.

Fons Trompenaars, Charles Hampden-Turner and Peter Woolliams continued this work and studied the way different managers and leaders from many different countries make a choice in regard to six particular dilemmas.

Six common dilemmas[64]		
(universal) Rules		Relationships (particular)
Group		Individual
Involvement diffuse		Involvement specific
According status – ascribed		According status – earned
Manage time – sequential		Manage time – synchronic
How we relate to nature (inner directed)		How we relate to nature (outer directed)

Their large validated database at the time of writing involves over 85,000 managers and executives, a 20-year longitudinal study of six dilemmas and the patterns of decision choices that characterise different national cultures. They also discovered an interesting correlation between individual ability to deal with the ambiguity of dilemmas and higher performance.

Cultural insights

Their data showed relatively consistent 'in-country' patterns of responses to their six dilemmas but showed variation between countries. The approach any individual has to a dilemma can be culturally determined. In Japan, for example, group achievement outweighs the interest of an individual's achievement whereas in the West the opposite is generally held to be important. The way decisions are generally arrived at will be shaped by this bias.

Different patterns of locally accepted ways of dealing with dilemmas help explain why people from different cultures misunderstand each other. Understanding different orientations can be especially helpful in the leadership of multinational teams as well as in negotiations across borders.

Ambiguity ability and performance

The three professors' data, complied up to 1998, involving 35,000 managers, showed that only 35 percent of a wide sample population of middle managers opted for the more integrated, complex reconciliation choice.[65] Subsequent, more detailed investigation of 85,000 managers in different countries AND in different job functions indicated different levels of a tendency to integrate and reconcile a dilemma. For example, accountants generally score very low whereas those in sales and marketing score much higher. The data indicates that experience of working with external suppliers/customers and years worked abroad also correlate with higher cultural awareness and the likelihood of an ability to reconcile dilemmas.[66]

years worked abroad also correlate with higher cultural awareness

Peter Woolliams says that the important issue is **that managers and leaders who score higher on reconciliation are much more effective.** Importantly, he points out that this reconciliation process can be learned.[67]

Impact on the bottom line

Interestingly, these acclaimed business school professors also detected a statistically significant correlation for individual ability to reconcile a dilemma and bottom-line commercial performance.[68] In addition, they demonstrated a high correlation between an ability to reconcile a dilemma and executive ability (the latter being validated by independent peer assessment).

a high correlation between an ability to reconcile a dilemma and executive ability

This observation makes sense since much of what an executive has to deal with is located 'above the ambiguity ceiling' involving work on complex uncertainties but still getting something certain done.

Taken together, Hofstede and Trompenaars' validated research provides leaders with really helpful insights. Hofstede identified uncertainty as an important cultural issue. Also Trompenaars, v and Woolliams identified that an ability to reconcile dilemmas had an impact on commercial performance.

Measuring individual tolerance for uncertainty

Phil Hodgson and Randy White in 2001 declared, 'Relax it's only Uncertainty!'[69] Hodgson and White are two deeply experienced, hands-on, top-class business consultants, authors and academics from Ashridge Business School (UK) and Duke Corporate Education[70] respectively. They have developed a practical interest in 'uncertainty' for considerably more than a decade, resulting in two books,[71] many papers and notably, The Ambiguity Architect®,[72] a psychometric instrument. Hodgson and White make the point that uncertainty is something to be embraced, not feared. They say, 'Uncertainty is normal. Get used to it!'

Interestingly, research based on data provided by the Ambiguity Architect® from increasing numbers of senior executives anecdotally suggests a correlation between the ability to reconcile dilemmas and executive ability.[73] Their observations complement similar findings by Professors Trompenaars and Hampden-Turner.

The Ambiguity Architect® delineates eight styles of behaviour seen in people who function effectively when faced with ambiguity.

- Mystery seekers
- Risk tolerators
- Future scanners
- Tenacious challengers
- Exciters
- Flexible adjusters
- Simplifiers
- Focusers

In addition, they categorised a further eight sorts of limiting behaviours displayed by people who may struggle with ambiguity.

- Narrow thinkers
- Muddy thinkers
- Complex communicators
- Conflict avoiders
- Wet blankets
- Poor transitioners
- Detail junkies
- Repeaters

Their work can create valuable insights into individual orientation and team composition.

Let go to gain traction

For some the meaning of leadership hinges on 'control' or 'direction' particularly when things become uncertain their dilemma, however, is that one person cannot possibly have all the answers. Researchers reckon that during difficult times there is still a desire to try to take greater control. The authors of one particular study[74] say, 'Letting go of some authority and giving employees considerable autonomy can boost innovation and success at knowledge firms, even during a crisis.'

CSC discovered that increasing control to turn around declining performance only led to further declines in performance. Handing down authority to non-hierarchical teams that focus on various issues allowed those teams to make significant company decisions. When leaders let go of the controls, performance increased. CSC Germany had great success with this approach.

Importantly, the researchers say, 'We've found that contrary to what many CEOs assume, leadership is not really about delegating tasks and monitoring results; it is about imbuing the entire workforce with a sense of responsibility for the business.'[75]

In other words a shared sense of 'meaning' and a collective 'focus of attention' adds value. The advantage of empowerment with responsibility AND accountability is that a wider intelligence is engaged.

Loose AND tight

You are there to lead? Right? Yes AND no. Leadership can involve contradictions such as the 'loose-tight' dilemma. Some things need a tight grip AND others need openness. When it comes to mission-critical information, leadership emphasis should be on getting other people to be open and free to challenge and be willing to point out critical errors or anomalies, not just in a crisis but also **as a routine**.

As a leader employing consensus, you retain the right to decide on some courses of action and this needs to be respected, **but** your decision needs to be the best it can be, employing all the weak signals picked up by the rest of the crew and fearlessly fed back. You need the group mind.

NASA studies created by Robert Blake and Jane Mouton from the 1980s involving whole crews using flight simulators showed that pilots make better decisions if they ask their crews for ideas in the critical 30 to 40 seconds prior to a crisis event before deciding. Less inclusive 'take charge flyboys' failed more than the pilots who sought advice.

pilots make better decisions if they ask their crews for ideas

Of deeper concern was an observation that crew who had worked with pilots who did seek advice tended to **keep** their restricted role behaviours – even when they had information that might save the plane.[76] So take care to make sure new recruits really do understand and practise your way of working. Make sure they experience your way of doing things AND adopt the norms you prefer.

In an increasingly complex and uncertain world it would be peculiar if a leader routinely assumed they had all the answers. **Not** having the answers actually allows everyone else to contribute. It therefore makes a lot of sense to create a habit of openness, confirmed by right behaviour – as a routine – so that virtuous behaviours become a regular working habit modelled and **led by everyone**.

Organisations that can cope with uncertainty will probably foster 'communitarian' ideals (this is not communism) in the form of networks of committed communities of practice working through consensus, ultimately led by small groups of people who possess fluent 'above the ambiguity ceiling' skills.

Chapter 10 Section 2

Future-ready leadership

The trend of life towards increasing complexity and uncertainty is not likely to ease up any time soon. So how could you get ready for more uncertainty and ambiguity? I would want to know how well my peer group and I coped in different conditions and how well we used our energy. Then I'd want to know how many members of staff were capable of dealing with ambiguity and just how flexible or resilient were the teams, leaders, systems and processes currently employed. Then I'd want to discover how all of us could improve as an investment in our strengths for an uncertain future.

No matter how clever the hardware or procedural systems, organisational agility just won't develop without smart, aware, flexible, intelligent people working together in integrated ways. When it comes to dealing with complex uncertainties, higher performance can be better established by developing whole teams as well as individual training. Don't wait for someone to help you upgrade though. Individuals can still take the initiative and lead by example. It costs nothing to adjust your own attitude.

Who and what can you tolerate?

In terms of tolerance of uncertainty, there are wide differences between situations and between individuals. Individual tolerance may be stretched; however, there are natural limits. You will lose credibility if you try too hard to be all things to all people. My experience is that teams are able to tolerate people from their own reality realm plus one adjacent zone (see the funnel model).

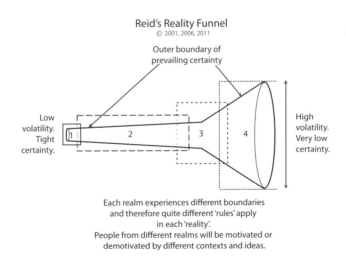

Reid's Reality Funnel
© 2001, 2006, 2011

Outer boundary of prevailing certainty

Low volatility. Tight certainty.

High volatility. Very low certainty.

1   2   3   4

Each realm experiences different boundaries
and therefore quite different 'rules' apply
in each 'reality'.
People from different realms will be motivated or
demotivated by different contexts and ideas.

Funnel people

Funnel map type	Core preference/Orientation towards uncertainty
1	Very deep, very well-ordered detail. High certainty required. Clear rules and procedures. High control.
2	Clear rules and procedures. High control with moderate variation within known parameters. Moderate to high certainty required.
3	Ambiguity merchants/brokers/ translators – enjoy the novelty of uncertainty but are not completer-finishers. Rules and the truth are seen as variable. Some elements of certainty needed.
4	Visionary novelty addicts – out there at the very edges, creating the future, – if people will listen or follow. Certainty is regarded as ephemeral. Too much certainty can feel uncomfortable.

Remember this is just a map. People can and do bridge two realms, rarely three but never four. Moves out of a familiar preferred certainty zone demand huge effort and higher expenditure of mental energy. Such stretch moves can be immensely draining. We are therefore biologically inclined to stay close to what we know and feel most comfortable with.

Leading complex teams

People at the extremes, i.e. realm 1 vs realm 4 can find each other intolerable since the other's beliefs and behaviours undermine a particular view of what constitutes 'the right reality'. Simple organisations will not engage all four realms. In more complex organisations it may be smart to work out how to bridge the differences of perception and decision-making.

Bridging all four realms will be especially important for people working on high uncertainty transitions such as radically new product development, new business development, business process re-engineering, true innovation and strategic leadership.

Building an intellectual food chain

For those that wish to get a complex job done or to retain leading edge the funnel map highlights the social and practical difficulties of building a working 'food chain' that encompasses all four types of intellectual resource. You require very different people who can agree a shared focus of attention, despite their intrinsic differences. The whole food chain falls apart if the linkages and hand-offs between quite different people are poor. This is most difficult between people at the extremes.

Working out the best team composition according to task and desired outcome as well as setting up social bridging mechanisms across all four realms will be operationally and commercially important. If the skills are not present, some team members will need to flex out of their usual comfort zone.

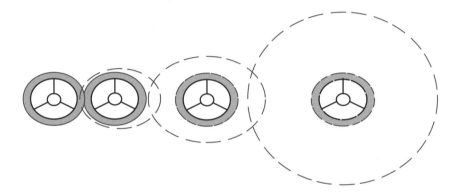

Leading through uncertainty AND progress

When developing new ideas from scratch, there will always be challenges and lots of uncertainties and frequent setbacks. The question is how will you deal with protracted uncertainty AND more importantly how will you react to reversals? As development of a novel concept moves forward, decisions with incomplete data are often demanded in order to progress ahead of a competitor.

Decisions are an art at level 3 or 4, not a science. With heightened uncertainty and ambiguity there is a lack of clear precedent or rules and the boundaries and reference points are volatile, elastic and subject to change.

Errors will naturally occur more frequently here; however, any actions and reactions create new information. A right attitude towards 'error' is therefore crucial. A positive learning culture is more likely to prosper in a volatile space than one that is rule-bound and hot on blame. Recall Randy White's executive delegate response: 'Fail forward and fail fast!' Blame simply gets in the way of learning, curiosity and experimentation. Orienting people towards desirable behaviours is therefore extremely important if you seek productive outcomes.

Managing the differences

The basic chemistry is against some people collaborating. There is a strong possibility of explosive difficulties between people who occupy the extreme roles of the funnel simply because of vastly different norms and expectations.

Well-developed thinking skills and a mutual recognition of abilities may not be enough.

Managing the flow of information, decisions and ideas between different parts of the food chain will be important. The trick, if there is one, is to facilitate the necessary routine creative conflict and challenge that provokes progressive adaptive responses, as an everyday natural habit, right along the chain.

A shared team philosophy is important and can be sustained by the repeated evidence of the team's adopted daily habits. The beliefs established by a shared team philosophy can accelerate and simplify decision-making, especially during difficult or uncertain times or in the absence of line managers.

When subtle behaviour systems regarding 'how we do things around here' fail, turf wars break out and energy is lost unpicking ego from material business issues. A shared philosophy helps to makes sense when things are complicated but it requires a willingness to trust.

Faith and trust

Because of higher levels of uncertainty, faster pace and change, faith, trust and a good helping of optimism are definitely needed. It can be quite difficult to build faith and trust between people with diametrically opposed views of reality.

Faith and trust have to be routinely experienced as a matter of consistency and habit. The same trust and faith needs to be demonstrated during times of positive AND negative challenge. Faith and trust should be established long before they are called upon. You can't mandate for trust.

Constructive behaviours emerge naturally from deeply held beliefs and philosophies, not from a rulebook. When people trust each other the energy of differences between people produces powerful forward movement and lots of tension but **not** a blow-out. Tough, resilient, adaptable, humorous leaders are required for this new sort of 'game'.

Your uncertainty vs their certainty

It is a fundamental mistake to assume that other people have the capacity or the wherewithal to think and make decisions the way that you do or at your speed.

One problem of perception in organisations is that above-ceiling managers and executives regard decision-making using incomplete information and high uncertainty as perfectly normal, whereas others below the ambiguity ceiling definitely do not.

Front-line staff tend to deal with the relative certainty of here and now. Grounded people do a fantastic job of getting high-quality goods and services delivered fault free, on time. They are likely to regard working with 'suspect' incomplete information as a dark art, gambling, betting or unnecessary risk taking. Working within a highly ordered world, they may not understand or appreciate how instinctive or intuitive decisions are arrived at. Exposure to instinctive or intuitive decisions may indeed alarm them, so don't frighten them!

Once you make a decision with incomplete information swallow most of your uncertainties and give it your best clear shot. Communicating your 'certainty' includes your facial expression and your body language AND the body language of the associates and support staff nearest to you. You have to be able to put on a convincing act! Acting with confidence and inner certainty where none exists does not involve telling lies but it may involve holding back selected parts of the story for a while.

The people that work with you can feel certain about an uncertain situation if they have faith in you as a 'strong' leader. At an executive level, inventing solutions from nowhere is what you have to do some of the time. Don't brag about 'making it up as you go along' though! Keep that just within your peer group. Let people learn to trust you. Do not break the illusion.

Loyalty

One thing a leader needs during uncertain times is the loyalty of the team. The skills of a leader are called to a high point when everyone else is at their low point. A leader needs to find something for others to trust or put faith in to carry them through uncertainty and prevailing difficulties.

a leader during uncertain times needs the loyalty of the team

In neat and tidy logical situations the context is predictable, but when matters become uncertain, then leadership and the willingness of people to follow can become highly subjective and open to question. If a leader is 'in credit' and has goodwill already banked with the team, he or she may carry the day. Phil Davies neatly describes the difficulty of loyalty between a leader and his or her followers:

1 Leader	2 Followers	3 Context	✓ = positive ✗ = negative
✓	✓	✗	Leader exhorts team to fight
✓	✗	✗	Leader considers his own safety
✗	✓	✓	Leader is carried by his team
✓	✓	✓	Harmony
✗	✓	✗	Leader most likely sacrificed by followers

Reproduced courtesy of Phil Davies PhD MBA MA Oxon. Bedford Business School.

Cracking through the ambiguity ceiling

One of the most challenging difficulties encountered by someone adopting a senior role for the first time involves a big adjustment in regard to 'the ambiguity ceiling'. Getting used to the idea of living **with** instead of fighting off ambiguity is important. Think of uncertainty and ambiguity as a lifelong 'tease'.

Your adaptation will involve a habit of mind, recognising that when one group of ambiguities or dilemmas fades others will soon emerge. Getting past an ambiguity ceiling is a lesson that is easier to understand only **after** having surmounted the difficulties involved. It is a bit like being a parent in that you cannot really describe the experience to a youth who has not yet come close to parenting. Trust me, the ceiling is there.

getting used to the idea of living with instead of
fighting off ambiguity is important

You cannot be all things to all people. Growth requires personal adjustment in response to the signals you select.

You will need to reconcile yourself and your role within revised, more flexible boundaries from time to time. Remember, you add the most value when situations become vague and uncertain. People will look to you for answers. At that point you need to be fresh and ready. As a leader you will need to embrace a belief system that will sustain you during foggy times and, along with your other skills, will help you create a positive sense of purpose, direction and meaning for yourself and for others.

Visibly, your actions outwardly define you. Actions are what people pay attention to. Act with virtue in mind. Your virtue has its foundations in what you believe, since your beliefs shape your perceptions, your thoughts and what you choose to do. Your resilience, tenacity and adaptability will be sustained by these deeper beliefs. If you do not know what these are, how can they help you?

Reflection

- How will you cope AND be productive with higher levels of tension, especially between people with very different world views from realms 1, 2, 3 and 4?
- How will you cover the gaps that intolerance will open up?
- How will the type 1s and 2s on the funnel discover when they are tenaciously doing the dumb thing?

When you envision a solution but don't have the evidence to back it up how will you convince more 'grounded' people to follow you?

Chapter 10 Section 3

The uncertainty of politics

Where there is power and influence you will find political activity. Families, teams, and, of course, organisations all have the potential to be quite political places. Political activity for some can be a source of huge discomfort, whilst others take political tension easily within their stride. How do you see politics?

Leaders need to be proficient with political issues. Political activity is expected and considered normal. There are two particular aspects of politics that are very important to leaders, namely the possession of power AND a reputation. Let us assume you have power already and turn directly to reputation before we look at the basics of exercising power and influence during uncertain times.

Reputation is everything

In a highly uncertain world transactions are based on trust, therefore your reputation is everything. It is one of your most valuable assets alongside power and influence. A reputation is difficult to build and maintain, so be careful what you commit to. Look after it well. If you must commit to something, follow it through and deliver your promise to the best of your ability.

There will be occasions where you will be damned if you do and damned if you do not follow a course of action. If you cannot find a third or better way, if you cannot deflect, avoid or defer then use your moral compass and your values and do the best you possibly can with as much grace as you can muster. The experience will provide good exercise for your humility muscle!

Careful conversations

As an extrovert you may feel a quite natural need for conversation to improve and round out your ideas. As you rise through an organisation take careful consideration of who you share these nascent thoughts with. Your way of arriving at conclusions may appear very ill considered to those who think through their positions clearly long before they open their mouths.

take care of your mind and your mouth

Enthusiastic young extroverts take note. Take care of your mind and your mouth. Think quickly **but** speak slowly. It doesn't work the other way around! From a less hurried position, one has more time to think. Natural introverts know this already. Introverts routinely reflect first, and then speak. Extroverts can learn an introvert's reflective approach, just as introverts can master extrovert behaviour.

think quickly but speak slowly

- Do you have a sense of appropriate humility?
- Do you **always** speak first in groups? Why?
- Do you have a 'pre-conversation' in your head before you speak?
- Have you ever tried gently biting your tongue to hold your impulse to speak long enough to hear others?

In uncertain times take care what you say

What you say or promise during a crisis or when faced with uncertainty can come back to haunt you. This is also particularly true of your early days in a new role. Remember that when you speak you **are** the voice of the whole organisation. Even with good intentions, a simple promise or comment can backfire harshly. The ability to create a positive impact is a consequence of a well-practised and disciplined habit of mind, namely, having '**always on** awareness' of yourself AND the wider contexts along with an ability to respond in a timely, **proportionate** and graceful way.

Lost in translation

'I want my life back,' said Tony Hayward, BP's CEO, on 31 May 2010. It was a most unfortunate choice of words given that thousands of Americans living on the Gulf of Mexico had lost their livelihoods and several rig workers had died following the Deepwater Horizon disaster. There were thousands of messages from BP during the crisis but only one or two will be remembered.

At one point in the whole sorry affair, the BP share price plunged to a 14-year low, led down also by BP suspending the dividend and setting aside a massive $20 billion fund for potential damages.

On 16 June 2010, BP's Swedish Chairman, Carl-Henric Svanberg, conspicuous by his very low profile, addressed the American media from the front of the White House and sincerely apologised for events in regard to the Deepwater Horizon catastrophe. Perhaps something got lost in translation when he said, 'We care about the small people.' Investor and political sentiment cannot have been helped by the chairman's PR gaff.

The chairman kept his job but a few months later Tony Hayward lost his. A top job is accountable. The buck does stop with you. Given their two quite different roles one wonders about the merits of being heroic AND conspicuous.

Be extremely careful, thoughtful and 'present in the moment' if and when you step up to a public challenge.

Reputation and humility

Gerald Ratner's much-reported attempts at humour emphasise the risks of seeking the limelight. Gerald certainly had a lot to be proud about. He had built up the family firm Ratner's into one of the world's largest jewellery retailers. Under his stewardship, the share price of his company grew quickly from 27p to £4.20.

A late addition of two jokes to his speech at the Institute of Directors in 1991 did significant damage though. 'We do cut-glass sherry decanters complete with six glasses on a silver-plated tray your butler can serve you drinks on, all for £4.95. People say, "How can you sell this for such a low price?" I say, "Because it is total crap". 'Plus: We even sell a pair of gold earrings for under £1, which is cheaper than a prawn sandwich from Marks and Spencer. But I have to say that the sandwich will probably last longer than the earrings.'

The limelight bites. The loss of customer confidence in the group led by the media wiped hundreds of millions of pounds from the value of the company. Mr Ratner left the firm. This unfortunate story is used as an example of the need for quality, careful, long-term PR.

What I suspect gets overlooked is that it would be difficult not to learn humility from such a harsh lesson. One should be able to find a good deal of admiration for anyone who demonstrated the resilience to successfully bounce back from such a low point, as Mr Ratner appears to have done, this time discreetly and progressively building another company. He recovered, quietly.

Recovery

Reputation and credibility are foundation stones that need to be constantly and vigilantly sustained and reinforced. One very big uncertainty that needs to be managed is 'the political you'. You should really consider why you would want to step into the limelight. Why would you seek media attention? Big visible roles come with big decisions, big moves, big success AND because we are human and fallible, big visible mistakes too. If you still want to seek the limelight, get ready for the inevitable hard knocks and get a lot of PR training and support before you venture anywhere.

> *Life is unfair!*
> From the opening sequence of the sitcom *'Malcolm in The Middle'*

You **will** make mistakes in life, so be aware that the damage you do by your own actions can inflict the greatest hurt upon yourself. You will most likely beat yourself up harder and for longer than anyone else will. The smart thing to do is put the beating stick down once you have found use or meaning in your error, then get up and get on with living.

Move on. Learn, hone self-awareness and presence in the moment, but remember that if you don't fail once in a while, you're probably not trying hard enough! Humour and learning to forgive and forget are absolutely essential.

Political fix AND flex

Every leadership job involves political behaviour. Politics almost always involves uncertainties. Politics involves the art of the possible as opposed to the science of the definite. We could therefore cut everyday politicians some slack and be grateful our own decisions are not televised or scrutinised in the manner that theirs often are. A good example of difficulty is Nick Clegg's televised pre-election promise to cut education fees for college students.[77] A matter of months later the government he joined (as Deputy Prime Minister) increased the same fees by as much as 300 percent.[78] The economic reality was the money wasn't there, hence the volte-face.

Politicians make practical lessons available to us for free. Spend a little time observing how your elected officials deal with difficult clear-cut, much-simplified questions posed by journalists. A good politician will almost always stick to their preferred side of an ambiguity.

ambiguity is both a curse AND an ally

The minimum political lessons are:

- in most businesses there will be political activity.
- politics **is** a slippery business.
- occasionally you will need to perform your own volte-face.
- absolute positions leave absolutely nil wiggle room.
- absolutes can be a hazard. It can be a mistake to tie your hands with absolutes. Almost 'always' have caveats and get-outs available.
- ambiguity can be both a curse AND **an ally**. It creates wiggle room.

Politicians, middle managers and senior leaders, generally need some wiggle room in order to get results simply because circumstances do change.

Man is by nature a political animal. Aristotle (384–322 BC)

Politics is the art of the possible. Otto von Bismarck, 1867

Power dilemma

Power is almost always political and creates uncertainty because someone else either covets or fears it. With increased uncertainty comes the need to exercise power and influence in a wider range of styles than might be the case during stable times, in spite of any skill gaps you may have.

power is almost always political

I recommend that a leader gains valid experience in the use of power right across the range, namely from highly assertive directive control to low-impact influence engagements.

Failure to exert firm directive authority can, for example, lead to confusion and a breakdown of cohesion during the uncertainty of a crisis when clear direction is most needed. Too much command and control, however, can throttle the life out of entrepreneurial explorers who need uncertain boundaries in order to engage novel solutions. At the other end of the scale is a low power, yet quite influential, coaxing style found at volunteer events such as a village fête or a street party. If you have not experienced this more subtle form of influencing, I recommend you do. It can be most enlightening.

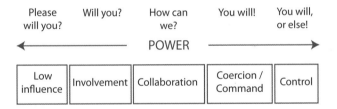

Leadership is a matter of contingent balances applied judiciously in a timely manner. It is very important that when it comes to the use of power, great care is required not only regarding the encounter but also the consequences that follow. Think through carefully whatever you intend to do, if it is in any way political.

Better than the boss dilemma

Sometimes the senior role holder has gone past his or her 'best use by date' or a younger, sharper subordinate already has skills and experiences that surpass those of an incumbent leader. The dilemma is what is to be done for the best. Naturally, this will be political. Having worked hard to get a leadership role do you, as the incumbent, volunteer to step aside? Unlikely. If you are the incumbent, how do you deliver a suitable learning experience for ambitious subordinates? As the young, new, potentially better leader, what do you do, challenge, leave or adapt?

The 'best' man or woman doesn't always win. 'Best' can be a matter of opinion, personality or blood line. In some family companies a family member will play the card that says, 'Family always comes first', irrespective of commitment, merit, tenure or service. There are some hoops you just can't jump through.

your career is a long game

At the end of the day, it is important to see that the whole of your career is a long game. If a contested idea gets too personal, your clarity of judgement will diminish, so:

- step back and reflect on what outcomes are most likely.
- what are the games in play in your context?
- how could the rules be tipped in your favour?
- is everything that matters in line with your ethics and values?
- is there a better opportunity elsewhere?
- are you being 'played' on false or cheap promises?
- who is your champion? If they leave what will you do?

Summary

Increasing volatility will differentiate people and organisations. Commercial experience and academic research are beginning to show just how important ambiguity skills are. The need to be 'ambiguity enabled' will rise to the extent that not only leadership but also a larger percentage of a workforce will need these skills to thrive during times of high volatility and uncertainty. This may involve new and potentially ambiguous ways of organising for productivity and different ways of leading and decision-making.

Your role as a master of uncertainty, ambiguity and dilemma is to lead other people with clarity and relative certainty even though deep down you know the next few steps are invented, uncertain and may not go the way you expect. Those who are unable or unwilling to work with uncertainty need your sense of clarity and decisiveness. They will trust your ability to turn things around.

Trust is required more than ever where distance, isolation or remoteness becomes a routine feature of relationships. Remember you and other people are not task/purpose machines and you will perform better if hearts and minds are engaged. Toughness AND tolerance, humility, forgiveness as well as human warmth along with faith are also important features of good leadership.

Fear, shame and guilt have a place in a moral life but play only a very limited role in a well-run ethical business or organisation. Generally, fear benefits no one and closes down the sort of decisions that help differentiate higher performance from mediocrity.

Resilience can be built out of a 'failure'. In other words, failure can be just the preparation you need for something better.

Exercising power requires skill, honesty and restraint. Positions of power are always political and you need to be vigilant about what you say, promise and do. The world is watching you. You set the tone that others follow so know what you stand for and walk the talk. Turn the words you employ to express your sense of direction and purpose into actions that are consistent with what you believe, especially during tough times. Don't disappoint.

Last but not least, your role as a leader involves directing **not** doing. Other people 'do', you do not. When things are quiet and 'normal' learn to sit back, relax and read the paper until you are really needed.

Reflection

- When did you last audit the behaviours of key standard bearers to locate evidence that you are on or off the rails your founders put in place?
- How often do you develop political skills in rising stars?
- What stories about you and your organisation are in circulation? What do they say about what is held to be true?
- Who in your organisation demonstrates 'grace' and how do you foster that particular virtue?
- How do you and your people cope with error and when things go wrong?
- What are you doing to build in resilience in yourself and your organisation?
- Could you start again and set things up in a better way? If yes, what is stopping you?

Chapter 11
The uncertainty of innovation

I have addressed the uncertainties of innovation in four sections: -

Section 1: Wrong question, wrong start

Section 2: Right perceptions of innovation

Section 3: Organising people

Section 4: Academic and practitioner insights

Logical frames of reference are fantastically helpful for dealing with subjects that are known or knowable, but they are of limited use with subjects that defy definition or capture.

Innovation is the sort of subject that is literally open ended and involves lots of uncertainty and high ambiguity. Innovation, like love, ultimately defies closure to a reliable, definitive set of answers. Seeking the perfect answer in regard to innovation is therefore futile, but like love it is worth a try!

Section 1

Wrong question, wrong start

The problem of embracing innovation is compounded by substantial differences in, and errors of, perception. Differences of perception arise because our individual frames of reference of what we believe constitutes reality varies substantially from person to person. Some see the world from the ground up, in remarkably fine detail, whilst others see reality from a lofty viewpoint in very broad-brush terms. Gaining agreement from such extreme viewpoints on a slippery subject such as innovation can be taxing. Let's look at some of the problems.

A wrong start

If we find the answers to a particular question confusing, perhaps we are asking the wrong question. Perhaps there is something about our perception that fails us? For example, if you begin with a narrow or erroneous perception or the wrong question, how could you possibly hope to uncover anything meaningful, especially when dealing with a slippery question?

Some of the biggest problems in regard to the slippery subject of 'innovation' are to do with wrong definitions and misguided expectations. Given that innovation belongs to a class of subjects that defy definition, a series of clues are more likely than a definitive answer.

- What do you believe innovation is?
- How do the people you serve define innovation?
- Who determines if something is genuinely innovative or not?

Is 'innovation' a redundant word?

Individual perception varies so much I have found that the word 'innovation' has been rendered almost useless. The word fails to convey consistent meaning. It means very different things to different people. Compare and contrast what is said and understood in regard to innovation by those who generally take a high-logic, ground-up position and those who see things from lofty clouds. There are all sorts of 'understandings' in between.

people do seem to agree that genuine innovation involves a substantial step change

In general, people do seem to agree that genuine innovation involves a substantial step change. The problem then is that what feels like a major step change for one person may be a minor hop for another. Getting the right perception of what innovation actually involves, in an honest way, allows a more effective allocation of people and resources. To some extent the meaning of the concept has also been corrupted, incrementally.

Incremental, faux innovation

Starting with a wrong question or a wrong perception, we leave ourselves open to false starts. When something is misunderstood we are at greater risk of deluding ourselves. When it comes to the notion of 'incremental innovation', let's put the king's clothes back on! Over the last couple of decades we have somehow come to generally accept definitions of innovation that are comfortable rather than true. The definition of true innovation has drifted.

Leadership teams like the idea of 'innovation' because they believe that is where profits, high status and kudos are. One easy response for pressured managers when they fail to come up with the genuine article is to rebadge NPD (new product development) as innovation. The word innovation has become so abused that any modest improvement, any ground-up, incremental NPD move, any minor novelty or otherwise worthwhile advance, has been bagged and tagged as innovation, and no one objects.

In many cases 'business improvement' would be the more honest term for what is often described as 'incremental innovation'. Attrition of a competitor and incrementally growing market share are part of regular business warfare and not innovation.

The lesser component parts of an innovation may contribute to, but in isolation do not constitute, true innovation. Half an elephant is not half an elephant; it is a large amount of dead flesh and bone. Some things are just not divisible. Use the right words. Be honest, increments are not innovation. Increments do not lead to fundamental changes in behaviour.

Honest perception counts

Wrong definitions and corrupt meanings increase the uncertainty of what is expected of innovation and allow people to be comfortable when they should not be.

The true definition of innovation for me involves a level of originality that fundamentally changes established behaviours by others in a really significant noticeable way in your favour. 'Incremental innovation' does not accomplish this. It is a corrupt term. Incremental improvement **does** have a valuable contributory role during the development of a true innovation but does not provide an alternative route.

For example, the Dyson cyclonic carpet cleaner involved a truly innovative concept and was completely new in category technologies. This was a product from realm 3 or 4 thinking on my funnel map. **It broke the rules** and created new ones in the carpet-cleaning market with a bag-free, colourful, attractive, design-led, fashion item, with high functionality and high novelty value at a premium price, all to Dyson's commercial advantage. For sure several thousand iterations – as component contributions – went into the original innovation. Once a product is established, iterative product improvement is no longer innovation. It becomes NPD of an innovative legacy. Using the funnel map, once a new product or service gets down to mass manufacture in realm 1 or 2, any further development is NPD.

talk of innovation successes in the past tense

Innovation is a consequence of historical actions and decisions. On that basis it is dangerous to self declare that you **are** innovative. It is better to talk of innovation successes in the past tense to keep employees' attention on the whole 'food chain' and not just the success of delivery at realm 1. If innovation is a consequence of historical actions and decisions the seeds of your innovative capability may be present but unrecognised or supported.

Good intentions, limited capability

With regard to innovation, there are multiple uncertainties, one of which is **where** to begin and **who** to begin with. The ability to innovate is in large part about the ability of interesting combinations of people and the way they are encouraged and allowed to think and take decisions. It's easy to get it wrong **even when talent is abundant**. IBM found this to its cost before the behemoth successfully reinvented itself.

Starting with people seasoned in research methodology is unlikely to create a revelation. There simply isn't enough money, time or resources available to be so completely thoroughly logical to get to the discoveries needed by a ground up, deductive, logical route.

John Kearon, founder of BrainJuicer,[79] an innovative, global research agency, agrees. He says large corporations '*marketing science … has actively hindered their ability to create the new category "blue ocean" innovations that made them big in the first place*'. The thrust of his article is that new thinking and new behaviours (realm 3 and 4 on my funnel) are required to give birth to innovation.[80]

Leading-edge research involves dealing with the unknown and the uncertain and inspired thought. This is not the territory of typical realm 1 and 2 thinkers. Having an ability to locate breakthroughs based on inspiration and unusual thinking skills is a hallmark of leading innovators. Einstein imagined riding a beam of light as a prelude to $E = mc^2$. In the mid-1800s the German chemist Friedrich August Kekulé's dream of a ring of snakes biting their tails inspired his discovery of the structure of the benzene ring, a fundamental breakthrough in organic chemistry. People who can make leaps of inspiration are needed for breakthrough thinking. Innovators generally operate above, not below, the ambiguity ceiling. Starting 'the process' with grounded, structured, disciplined thinkers would therefore be wrong.

Uncertainty as to process

Innovation cannot be codified. A 'process for innovation' is an oxymoron. Generally speaking, it is a fruitless task to look for deterministic answers to 'open-ended' problems such as innovation – or love, for that matter. Both are elusive.

Neither is ever really mastered. There is no one right way to love, to innovate or find wisdom. The best you can do is to locate the most likely stepping stones, obstacles and pitfalls, to pay attention, learn and adapt as you find a unique way forward. You need to find your own unique truths.

Even when you discover your unique solutions, there are multiple dilemmas that can frustrate successful implementation. You can still fail even after you have developed an innovative product or service. There are uncertain gaps of technology, expectations, finance, personalities and opinion. The next big hurdle is then to get them widely distributed. Being innovative is not necessarily a guarantee of commercial success.

Summary

Reconciling the extreme differences of perception and reality of grounded, focused, hard-edged, rule-bound, no-defect thinkers AND rule-breaking, creative, lofty thinkers with their heads in the clouds is not easy. Winning through innovation is not a question of either/or but of AND. In other words, both classes of thinking and behaving are needed, along with hand-offs and linkages to build true innovations. Returning to my funnel model, this means realms 1 and 2 **plus** 3 and 4 thinking and action to create a viable intellectual and production ecology, an intellectual 'food chain'.

Chapter 11 Section 2

Right perceptions of innovation

An innovation is an outcome, not a process. Ditto love. No formula is involved, but you can increase the odds by understanding the journey, various expectations and obvious pitfalls. Think of true innovation as an attribute and a virtue defined **not by you** but independently by your customers and peers. It is a brief, valuable accolade easily seen '**after the fact**', yet is difficult to produce or predict. As with love, there are no absolute rules with innovation.

With innovation, you have to find your own truths, your own originality and your own 'heart of the matter'. What is discovered during your difficult journey becomes an important part of your evolution towards being an innovative team.

with innovation you have to find your own truths

The acid test for locating or defining an innovation is simple: 'As a consequence of your new introduction have the rules of your particular game been completely upended and changed in your favour so that you gain substantially?' If you answer, 'No', then there has been no true breakthrough, merely improvement at best.

Uncertainty mindsets and mapping opportunities

If the core difficulties to do with innovation are to do with different and often misunderstood perceptions, then my reality map can help us understand how and where potentially productive interventions may be placed.

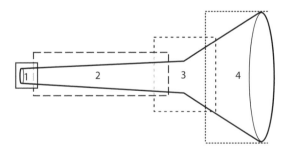

Future backwards

Consider **who** leads the operation and who they report to. Which of the four domains do they normally inhabit as suggested by their most frequent behaviour? Then consider if they are static or in which thinking/acting direction they typically move.

Revelation

Revelations involve a synthesis at the uncertain margins of our perception where reality has not yet fully formed. (4←→3) We also need to be aware that this is an emotional space where multiple uncertainties are engaged. Words, feelings and images may be involved. From a future backwards standpoint, travelling from 4 towards 3, there will be no hard data, no market research, just a difficult-to-explain gut feeling or intuition. Embracing uncertainty is therefore a very important first step. It involves risk at several levels.

An innovation 'food chain'

For me, an innovation 'food chain' involves an evolutionary, often messy non-linear progression, eventually from 4 to 3 to 2 to 1. In other words, there is an overall progression right to left along the funnel.

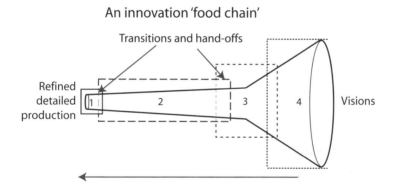

An innovation 'food chain'

It starts with a revelation or an inspiration (4) that may be riddled with faults and shortcomings, but by the time the starting concept has been reworked and adapted multiple times (3) it, or something totally unexpected, emerges out of ambiguity into development (2) and then enters high refinement (1) as a finished product or service. Along the way, the pattern may be reversed as new problems emerge, but the successful product, service or behaviour eventually becomes something tangible that can be used.

The origins of the flash of inspiration can come from anywhere along the food chain **but** they then need to go through the same overall development sequence in order to extract full value. Attempting an exploratory journey that starts at 1 and 2 and attempts to project rigour onto the uncertain, unknown spaces is of dubious value. Forward projections based only on past market research and deductive reasoning are equally unlikely to deliver a revelation.

A team that lacks original thinking and the ability to work in realm 3 or 4 is unlikely to produce a revelation. Locating a true innovation involves dealing honestly with uncertain futures AND an original, interesting, unanswered question about something significant that will eventually have scale. The outcomes then depend on the quality of the minds engaged at each stage of the intellectual food chain.

outcomes depend on the quality of the minds engaged at each stage of the intellectual food chain

Hand-offs and interactions

A sure connection needs to be made between all parts of the 'innovation food chain'. The right kind of thinking and awareness of direction of travel, in addition to well-managed hand-offs and interactions between different domains are needed. This requires a humanistic element at the sensitive end of development because cold machine-minded efficiency (1) is likely to kill off nascent thinking at 3 or 4 as flawed or 'risky'. Working out how people can safely interact AND value each other's way of making progress by different and sometimes alien methods requires a good helping of faith and trust.

Useful volatility

A huge uncertainty involves getting seriously different types of people to get along with each other. When the passion for freedom of expression and novel innovation clashes with the passion for rigour and control, the obstacles to progress can be magnified. Getting beliefs aligned is therefore an important prelude to bridging the gaps.

One very easy to predict source of conflict occurs when grounded and airborne types fail to acknowledge each other's value. Vijay Govindarajan and Chris Trimble caution entrepreneurial people that if passions are misdirected, the person on the fringes loses out when it comes to a fight with people in charge of big operational units.[81]

This is a problem, but such differences could be usefully employed as an opportunity to build a dialogue to negotiate boundaries and hand-off mechanisms. For example, Apple has gone through several cathartic learning periods. During its history, Apple has swung from a high of great design-led, free, youthful, contemporary ethos, to a low of tie-wearing, efficiency-focused, leadership. Neither seems to have proved sustainable. Steve Jobs now heads an organisation that **combines** great design freedom AND strict financial and production discipline. Both are required. Apple owns its 'innovation food chain' and is close-coupled to a mega-market of hundreds of millions of loyal, mostly pleased customers. Apple appears to segment the way it develops its business by fiercely guarding a freethinking, experimental product zone AND at the other end of the scale fosters relationships with highly efficient, low-cost manufacturing sites in Asia. This configuration allows Apple to focus on what Apple does best and to generate and capture substantial profits along the whole system.

Uncertainty tolerance

The front end of the 'innovation food chain' needs realms 3 and 4 ability. There is a very high requirement to tolerate uncertainty because a lot of the work involves grappling with complex and ambiguous environments. At Innocent Drinks, Richard Reed tells new recruits to take 70 percent as good enough to go with a decision but at the same time instils the imperative to speak up and say something is rubbish (to anyone including the directors) if that is what they honestly think.[82]

> ### take 70 percent as good enough to go with a decision

Turning to your situation, how 'elastic' or tolerant are you and your colleagues? Low tolerance of uncertainty in a leader or a key team player can present a fundamental barrier to innovation if applied at the wrong place in the food chain. The value-adding skill is to create an 'innovation food chain' where the level of certainty involved suits individual temperaments.

- As an organisation, how well are you configured to cope with the four realms and the personality types involved?
- Do you have enough or too many of a particular type?

Status issues

One of the obstacles that needs to be removed involves a perceived difference of status associated with being an 'innovator' versus being an 'improver'. Both are extremely valuable roles but are in nature substantially different. Confusing the two or failing to differentiate them clearly does not serve anyone and may perpetuate a culture of self-deception. Senior managers need to understand, risk-assess and reward the two different skills. Strategically it's a good idea to decide which of the two you are individually and collectively better at.

Fickle serendipity

Innovating at a leading edge can be misleading. The outcome may not work in an expected way and serendipity may come calling. It takes imagination, curiosity and adaptive, responsive minds to get her to stay long enough for you to capture value. Imagine what would have happened if Fleming had thrown away those mouldy agar plates. Billion dollar profits would not have been captured if Pfizer scientists had completely closed down a heart-drug research study that failed, where trial volunteers were reluctant to return their unused pills that seemed to have a rather pleasant side effect on their sex lives.

The uncertainty of time to market

A perception that your proposed innovation will ride in, just in time to save or make the day is generally a question of misplaced faith. Practitioners say that getting an innovation to graduate into a fully fledged beneficial, rule-breaking, market-changing position often takes much longer than anticipated.

Adam, Jon and Richard found that their new drinks were very popular with their friends and expected quick success. Despite having a great new product, finding financial backers and launching their products took substantially longer than expected. The three founders of Innocent Drinks had expected to get their great new healthy drinks onto the shelves of major outlets in a matter of months.

Concept	Years before commercialised
Ballpoint pen	58
Continuous steel casting	25
Fluorescent lighting	37
Helicopter	32
Jet engine	13
Kodachrome® film*	14
Nylon	11
Penicillin	15
Radio	18
Television	13
Zipper	32

* Kodachrome® is a registered mark of Eastman Kodak

The uncertainty of keeping up

Repeating and sustaining the ability to generate revelations and a stream of innovation requires real talent and retained unique knowledge. Can you sustain your ability to innovate again and again or will you be a one-hit wonder? Whatever you do will require organisation and good people.

Chapter 11 Section 3

Organising people

A fundamental problem with high-performance, innovating teams involves the intellectual stretch required to reach from a feathery dream (realm 4 in my funnel) right down to the tiniest picky detail (realm 1), so that a dream becomes a working reality that results in significant beneficial change in previously established behaviour.

Organising people and systems into an intelligent 'food chain' presumes you already have the right talent on board. That's unlikely. Tribal behaviour tends to push out people who are 'different'. Often the people who generated the existing generation of revelations will have left your organisation some time ago or are hidden. Locating and acquiring the right sorts of talents is critical. Given the challenge of getting vastly different types of minds to work together ,retention is the next major hurdle.

Tapping internal talent

Gifford Pinchot III coined the term 'intrapreneur',[83] meaning entrepreneurs that already work for you. In all probability there are only a few intrapreneurs in large corporations, possibly as few as one per thousand. Finding and fostering them, whilst difficult, could be disproportionately rewarding because they can, in the right conditions, push the boundaries and help you locate valuable, original opportunities. If you track current successes and then look for who pioneered them at their origins it is probable that your early intrapreneurs have moved on and taken their magic somewhere else. Retention of awkward talent is a real challenge.

Short rides on the innovation bus

Novozymes is a successful Danish Biotech firm that holds more than 6000 patents and has built an internal network of entrepreneurs. The company took a smart decision to recruit into this team **external** people who showed entrepreneurial spirit.[84] In many cases the new people had prior experience in developing and building up their own businesses.

Novozymes were aware that this sort of recruit could be very different from existing employees and would probably want to leave after a short period of time. Despite this Novozymes decided that even a couple of years of their time would be enough to provoke inspiration and learning that would benefit the organisation.

Challenging uncertainty

British Airways had, for a brief period in the mid-1990s, a 'corporate jester', a role applauded as a management innovation in the *Financial Times*. Unfortunately, the role did not last. Pity. I found him to be an imaginative, talented, strategic, thinker.

Adopting such a role is not for the faint-hearted. Without the king's support, a wannabe jester is likely to get shoved off the top of the nearest tower by any number of henchmen. Any takers? If not, then responsibility for honest challenge falls to **whole teams**, or better still **everyone** gets into the habit of fearlessly and respectfully telling the truth. How would that play out in your organisation?

My primary point is that innovation can be just as much about developing original new employee and leadership **behaviour patterns** as it is about creating new products and services. Do you currently have any change behaviour programmes linked to genuinely innovative activity? Have you won any awards for this?

Team intelligence overcomes uncertainty

Innovation of **leadership behaviour** is bound to happen as a response to increased uncertainty as environments become more complex. As the content of work becomes ever more complex it is becoming less likely that any one individual will possess all of the required skills and experience to complete a project alone to a high professional standard.

Even if you do locate such a superhuman mind, additional team support will usually be required to complete and finish his or her concepts, and to mop up unfortunate outcomes.

Small teams, as opposed to individuals, are more likely to be required to locate solutions AND take important decisions when faced with increasing uncertainty. I foresee the future as likely to involve core team leaderships replacing the top man (more often than not, it's a man). This would involve very small teams (three or five individuals) of intimately connected people replacing the authority vested in just one individual at the top.

Chapter 11 Section 4

Academic and practitioner insights

Glossed-over, sanitised, oversimplified textbook versions of success often provide the smell of a dish but not the meal itself. Even if you did detect the author's truth about how an organisation innovated, their particular truth cannot realistically become your truth. The way you love or innovate cannot be imitated. There are only clues to be detected and assembled into your own meaning of what it is to innovate.

Not everyone survives the challenge. Innovation can be very expensive. Relatively risky exploration work can sometimes lead up a blind alley. Some seemingly blind alleys do eventually lead to a payback, but only those with very deep pockets, tenacity and patience reap the benefits.

Below are some real-life examples of what other people are doing. This is not an exhaustive or comprehensive oversight; however, the examples do suggest some valuable clues to what may become your truth, your own frame of reference about the uncertain subject of innovation.

Don't innovate, be a fast follower

Follow a completely different frame of reference. Don't innovate. Often a lower cost route to market is to be a fast follower. If this particular route is available but not chosen, ask, 'Why do you walk past the easy pickings?' Copying to create 'me too' imitations need not be a low-status move. This route to prosperity has been successfully adopted by several emerging economies, including Japan from the 1960s onward, to gain footholds.

Adopting a strategy to be a fast follower is a valid commercial proposition that carries significantly less risk than innovation does. The key to success using this route is a better understanding of customer usage and needs and being able to add value or utility or ease of access or use in a timely and responsive way so that **your** competitive advantage is created. Sometimes added value is a matter of figuring out the 'food chain' in which the product or service sits and recrafting your offer so that your part in the chain flows better for those connected to you. This is not innovation. No fundamental rules have changed, but it can be a good faster route to improved performance and profit at lower risk.

R, R and D

The long game involves generating sufficient sustainable surpluses, profits, knowledge and talent to develop your own revelation, research and development (R, R and D) so that if you choose to innovate you are decently funded and resourced. Some fast followers have done just that. Professor Oded Shenkar's book *Copycats*[85] provides a wealth of examples of companies that have copied and adapted the work of others to produce and distribute acceptable AND profitable products and services. Imitators, though derided in literature, can sometimes surpass original innovators in terms of added-value, long-term customer preference, market share and ultimately profitability. The other side of this particular insight is a warning to innovators to watch out for a competitor who has decided to eat the innovative lunch you invested in!

Real world examples

This next example pulls together many of the important themes covered so far in this book. It is based on a recent interview. Almost every aspect of the inner/ outer world/ wider context/ model are encountered here, including a clear frame of reference, acknowledged feelings, capabilities and values. The way projects and teams of people are configured is carefully considered. Success as well as some failure is factored in. Scale is considered from the outset. Rational AND non-rational ideas, ambiguities and contradictions are accommodated along a well-thought through intellectual and commercial 'food chain'. The Teams develop character and resilience by virtue of being aligned. This is a rewarding environment for individuals and the organisation in terms of performance.

Passion AND patience

Eric Peeters,[86] Business Vice-President of Solar Dow Corning Corporation, says, 'At Dow Corning we have continued to evolve our approach to innovation. Our innovations have sustained double-digit growth over recent years and our pipeline is set to continue that trend.'

Incremental AND breakthrough

Eric makes a clear distinction between incremental and breakthrough innovation. Incremental innovation, he suggests, involves steady annual improvements of 5 percent; 'We focus on both. We established a business incubator where our strategy for innovation can differ depending on life cycle positions. Within established businesses, growth tends to be incremental. We drive current profitability to fund investment in future breakthroughs. We've focused on high-level portfolio management projects beyond three years AND on short-term cash management. We cannot take our past success for granted.'

Seeking mega-trends

'Strategically we look for five or six mega-trends that we believe will be important to us. We aim to detect class level innovations and then form a portfolio with sufficient critical mass. Within each mega-trend we spend two or three months discovering projects and looking for major market and profitability potential that must surpass a one hundred million dollar annual revenue hurdle to be included.'

Right people

'Our business incubator has strong leadership backing. Four years ago we created a new leadership role called a "business builder". Given that some projects run to seven years, we expect there will be more than one business builder on a project. We also use a lot of external inputs such as design studios, universities, technology experts and so on in the early discovery phase and again just prior to graduation.'

Right mindset

'One absolutely key skill involves **passion** AND **patience**. Too much passion and people burn out, but not enough patience means you kill the project too soon. We have a high level of passion and belief. This requires managers to be skilled in dealing productively with this energy. Occasionally there are conflicts but the majority of the energy goes into getting results. We also couple **passion** AND **objectivity**. We are always ready to be confronted by the brutal facts. This means we generate energetic breakthrough ideas but our decisions are also tempered with rational common sense so that we do not get carried away.'

Tolerances of ambiguity

'Having a high tolerance of ambiguity and uncertainty is very important as there is a huge difference between those people who can foster incremental benefits and those that pursue breakthroughs. We have learned how to spot individuals who can cope with the high levels of uncertainty and ambiguity involved in breakthrough innovations. In just a few questions I can usually spot the tolerance level.

'We need people in the breakthrough teams who can get along using the minimum of data. We know that probably three out of ten projects will come good. That means the individuals leading one project either succeed or they do not. For them it is all or nothing.'

Resilience

'There is an almost daily onslaught of reasons to give up on a project, but the special individuals who carry on are those who have the tenacity to hold on to the passion that their project will come good. They will only stop when the hard cold data flags up that the project cannot continue. We value people who have the resilience to keep going when it gets tough, because developing breakthrough ideas is almost always tough.'

Innovation is a marathon NOT a sprint

'Over the years we changed the people involved and learned important lessons along the way. We also learned that it takes a lot longer than we expected to get a breakthrough to market. It took seven years to graduate our solar business into a real business. Innovation is **not** a sprint but a marathon. If you are breaking new ground it means completely new ways of doing things, new ways of manufacturing and so on. Going the distance requires tenacity.'

Difficulties in developing innovation

- 'People. Getting the right people with the right attitude, skills and experience.
- Managing the balance between passion and patience (tolerance of ambiguity).
- Confronting the facts quickly means finding people who can in five minutes, on the back of an envelope, evaluate the key issues and success factors. This prevents projects from going too far before someone realises the basic business model is flawed.'

Opportunities for developing innovation

- 'Detecting and exploiting mega-trends.
- Resolving the difficulty with the transition from programme to business. There is an issue at the hand-offs between horizon 3 and horizon 1. The different types of people involved have very different viewpoints.'

I suggested that four out of these five key issues involved the philosophy of what people believe and how they think about things and how people relate to the issues and to each other. Eric replied, 'You are absolutely right and do you know, the philosophy and psychology of it all are not taught skills in schools or business schools. We picked up our philosophy and psychology on the job.'

> ### we picked up our philosophy and psychology on the job

Insights from innovation at IBM

An organisation as large as IBM is not and never has been short of talent but even bright people can fail too. IBM employed 400,000 people worldwide in 1986 but halved to 200,000 by 1994 along with declining revenues.

Matching talent with opportunity

A turning point was reached in the mid-1990s.[87] The company's brush with failure led to a deep understanding of several shortcomings that needed to be fixed. They recognised a failure to reap commercial rewards from innovations that IBM pursued. A pervasive rational, but quite short-term, risk-averse company psychology had led to undue focus on just one of several possible business horizons. The company reorganised to fully capture the benefits of innovation. Senior management began to appreciate that different mindsets and philosophies were required in order to run and exploit different opportunities at each of several horizons.

IBM needed to grow its own entrepreneurial culture to take advantage of several 'future horizon' business opportunities. From the mid-1990s, IBM regained stability and as part of a wide range of initiatives then set up the 'Emerging Business Organization' (EBO) in 2000. In the following five years the EBO added more than $15 billion to IBM's revenues. This organic growth was more than double the growth achieved through acquisitions over the same period. Six years later new revenues from EBOs accounted for more than 20 percent of sales.

Part of the answer to enabling productive and profitable innovation lay in resolving the dilemma of a mismatch between power and status. Do you put youthful talented energy ahead of deep commercial experience and depth? Apparently no. The company discovered that young bright minds were **not** necessarily the best recruits for their huge new business growth projects, simply because capability alone was not enough.

The thresholds for these new businesses were sustainable, profitable sales in excess of one billion dollars in three to five years' time. This required not only intellectual capability and business competence but also deep commercial experience coupled with **a wide network of internal and external relationships**. Senior execs had this. All they had to do was adapt. EBO champions observed, with some humour, how IBM executives seasoned in directing huge operations would enter the process '*so pent-up and tight*' and would then have to adapt and struggle with completely new beliefs and behaviours.

Building a brand new business from scratch as opposed to managing and running an established organisation presented a very high risk for a successful IBM executive. IBM recognised this and provided CEO support in the beginning. High-profile, high-risk, new roles need to be closely aligned with the most senior champions, if they are to have any chance of survival.

Other findings

High-tech leading-edge myth

There are low-cost ways of innovating, e.g. changed behaviour and revised allocation of responsibilities and locations. Some believe that high technology holds all the answers. That can be true but less so than you might imagine.

One of the world's very best car makers intentionally does not install the very latest electronics technology, not because of price but because their primary concern is with rock solid, proven reliability. This prestigious car maker is not alone in adopting this policy. Low tech makes really good sense. What they want are high-volume, reasonably priced, but most of all, they require the reliable supply of fault-free, proven, durable parts.

Good enough will do

The key lesson is that when it comes to technology 'good enough will do'. Clayton Christensen discovered a trend in which technology companies eventually overshot what customers actually needed and often over engineered their products.[88] A technocentric approach costs more and adds no benefit, creating a gap for lower-cost, dumbed-down, new entrants to exploit.

Low tech works too

Take a fresh look at some of your old cash cows. Even the simplest of products can benefit from an innovative approach. Who would have thought 20 years ago that the concept of bagged, washed lettuce leaves would quickly lead to a multi-billion-dollar market? The product looks simple now but consider, at the outset, how many glasshouse lettuce growers were aware of, let alone experts in, sealed bagging, cut food, gas management and rapid distribution to produce this form of table-ready food.

The bagged lettuce example illustrates that a novel idea often demands that brand new relationships be formed. Sometimes a new partner can bring in radically different ways of thinking AND new technology that creates a substantial advantage. Sometimes it's just 'old thinking' that gets in the way.

The new guard becomes the old guard

A core contradiction of innovation leadership involves **you**, as both a potential opportunity AND as the equally powerful source of future problems.

Clayton Christensen used an analysis of manufacturers of small disc drives as the business equivalent of drosophila fruit flies employed in genetics experiments. Both have relatively short life cycles, so changes that impact likely survival can be studied fairly quickly. He also studied how smaller, faster, scrap-metal recyclers eventually broke the rules of the big steel game by applying low volume methods in an industry dominated by high-energy and high-volume production.[89] Could this pattern emerge in your business?

Clayton Christensen's research describes the innovator's dilemma as a surprise: *'The logical competent decisions of management that are critical to the success of their companies are also the reasons why they lose their positions of leadership.'* Those that listened closely to their customers' needs, followed the market trends, logically allocated resources and invested heavily in new technology to provide their customers with better products **lost** their leadership positions.[90]

The tenor of the dilemma Clayton Christensen describes is that bottom-up, logically derived development loses ground to disruptive or to what I would describe as, true, innovation. Another way to think about the dilemma is that the challenging new guard succeeds and progressively becomes the resistant old guard.

This testifies to the ever-present need to maintain a flexible, adaptive mind. Accept that you will be wrong some of the time and show grace in admitting to a need to change your mind. Sometimes you need to do more than that; you need to start over and destroy what you already have to create something better.

DYB

Another challenge to conventional thinking and established wisdom originates from Jack Welch who was once referred to as 'Neutron Jack'. He had a number of constantly challenging remedies that kept very large numbers of executives on their toes at GE, a huge American-based global organisation. He led many initiatives that cut cost and administration. During his tenure, his company's share price zoomed along with performance.[91]

One particularly creative idea that is relevant to those who wish to engage disruptive innovation AND to protect themselves against active competitors is his philosophy of DYB[92] – **d**estroy **y**our own **b**usiness! Figure out how a competitor would disrupt and destroy your business by applying a better model and then do it to your own business quickly, before they do. How does that sound to you? Any suggestions?

Suggestion box saviours

A relatively common desire to access the latent talents of employees can lead to a proposal to start a suggestion box. Can an employee suggestion box help?

It is possible but unlikely. I'm not a great fan of the classic company suggestion box simply because my own research and that of others shows such schemes, no matter how well intentioned, eventually disappoint. Typically 80 percent of proposals are rejected. They become rejection schemes. Over time, employee engagement and enthusiasm for such schemes die off. I did notice that quick, short-run schemes performed reasonably well, as long as they were genuinely boxed off and finished and left fallow for a long period afterwards.

Different ways of thinking and behaving are required if you wish to engage and empower your workforce so that contribution of new ideas becomes natural and commonplace. This approach requires a whole new philosophy along with a history of authentic behaviours that flow from this.

Sometimes the answers your organisation needs don't come from within. They come from free thinkers outside.

Cisco's 'crowd sourcing'

Externally sourcing new business concepts has proved productive for Cisco. At the time of writing, the system is novel. 'Crowd-sourcing' has worked for them two years in a row.[93,94] They are now into their third wave of encouraging individuals and teams to pitch for a $250,000 'I-prize' for coming up with a new business concept for a Cisco target theme. Cisco gets all rights to the winning idea. Importantly, losers keep all of their IP.

What I like is that this process is not just a post and dump scheme. The scheme is potentially collaborative, and entrants are encouraged to network with other, so-far-unknown entrants, from around the world, using Cisco-supplied online web-networking tools. Teams are encouraged to progressively refine and judge ideas with others.

The first concept to win the prize, a sensor-enabled smart-electricity grid, was chosen from 2500 global entrants. The second 'I-prize' programme saw 3000 global entrants competing. The winning team of five young people submitted a concept described as a 'Life Account'. This is conceived as a combination of actual and virtual technologies that understands habits and behaviour patterns for the benefit of the user.

Cisco's approach is not innovation on the cheap because considerable cost is incurred in the allocation of full-time staff, web resources, filtering and concept testing. In arriving at a winner, Cisco's internal 'expert blindness' was purposefully mitigated by including external people and entrants as a part of the filtering process. They say that the winning concept is not the end of the line. It gets included in their new business concept process, added to, amended, adapted and further refined.

Last few words on innovation

There is an immense amount of research and practitioner insight on the subject of innovation. In 1995 I was given access to a British MBA lecture resource pack designed to help deliver innovation skills more widely. The pack was developed by several of our best business school professors from around the UK. The document pile was several feet thick and growing! Interestingly, nowhere within this divergent body of work was a clear answer, a distinct pattern or the right way. That made sense because 'innovation' is itself a divergent subject; the more you dig, the more you realise how the subject opens up. My conclusion then, as now, is that you have to find your own truths for the context in which you plan to produce a significant change.

A large part of my particular truth about innovation comes courtesy of a British 3M strategist who in 1997 told me, *'Our strategy for innovation is simple. It's all about relationships.'*

If you want to innovate:

- get a good philosophy for your ambition.
- understand valuable differences between people. Form an intelligent 'food chain' AND hand-offs linking all four bases in my certainty funnel.
- collaborate. Use 'fun'. Ensure you engage feelings and encourage laughter.
- get into creative conflict when required.
- orchestrate what you all do.
- fail a few times and exercise appropriate humility.
- be patient but pushy too.
- build resilience and keep learning from others.

Innovating and careful husbandry of an organisation leaves a positive legacy for others and their children's children. There is no room for greed and/or dishonesty. Be honest about your ambition. If you are, other people will be inspired.

Summary

Any relationship in life or business built on a lie or a mistaken perception is unsafe. Starting with honest perceptions and hanging on to them is the best place to begin to truly innovate. Getting perceptions right from the outset allows a more effective allocation of people and resources. Before you embark on an innovation quest, ask yourself:

- why are you doing this?
- what do you hope to gain?
- when do you hope to gain from your innovation?
- what alternative lower cost options are available to achieve the same, better or similar ends?

The subject matter of innovation is really open-ended and quite slippery. Many aspects of innovation therefore defy definition. Consequently you need to be aware, to reflect on your needs as well as the capabilities and resources available. Then you need to consider how people think and interact when faced with volatility and divergence of opinion **before** you start. Also just because you want something it does not necessarily follow that you will get what you seek. Above all you will be changed by your journey. You will need to adapt, many times over.

Reflection

- What part of these notes made you think? What ideas or comments rattled you the most and what, if anything, made you laugh?
- When were you surprised?
- What subjects or perceptions of change and innovation are you open or closed to?
- When was the last time you 'experimented' or had some fun exploring?
- Is your next 'big thing' a genuine new game or an old game re-enacted in new garb?
- Would a representative, independent, outsider panel agree with your internal analysis of how good you think you are?

Chapter 12
The ambiguities of strategy

My objective in this book is not to suggest the right answers but to get you to think for yourself to locate your own interesting questions in order to arrive at a better perception of what is possible. The way you think is an essential part of strategic thinking.

I have addressed the uncertainties of strategy in three sections:

Section 1: Wrong question, wrong start

Section 2: Better perceptions of strategy

Section 3: People, systems and implementation

Section 1

Wrong question, wrong start
Smoke and mirrors

When it comes to working out a grand strategy for yourself or your business, there are sufficient uncertainties and ambiguities to start a mystic priesthood! Good ways of strategic thinking and execution remain difficult to establish, despite a plethora of consultants offering advice and professors suggesting neat models. This is because the subject of strategy opens out and diverges in many directions from relatively few, simple questions:

- Where are you now?
- Where do you want to go?
- Why particularly do you want to get 'there'?
- How do you intend to get there and who or what will obstruct you?
- How will you know when you have arrived at your goal?
- A vital question, often overlooked, is 'What will you do afterwards?'

The family of difficulties associated with strategic planning are similar to those with innovation. Different perceptions of reality and tolerance of uncertainty have a strong influence on the people doing the planning. This leads to several difficulties. At one extreme is the perception that the future is an extension of the past, perhaps plus or minus a few percent. At the other extreme is the view that a vision is required. Then there are problems of insight and suffering the fate of Cassandra of not being believed by those who have power and control.

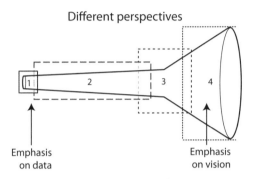

Different perspectives

Emphasis on data   Emphasis on vision

Single point forecast

A major uncertainty is the false sense of security engendered by reducing important forces or intentions to linear graphs. Charting the future is popular with people grounded in deductive logic (realm 1 or 2). In times of slow change or enduring stability, this approach might work, for a while. But who believes we live in certain times? I don't. Even in stable times, a single-point future projection makes far too many risky assumptions. A belief that the future is a simple extension of the past, plus or minus whatever percentage, is nonsense.

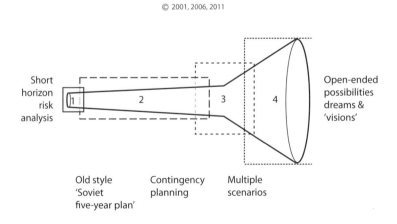

Strategy and
Reid's Reality Funnel
© 2001, 2006, 2011

Short horizon risk analysis

Open-ended possibilities dreams & 'visions'

Old style 'Soviet five-year plan'   Contingency planning   Multiple scenarios

The new old plan

Forward projections based on history regarding an uncertain future can feel a little more 'secure' and reassuringly robust if they passed scrutiny by senior executives the year before. Such rationally derived results run the risk of becoming a serial iteration of what is hoped for rather than what is likely. Leaders then run the risk of repeating old mistakes by following old, unquestioned habits.

Faulty logic and untested assumptions do not improve with iterative regurgitation. Think of this approach as a serial repeat showing of *The Emperor's New Clothes* by Hans Christian Andersen. A brave youth is required to give voice to honest observation; that is, if you haven't screened them out or frightened them to death already!

The vision thing

Imagination is valuable but runs the risk of becoming disconnected. Creating a vision is a step in the right direction. The problem remains: what if your vision of the future turns out to be wrong?

Misplaced optimism

Another strategic uncertainty that gets overlooked is longevity. People wrongly assume a business has an infinite life, when most evidently fail to last. Not many enterprises make it past 100 years. According to one Japanese research house only 11 made it past 1000 years.[95] Being honest as to where your business actually is in its life cycle together with a realistic assessment of the remaining life it has in it will be essential if you want to produce a decent strategic plan. Also planning for a new business is quite different from one that has topped out or is actually on the skids. Resource allocation and effort can be wasted if you get this assessment wrong or if you are overly optimistic or too pessimistic. Who will tell you the unpleasant truths when you are powerful?

Uncertain starting points, models or mindset

People who are new to the subject want to know what the best models are. You will find there are lots of models. Real strategic skill involves a peculiar combination of thinking and sensing skills involving both logical-rational AND non-rational skills (i.e. feelings!). The way information is intellectually processed and synthesised is really important too. If you are new I suggest you try out and locate several quite different models. If you are not new to the subject, I'd still suggest you locate some new models and experiment to test for complacency. Find the ones that work for you and your team. By 'work for you' I wish to imply that the models provoke curious and interesting questions that lead to insight or a rich dialogue. Then consider the manner in which you choose to think.

Your success, and if you are a soldier, your life, pivots on good thinking, smart questions and a smart strategy. The output from any model, framework or dialogue depends on what you push through it. Pearls in, pearls out. Rubbish in, rubbish out.

Dodgy time lines

The standard planning period for a lot of companies was the old Soviet five-year planning cycle. Five years is about the length of the average government election cycle in democratic countries. Alternatively it is about two job changes of a middle manager. Whatever the reason, a one-size-fits-all strategic time line of five years makes no sense at all. It doesn't help.

The other problem is that when forward planning falls into disuse busy managers choose to substitute strategic planning with two or three-year budgeting periods that are linked to performance targets and bonuses. This is not wise. Long-term strategy should not be pushed off radar by greed or a lack of long-term planning skills. The question is, 'What is long-term?' Getting the time line right is important.

> When asked, 'What do you think of the French revolution of 1789?', Chairman Mao, former leader of Communist China, replied, 'Too soon to tell.'

Narrow context

A common limitation that leaves large uncertainties unexamined is that management's focus of attention can be too narrow or has significant blind spots. For example, have you considered the availability and price of oil, world population growth, climate, the availability of basic resources or the sudden impact of 300 million new-to-market wealthy people or the gradual impoverishment of parts of first-world countries, as economics shift in favour of global trade?

Ego tripped out

In spite of George Bernard Shaw's observation that all progress depends on the unreasonable man, a major strategic uncertainty arises when top management egos get in the way of intelligent sense. It is important to remain vigilant. A foolish presumption would be that because someone in a top job has a self-generated map, they know the future. It's too late now but we should have expressed much more concern when bankers and people in positions of economic power started to describe themselves as 'masters of the universe'. Collectively we have to be concerned, not just about their mental health but also about the ripple effect on the rest of us of their faulty decisions and crushingly wrong assumptions such as, 'we are too big to fail'. Send for the men with straightjackets! No matter how much these monster egos shout or bluster from on high, no one can know what the future holds; it's uncertain!

Chapter 12 Section 2

Better perceptions of strategy

Strategic planning can be about a personal future, the future of an organisation or a nation state. The basic concepts arise out of the same principles. Be as rational as you like AND keep your eyes and mind open to the possibility of surprise and a little magic.

several equally plausible futures may be possible

Good strategic thinking precedes formal planning. It starts with clear and honest perception in those who have an orientation and an ability to think on several levels at once. Essentially, smart strategists are aware that **several** equally plausible futures may be possible. Also, an important way of thinking involves detecting weak signals that may suggest an increased or decreased likelihood of one or more far bigger patterns beginning to play out. They know single point planning is dangerous. They also know that life will not play by their rules or expectations and that they will have to adapt as they proceed.

Why are you here?

Rookies often overlook the simple strategic question as to the purpose of why you are where you are presently. Do you collectively/individually understand your reason for 'being', for your very existence? Are you sure that the reasons for 'being' as you are now will be the same in the future?

Central to any strategic thinking process are your intentions.

- What are they and what will they be as time passes?
- What would disrupt your original intention?
- Have you been distracted from your original intention and if so why and what do you intend to do about it?

How long will you be 'here'?

I mentioned earlier that people overlook the overall lifetime expectation for the organisation. Having an idea of the genuine life cycle position of your organisation can aid decision-making and guide investment and leadership behaviours. Assuming you have thought through 'why we are here and for how long', the next step is to consider the fundamental assumptions behind choosing an appropriate time period for your planning.

Ambiguous scenarios

The Shell Oil Company profited considerably from using this approach. Scenario planning is a valuable antidote to myopic, single-point forecasting. The primary intention of scenario planning is not to generate an accurate future estimate but to create several equally plausible futures based on group intelligence and outside resources. A well-composed and memorable set of working scenarios then act as a decision-testing framework that embrace a variety of future contingencies. This encourages adaptability and the retention of sufficient flexibility to respond to future major shocks and opportunities. It also keeps managers alert to faint signals of bigger changes looming.

Scenarios can be produced in a variety of ways. Some methods are overly indulgent and perhaps that is one reason why the technique fell out of favour for a while. There are other ways of developing insights on a faster basis. A central requirement in producing valuable scenarios is locating key, high-impact variables. These variables are tacitly held in the collective mind of the organisation and can be teased out into the open. A simple scenario archetype might look like this:

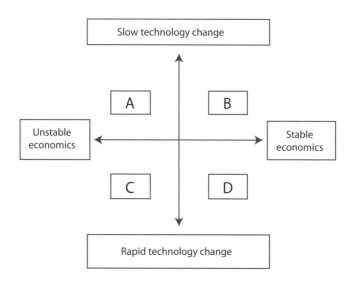

Assuming we had found the major variables, four quite different situations A, B, C and D are then synthesised. A summary name is developed to identify each segment. Ideally these segment names should then enter everyday discussions and decision challenges. For example, depending on who is involved, B might be labelled 'Sludge world' or 'Comfy chair', whilst C might be described as 'Techno fire sales' or 'The rapids'.

It is not a matter of which scenario may come true. Instead, what is important is that influential middle and senior executive minds are held open to the realistic possibility of multiple equally plausible futures. Intentionally, no single future is allowed to dominate. Using scenarios helps you develop far more realistic plans for uncertain futures.

Multiple horizons

Strategic planning needs to capture several time horizons. This involves allocating people who are good at dealing with each horizon in practical terms. Mapping out multiple forward future horizons and matching the required thinking, people and behaviours to each is important. IBM did exactly this as part of its turnaround strategy from the end of the last century. (See Chapter 11.)

Contingency planning

Even with good planning, uncertainty remains. A military friend of mine once said that if you locked a monkey in a room and made contingency plans for the four ways out, the monkey would invariably leave by a fifth. Adaptive ability when faced with inevitable change is key.

The route to your goal will most likely be changed or at least be influenced by other players. Sticking to a fixed prescriptive recipe can be a formula for failure. Local people should have sufficient discretion to adapt and respond in a way that enhances chances of achieving the intended goal. Are your people and systems configured to allow such discretion?

The uncertainty of beneficial obstacles

Richard Branson says, '*Do the best you can approach and don't give up!*'[96] In his case, doing your best involves a generous helping of flair and lots of imagination. For example, when Virgin Atlantic was a young company operating a limited number of relatively old jets Richard decided that customers would respond well to seat-back media, with video delivery on demand at a time when the most common in-flight option was a fixed-time, fixed-choice mid-cabin video projection. Installation would cost $8 million but the banks refused to loan his company the money.

So Richard asked Boeing if they would supply brand-new jets with the seat-back video system pre-installed. The irony was that the banks wouldn't loan Richard Branson $8 million for seat-back videos, **but** they were willing to advance $2 billion to buy a new fleet of jets. Scale counts, especially if there is a promising payback. Imagination and flair count too!

The strategic value of big failure

Acute failure can be a 'cathartic learning' opportunity. The lessons that are deepest etched on your mind and on an organisation's psyche are those derived from genuine hardship or harshness.

> To err is human … Alexander Pope

Failure and disaster can have potent upsides, if you can locate and tolerate them. Such experience builds resilience. Error is normal. Sometimes our reactions to failure or error can become counterproductive. Employees should not be afraid to fail, assuming they have the intelligence to learn and not repeat the same class of errors again. Senior managers should not be afraid to fail either. Fear inhibits people.

> Alexander Pope's full quotation reads:
> To err is human; to forgive divine.

Strategically, it is important that the organisation and the people get into the habit of forgiving errors and mistakes and moving on.

> No one should be ashamed to admit they are wrong,
> which is but saying, in other words,
> that they are wiser today than they were yesterday.
> Alexander Pope

Contradictory strategy

From time to time you will have to perform a strategic 180-degree turnaround and do the opposite of what you originally set out to accomplish or to pursue something totally different. You won't be on your own. This sort of dilemma is not unusual. Bill Gates and Microsoft initially totally underestimated the web-browser market but turned around relatively quickly to catch up when they spotted the strategic error.

Sometimes you can be just plain wrong, which should be forgivable, if you are human that is! The trick is to admit the error as soon as possible and then to act with renewed determination to put things to rights.

A classic leadership contradiction that makes the necessity of AND-type thinking a standard requirement is to prepare for the worst when times are great and to get ready for growth when times are bad. Team members and leaders who assume there will always be good times are naïve or just too young. It is important to be ready for both. An optimist and a pessimist are needed.

> In times of war prepare for peace AND in times of peace prepare for war.

Are you 'fixing the roof whilst the sun shines' or getting a suntan?

The uncertainty of strategic change

In the past 100 years the engine for many innovations in technology, economics, social behaviour and medicine has been led from privileged, mostly Western economies. The relentless rise of Chinese engineering and manufacturing success along with other BRIC countries should provoke your thinking in regard to deeply embedded business, political and social assumptions. (BRIC= Brazil, Russia, India, China.) For example, over the last 50 years BRIC countries have built up a capability to make things at low cost that are fit for purpose in a low-cost economy. BRIC country psychology and philosophy may yet turn out to be sufficient to create high-volume, even lower cost, genuinely disruptive approaches to our high-cost, Western ways of doing business.

Having readily accepted their manufacture of low-end goods and services, who is to say the BRIC countries will not follow Japan to become the next source of leading-edge premium-value technologies needed by the West? China is already the worlds' second largest economy in real terms and continues to grow rapidly each year. When looking at strategic comparisons of economic leverage look at purchasing power parity. It takes out currency distortion and allows an appreciation of latent power.

Disruptive change usually originates and grows unnoticed, off radar. Alternatively the nature of the emerging threat goes unnoticed or is seen and regarded as insignificant. Netscape, an early web browser technology, developed a leading edge until Microsoft woke up to the notion that the future was the Internet and developed its own browser at speed. From where we are now the move looks logical but that was not the case 20 years ago when the Internet was not a major factor to most people. Are you underestimating a challenge hidden in plain sight; for example, BRIC psychology and orientation?

Foxconn, already one of the world,s largest electronics manufacturers, fuelled by the explosive growth of Sony, Nokia and Apple products, plans to install a million robots by 2014. When this news was announced mid-2011 they had 10,000 robots. The company currently employs 1.2 million people, with about 1 million of them based on the Chinese mainland.

Why are you special?

Are you certain what your best features are today? Are you using an outdated template or impression of yourself or your organisation? When will these expire? Your USP is your unique selling proposition and can be read at a personal, a group or a product level. It is the special something that differentiates you, your products or your organisation or your nation – it creates a preference in the mind of people that matter. Knowing how your USP will evolve and decline is an important forward-looking strategic uncertainty.

- Why are you special as an individual, team, organisation or nation?
- Is there another who could do a better job of what you offer?
- How will your USP change, erode or evolve over time?
- What constructively can you do about that?

Resources

Most strategic planning encompasses the acquisition of various important resources and the way these are utilised. It can be a mistake to assume that what is freely available or abundant now will continue to be so in the future. Oil, water, clean air, open distribution systems, raw materials, vital components AND relationships should all be considered.

One resource that can easily be overlooked is consumer tolerance. As the competitive forces for market share accelerate and companies allocate increasing numbers of sales people and spend more on media, markets can become fatigued/overworked. In Europe in the 1970s a representative working for a pharmaceutical company could expect to visit six or seven doctors a day. By the turn of the century, this had dropped to two in some countries as these highly profitable companies deployed increasingly large sales forces. In situations where profit margins are so high the temptation to be unorthodox, in order to gain access to promote products increases. As boundaries are tested, a backlash becomes predictable. Customer access is a vital resource that can be damaged.

Chapter 12 Section 3

People, systems and implementation

Let's not forget the high value of Nelson's volunteer. It is willing, engaged individuals and teams of people who will deliver your strategy. If they commit their hearts and minds you have a chance. But are they able to use their minds in the best way possible? Have you considered people in your plans? Having staff with the right orientation of mind who are open to several possible outcomes AND who are responsive and adaptable when it comes to implementation really matters. Without them any plan is nought but hot air.

Do your top management seriously consider 'people' as a key strategic issue as opposed to a 'cost'? Do you have a map of strategically important relationships for example? People matter. Relationships within networks of multiple stake-holders are important in a complex world. Having a personal or organisational strategy that hinges on 'relationships' is every bit as valid as one that rides on econometric goals.

Engaging differences

There are quite different and somewhat contradictory thinking styles involved in forming a good, workable strategy, namely the combination of free imagination AND tight pragmatic realism. If you lack one of these two headline skills then I would suggest you form a working relationship with someone who has the skill you lack. Then figure out how you are going to relate to each other **before** you start your work because the odds are you are quite likely to frustrate the hell out of one another when you are at your best.

People and skills

Good strategic planning AND strategic leadership ability is not a widely available skill-set. Strategic planning and preparation require experienced 'above-ambiguity-ceiling' skills and involves all the senses plus one or two more, just a little short of 'magic'.

Getting top managers ambiguity enabled should be a strategic priority. Organisational responsiveness in the future will be about the number of people employed who have above-ambiguity-ceiling skills and who can cope with the increasing complexity, volatility and uncertainty.

Cliff-edge and castrated futures

Finding enough individuals who possess above-the-ambiguity-ceiling skills AND who also demonstrate a willingness to tolerate the gifts and the curses that very different people bring with them is really important. Hanging on to talent is an equally big challenge.

A key strategic issue is to understand that the real powerhouse of your organisation is often hidden within informal networks and relationships. This is your golden goose. Understanding these relationships and networks is particularly important if you are going to have to let people go. You can unwittingly castrate the organisation's future by taking out some hidden key players including the people who facilitate the hand-offs along your more complex decision chains.

People who have an intellectual wanderlust resent being managed. Being creative they will try to wriggle into interesting loosely defined roles that allow them freedom of enquiry (type 4 on my reality funnel). Come organisational downsizing, several different consultants tell me that people like this can be the first to go or be dismissed. Also managers are often unsure what some of the networked fixers (type 3 on my reality funnel) actually do, so they get to see a premature career exit too. Consequently your internal/external ambiguity network gets unplugged when leaders talk of efficiency and 'cliff-edging' anything fluffy, or worse, 'back to basics'. The danger is that AND-type thinking gets collectively dumped to be replaced by harsh, far simpler, mechanical thinking of 'either/or', in the name of efficiency. Consequently any remaining discretionary effort evaporates. Energy is lost as people fear for their jobs or feel guilty about lost relationships.

without 'management magic' ... performance tends to continue to slide downhill

Efficiency and cost-cutting drives do work, but only for short time. There is not a lot of mileage on an efficient but dumbed down outfit playing an increasingly generic game. Without 'management magic' and the wherewithal to implement new ideas, performance tends to continue to slide downhill, despite the best intentions of methodical people, getting back to basics.

The real strategic challenge is not just to survive, but also to figure out how you are going to 'win before you begin'. That requires a sufficient number of people who possess imagination, insight, foresight and heaps of energy along with lots of leadership ability, character and resilience, as part of a well-aligned complete 'food chain' of abilities.

Strategic direction and structure

When it comes to developing strategy, senior managers need to think about people early on. One barrier can be an ingrained perception as to the ability of different functions to add value to the whole enterprise. Compare and contrast what your people think about finance and human resources (HR). Both are back-office, administration cost centres that support the efficient running of an organisation, yet often only finance tends to get a seat at the very top table and contributes to strategic planning.

In theory at least, HR should be the speciality best positioned to think through and make strategic recommendations regarding commercially vital future resilience of beliefs and right behaviours especially in high-service environments.

Getting structures and systems right

How certain or uncertain are you that your operations in the future will be fit for purpose? Often there is a basic philosophy that underpins why an organisation is shaped and structured the way it is. Will this belief system help you in the future? For example, some people are fixated on size. People operating larger systems argue that their collective efforts perform better than those performed by smaller units or by individuals. Is bigger always going to be better in fast-changing contexts?

Structure, rewards and accountabilities influence behaviour too. They may be fit for purpose now but could be very wrong at some point in the future. Who do you bonus and why? How will you collectively evolve? Adaptable responsive structures and systems that are fit for an uncertain future should be part of your plan.

Strategic resilience

'Resilience' is genuinely important but how often does the word crop up as a specific, formal agenda item? Any personal or business plan that does not 'begin with the end in mind' or fails to consider the strengths and weaknesses of the people tasked to implement the plan is unlikely to do well.

In an increasingly complex world you will need to be in a team, a gang or a tribe if you want to survive and prosper. Resilient people, systems and processes are better configured to withstand and respond well to the surprise and shock factors of evolutionary challenges. Building a collective resilience should therefore be a formal part of every team player's and leader's underlying working philosophy, conversation and visible behaviour simply because there is one certainty in life, namely there will be more uncertainty!

Summary

Strategic planning requires answers to five fairly basic questions and then the willing hearts and minds of energised, enabled people to make it all come to life. Strategy can be both extremely simplistic AND enormously complex at the same time. Good strategic skills are uncommon as they involve an unusual blend of abilities. Above-ceiling thinking is mandatory because strategy seeks to address unknown futures and multiple ambiguous probabilities. To be clear, there are often no simple, single, right answers available so the ability to adapt in a timely way is essential.

Strategy is not just about the models used to describe an uncertain future. Developing and implementing a strategy involves imagination, and despite the absence of sufficient information, the synthesis of original options and decisions in regard to several equally possible futures. Getting to a particular destination can be achieved by a variety of routes. As a leader you just might occasionally have to invent some certainty.

Consider the structure of your personal life, your team and, metaphorically speaking, think about who will travel with you and for how long. Think strategically about your own and their philosophies, beliefs, attitudes and behaviours as well as skills, capabilities and capacities. Can they deliver when it matters the most?

Keep your eye on the pragmatic issues but at the same time make sure that there is sufficient independent AND collective resilience to respond to challenges and opportunities. Ensure that there is frequent, open, honest, wise communication through varied networks. Encourage people to be responsible and 'uncertainty ready'.

Is your strategy for conceiving a strategy robust?

Make sure you and others think about **several equally plausible futures** in terms of volatile uncertainties by frequently challenging homespun assumptions about what is and what will be 'true'. Use some flair and think a lot bigger and wider than you normally dare, then go and do something about it!

Reflection

- Is your strategy for conceiving a strategy robust? (Surely you're not intending to use single-point, one-future forecasts!)
- What have you assumed to be 'true' or consistent?
- Do you have a genuine strategy for innovation, people, roles, beliefs and behaviours?

- Do you know where your organisation's informal power networks are and who is involved?
- How resilient is your organisation? When was the last major stress test in terms of access to resources and systems, thinking ability, philosophical orientation and decision-making?
- What weak signals do you seek out?
- Who might the equivalent of Cassandra be in your organisation?
- What forward-looking, creative, intelligent, synthesis techniques do you use?

Reading

The ultimate strategy involves one that actually embraces life and death decisions. It is not surprising therefore that strategic planning has long been an obsession of the military. There are very many books on military strategy, but I find they make depressing reading. In spite of this I have added a few books for those readers who may not be as squeamish as I am.[97] Two books that I do suggest as mandatory reading whether you are into strategy or not are Machiavelli's *The Prince* and Sun Tzu's *Art of War*. They can also be employed as rich sources of analogy.

Chapter 13

Business philosophy

Some organisations build their foundations for success on an 'objective business model' involving routes to market, chosen methods, cold key performance indicators, material critical success factors, resources, segments, channels and any number of rational, logical dimensions. A few, however, have as their fundamental strategic starting point, **an explicit philosophy** in which virtues, values and principles, as opposed to 'rules', play a significant role in creating winning products and solutions. Their success then flows as a consequence of doing the right things for the right reasons. Their philosophy is not a bolt on. It's part of the DNA.

Getting beliefs and values right can pay off. Authentic values can help you personally to hold onto valuable reference points during times of great uncertainty or ambiguity. Your deeply held values can help you develop a decision when reason seems to fly out of the window.

At an organisational level, agreed beliefs, values and principles can sustain employee cohesion, improve the quality and speed of decisions and help create a clear sense of collective purpose. All of this helps tremendously during times of great uncertainty.

Living according to good values can also lead to standout performance during the good times. Below are examples where values continue to make a sustainable difference to two very large and successful organisations.

Right values

Values and honourable principles eventually count for an awful lot on so many levels. Perhaps a monk or a nun should be a mandatory member on the board of every bank. This is not such an impossible idea. One of the world's biggest banks had for many years in the Reverend Stephen Green, a chairman who was also an ordained (unpaid) Anglican Church minister.

Stephen Green and his fellow directors steered a very steady course before and during the North Atlantic banking crash of 2008. HSBC have remained carefully ambitious AND prosperous for the long term.

In 2009 other UK high-street banks were playing catch up on HSBC's friendly meet-and-greet approach. I got the distinct impression HSBC were beginning to lead the way in more ways than one and I wanted to know more, so I visited HSBC to see if values really did contribute to their performance. They do.

Rules vs principles

Joe Garner has been promoted since I first interviewed him. He's now HSBC's Deputy Chief Executive with responsibility for UK retail banking. Prior to joining HSBC in 2004, Joe gained extensive retail experience in senior roles with Procter & Gamble and the Dixons Group.

I asked Joe a variety of questions in regard to strategy and if he believed values and principles influenced performance. Joe replied, 'Yes, definitely we are interested and we have been proactive in promoting good working principles and ethics. It really is quite interesting how people think and behave. Survey information suggested that our graduate recruits employ freethinking in their first three months with us. After that, they aim to "fit in". So in a sense the prevailing climate influences their choices and perhaps their decisions. The way our "internal climate" works is therefore important.

'I'm interested in helping improve how we perform. In 2007 I came across a useful book called *Ethicability*[98] and I asked the author Roger Steare to work with us to investigate how we think and make decisions. He worked with my division to identify the ethics and principles at work.'

Joe continued, 'Interestingly, Roger shared with us that there can be three ethical frameworks in operation. Curiously these happen to correspond to the three classic transactional analysis profiles of child (C) parent (P) and adult (A). Taking the philosophical development of individuals as an example, these three different patterns may be adopted at different points in a lifetime:

- (C) Rule compliance – as typically seen in individuals until the approximate age of seven.
- (P) Social conscience – includes the idea of the greater good and still involves dependencies as well as rules.
- (A) Principled conscience – 'tarnished by life' but guided by principles of fairness, honesty, trust – often seen as a mark of maturity circa age 50.'

I said that it is easy to appreciate the different operational and cost implications of team or group behaviours that each would produce. For example, teams and organisations don't always mature in the same way that people can.

Sometimes teams get bogged down in thousands of pages of rules when what is needed is the application of 'common sense' principles along with trust, instead of micro-management. Adopting guiding principles that would facilitate socialised growth to a mature team level would clearly add value.

Joe picked up the conversation saying, 'Yes, and having determined what principles we would like to adopt at HSBC UK we turned these into everyday operational practice. At HSBC's retail division we have employed the OCI® survey of culture[99] and Giotto®[100] value scores to gain an insight into cultural and individual integrity. Our ethics and principles are routinely applied at job interviews and as an appraisal tool right across the division I'm responsible for.'"Joe then enlightened me with the fundamental underpinning of the seven principles that are now routinely employed in his business unit. He mentioned that Roger Steare is supported in his work and his thinking by a wide variety of people including Christopher Jamison, the Abbot of Worth.[101] Both Roger and Christopher make reference to seven long-established virtues. The opposites of virtues are vices to be avoided.

Seven principles

The first four virtues of the seven were considered essential for the successful running of pre-Christian, Hellenic society. These are values that are thousands of years old.

1. **Prudence** (alternatively common sense): to be able to judge alternative choices as to what would be the more appropriate action to take at a given time.
2. **Fortitude:** having the courage to address what is important AND to act no matter what – this involves tenacity, resolve, resilience, forbearance and endurance, as well as a willing ability to confront fear and uncertainty, or intimidation.
3. **Temperance** (self-responsibility/accountability): practising self-control, abstention and moderation. (Staff at Dow Corning's incubator unit found the right word for themselves: 'Patience'.)
4. **Justice:** proper moderation between self-interest and the rights and needs of others.

Christopher Jamison points out that it is important to notice that all four virtues need to be operative at the same time. Each helps to define the other. These last three are theologically derived.

1. **Faith** (belief): The question is faith in what, or to put it another way, 'trust' in what? The ability to project forward towards something that could happen.
2. **Hope** (or optimism): Hope without faith would be short-lived. Hope needs faith in a projection, a wish or an expectation. Sustained hope needs something to keep it alive. Positive energy is important.
3. **Love** (or charity): This might also be reasonably described as warmth and practical goodwill.

Again each of the seven virtues support and reaffirm the others.

I left the meeting and reflected on Joe Garner's decisions to embed principles in practice. Interestingly, Joe had made sure that 'the walk matched the talk'. By making sure that everyday routines included the need to witness and evidence their collective values as action, the underlying principles came alive, were made real and, importantly, will become habitual.

Getting several thousand people to steer in a particular direction and adopt a set of principles is not easy. Joe seems to have embedded a set of guiding principles for higher performance that will last. When values become practice, they can create lasting virtue.

Virtue and value

A virtue is something other people ascribe to you. You have to earn a virtue based on what you actually do. If your actions are consistent with your beliefs then what you do will be delivered with authentic conviction. By acting in accordance with clear values and principles, virtue can be recognised and reinforced.

Creating evidence that affirms beliefs is important to ensuring a good idea becomes a legacy. Sometimes the desired behaviour can be achieved by insisting on the dogmatic enforcement of a wise but very simple habit. At Shell anyone at any status level can stop someone on the stairs and direct them to hold the hand rail if they are not holding onto a rail. A simple rule and entitled behaviour has embedded a high awareness of safety based on attention to the simplest acts in a company that deals in billions of barrels of dangerous volatile liquids every day.

Values underpin virtues. Different people connect values and virtues, probably in different ways; nevertheless adopting agreed shared principles is likely to help resolve uncertainty and take the tension out of many dilemmas faced by diverse members of a team. Selflessly upholding values for the benefit of others is one way of fostering their accolade that you possess 'virtue'.

I want to conclude this brief, and I hope practical, philosophical look at the benefits and potential pitfalls of a well-developed philosophy or collections of values with what I have found to be one of the very best examples of a working, pragmatic, enduring set of guidelines and beliefs. 'The Key Speech' makes this particular company prosperous and contributes to the happiness of the people in it.

Ove Arup: 'The Key Speech'

Sometimes a longer script is required to underpin short values statements. One of the best expressions of established values in practice I have encountered comes from Arup, a wholly independent organisation. Arup is owned in trust for the benefit of 10,000 employees and their dependants. With no shareholders or external investors, the firm is able to determine its own direction as a business and set its own priorities. Each of Arup's employees receives a share of the firm's operating profit each year.

the principles ... form a lasting guideline for good decision-making

The late Sir Ove Arup wrote 'The Key Speech' in 1970. His ideas clearly come from the heart and from genuine experience. It is well written too. The principles he outlined establish a positive attitude and lasting guidelines for good decision-making. More than 40 years later, 'The Key Speech' embodies current daily habitual good practice. It reaffirms his ideals across different teams in multiple international locations. 'The Key Speech' is a genuine legacy.

This document captures a living, working philosophy and that is why I like it. Sir Ove Arup presents a pragmatic 'way of being' that works for an individual AND for the organisation. If you get into a challenging or interesting conversation with an Arup employee they will recite a part of 'The Key Speech' to confirm or to counter what has been said. His ideas have clear day-to-day practical application.

If you ever need an example of philosophy that makes sense, makes money AND makes people happy, read his speech.[102] His five-page essay provides solid guidelines AND a higher goal regarding benefit to society, especially during times of great uncertainty.

Colin Harris sits on one of three Arup boards and shares the following insights.[103] (Italics used when quoting directly from The 'Key Speech').

The humanitarian attitude

The humanitarian attitude leads to the creation of an organisation which is human and friendly in spite of being large and efficient. Where every member is treated not only as a link in a chain of command … but as a human being … treated not only as a means but as an end.

Colin Harris says, 'I firmly believe the reason people come to work beyond the basic needs of paying the mortgage is to enjoy what they do, feel they are making a difference. I have particularly noticed graduates over a number of years genuinely wanting to create a better society but most of all to work with like-minded people in an enjoyable work environment. Many companies want to create this sort of environment but few can. It is particularly under pressure, in these economically challenged times, where if we are not careful an over-emphasis on the 'bottom line' can destroy the trust employees have in an organisation. The pressure of money is particularly emphasised by "The Key Speech": *the trouble with money is that it is a dividing force, not a uniting force … if we let it divide us, we are sunk as an organisation – at least as a force for good.*'

Colin continues, 'The balance of creating the right environment whilst making sufficient profit not only to survive but also, importantly, to invest in our future (not the pockets of external shareholders) is also encapsulated in "The Key Speech": *reasonable prosperity of members.* This balance is nicely emphasised as prosperity being one of, not the only aim. '*… for it is an aim which, if overemphasised, easily gets out of hand and becomes very dangerous for our harmony, unity and very existence.*'

Clients first or partners first?

'Many service organisations state that satisfied clients are the most important concern but I disagree,' says Colin. 'In my opinion *satisfied members* are most important because satisfied members practising the aims outlined in "The Key Speech" will ensure satisfied clients.'

The reference to *unity and enthusiasm* is perhaps less obvious but so important. Our success has in part been due to an ever-expanding knowledge of the built and natural environment – our challenge is to bring this together in a coherent way which invokes … *our point of view, which is in favour of teamwork rather than stardom* … A brilliant person is only one person unless he or she is a brilliant leader enthusing and motivating a whole team. I also believe enthusiasm and passion makes an ordinary firm special. ... *enthusiasm is like the fire that keeps the steam engine going.*

A membership of quality

'*When we come across a really good man, grab him even if we have no immediate use for him and then see to it that he stays with us.* Colin refers again to "The Key Speach" and the importance of members being attracted by the *opportunity to do interesting and rewarding work... to use creative ability ... grow and be given responsibility.* I have gained so much pleasure and personal satisfaction from helping people to grow by trying to understand them and giving them the opportunity to excel at what they are good at – the greatest growth is from a 16-year-old then community YTS (Youth Training Scheme), member who is now a director in a pivotally important role in the firm.'

Colin adds, 'Graduates who join us say the clincher came when they read "The Key Speach". It was not the money, they often say, but the higher goals and meaning of life that Ove stood for that resonated with how they wanted to conduct their life. So philosophy pays! Ove Arup's philosophy helps us recruit and retain great people.'

Finally, Colin says, 'I believe "The Key Speech" anticipates how to survive and sustain the firm in challenging times: ... *but what binds our membership together must be loyalty to our aims. And only as long as the leaders of the firm are loyal to these can they expect and demand the loyalty from members.*'

What makes Ove Arup's concepts endure is that he sets out a variety of reasonable challenges to associate with, to produce things of quality, to lead, learn, be creative, prosperous AND honest. Ove Arup's 'Key Speech' comments on long-term benefits to society and harmony with our surroundings pre-date by decades the idea of sustainability and corporate social responsibility. From this 1970 script you can also detect the underpinning beliefs of 'key performance indicators'!

Ove Arup reasoned that if you get the right people with the right attitudes about quality, social benefit and harmony then good products and services flow **as a consequence** of those great people doing the right thing to the best of their ability.

Colin remains vigilant. He says, 'We are already 60 years old and not many companies live beyond 100. I'm concerned that if our core values are allowed to drift or are undermined by a failure of oversight, our long-term viability and justification of our uniqueness will slip too. If we fail to live out those values and philosophies then we cease to be authentic and we will lose our best people and our performance edge. We will have lost our "meaning"' We need to make sure that doesn't happen.'

The dilemma of absolute principles AND flexibility

Colin is right to pay attention to the dangers of 'drift' and he and his fellow directors may perhaps decide to reassert the original intentions. At the beginning of the book I caution, 'beware absolutes'. This applies to principles and values too. It is important to keep watch on the moral outcomes of what you do or do not do to see if your values are honest, true AND humane.

The principles underpinning your values need to be fundamental AND a little flexible. One useful principle to hold in mind is of the dilemma created between wishing to apply absolutes on the one hand AND the need for flexibility on the other. George Bernard Shaw, the late Irish critic and playwright, expressed the dangers that emerge when principles are applied in a cold mechanical way:

> *An Englishman does everything on principle.*
> *He fights you on patriotic principles.*
> *He robs you on business principles.*
> *He enslaves you on imperial principles.*
> George Bernard Shaw, *The Man of Destiny*

Consider Shaw's cynical assessment of the use of principle as a caution. Whilst adopting values and principles can provide guidance they may not necessarily push you or other people past the ambiguity ceiling or produce virtue. Values and principles are merely a part of the answer. They are a very useful part of above-ceiling reasoning but do not constitute the whole of the required capability.

Engaging principles can also sometimes create a new set of quite challenging problems. Dilemmas can arise within and sometimes between values and principles. To illustrate how the boundaries of reality are elastic, the principles or values that I hold dear or have faith in may well differ from yours. Two faiths may believe in one God but may go to war over who has the 'correct' scripture, despite the basic injunction not to kill.

sometimes truths are partial, or change with context or time

Sometimes truths are partial, or change with context or time. Learning how to stretch your thinking AND stay true to your ethics, values and principles is yet another hurdle you will need to deal with.

Dealing with conflicting values and principles is perhaps the trickiest ground of all because the dilemmas they pose involve deeply personal consequences. Looking deeply into yourself and your motives can be a 'Pandora's box' experience. The good news is, at least if you are aware of who and what you are, you stand a chance of doing something constructive, hopefully virtuous. Recall or research what were the last remaining elements of Pandora's open box and you will find three of the seven virtues mentioned earlier.

What unites also divides

On a practical note, it is important when dealing with what people believe to hold in mind that as a species we actually pay more attention to tangible negatives and will join together for our collective survival, generally with considerable vigour.

> *Beliefs are what divide people.*
> *Doubt unites them.*
> Peter Ustinov, English actor and author (1921–2004)

Ustinov's insight perhaps informs us why people watch the news. The stories are more often sad and bad as opposed to good and uplifting.

In general our individual beliefs and values are personal and can be quite subjective at a personal level and etherial at a group level unless some sort of deep experience is shared. Attempting to bind people together through beliefs and values is no easy task.

People can be unified behind common beliefs if they feel a deep visceral connection to them. Deeper fears and threats will get people's attention however, individuals are quite likely to rebel for having been confined after the fear is removed. It is therefore a mistake for leaders to constantly build 'burning platforms'.

Support is less certain when it comes to getting people to sign up to higher aspirations. The imperatives are less compelling as our survival is not at stake.

> *There is nothing more difficult to plan, more doubtful of success, nor more dangerous to manage than the creation of a new system. For the initiator has the enmity of all who would profit by the preservation of the old institutions, and merely lukewarm defenders in those who should gain by the new ones.* Machiavelli (1469–1527)

Embedding a working philosophy is not at all easy; however, once engaged, higher order beliefs are ultimately more likely to last and be more rewarding in the long run. Evidence, stories, icons and legends then sustain the legacy.

Summary

Establishing a convincing working philosophy can create wealth and guide the best efforts of large numbers of different personalities through the toughest of uncertain times. Consistency along with adaptability is just one of several contradictions that are required to develop evidence that the beliefs and philosophies that people sign up to do add value and should be retained. The ability to hold opposing views and contradictions is easier if you possess above-ambiguity-ceiling skills.

A viable working philosophy is a legacy.

Chapter 14

Legacy

As one of this planet's physically weaker species our societies thrived during highly uncertain times only because many thousands of years ago we made a highly pragmatic decision to collaborate with each other in tribes and progressively bigger groups. This very simple philosophy that many were stronger than a few became a force for genetic selection. The fittest arrangements survived at a time when the planet could easily cope with what we asked of it.

A child born in the middle of the twentieth century who lives to be 100 will see the planet's population almost triple from around three billion people to nearly nine billion souls. At the same time consumer appetites have grown ever more voracious driven by intense media pressure to assert a philosophy of individual entitlement. It is easy to imagine the consequences but not the solutions of such explosive global demand and our seemingly unlimited appetites for growth within a finite space. Our option to wait and see most likely expired in our recent past.

From here on in our species will need to be very clever as critical resources become scarcer. I believe our imagination and capacity for compassion to create a positive legacy will help us find our way through a time of unprecedented uncertainty.

Just as humankind has survived in the past we will most likely be obliged to revisit many aspects of the way we make decisions and conduct our lives. We will need:

- new ways of thinking.
- more people with above-the-ambiguity-ceiling ability.
- new ways of making decisions.
- new ways of behaving.
- new ways of working together.
- lots of innovation.

Our most basic philosophies, our individual and collective sense of meaning, our focus of attention AND the way we think will need upgrading and revision if we are to continue as the planet's dominant species beyond the Earth's capacity to cope with our consumption.

This will mean fundamentally new frames of reference for the rise and fall of expectations and entitlement of generations to come. But what will you do? What will be your legacy? It could be something as simple as encouraging people to develop higher levels of awareness, thinking or decision-making skills so that **uncertainty becomes an opportunity** and not a barrier to be feared.

Scientific reductive logic employing either/or-type thinking will not be enough in a more complex world. Our societies will need a larger body of people capable of collaborating above AND below the ambiguity ceiling in integrated **minimal groups** to deliver elegant yet complex solutions to complex uncertainties.

In an age of uncertainty 'above ceiling' thinking and decision-making skills will be in great demand. I hope that the pragmatic experiences of the practitioners cited in this book together with the academic insights and the working models I have suggested will help you in many ways.

What comes next is, as it has always been, uncertain!

Recommended reading

Books on providing helpful viewpoints, points of influence and thinking skills

The next four books are must-read texts.

Difficult Conversations: How to discuss what matters most, Douglas Stone, Bruce Patton & Sheila Heen from the Harvard Negotiation Project, Penguin

Getting To Yes, Ury & Fisher, Random House.

The Third Way, William Ury, Penguin.

Influence Science and Practice, Robert B. Cialdini, Allyn & Bacon, Pearson Education.

Thinker Toys, Michael Michalko, Ten Speed Press.

Synectics, W. J. J. Gordon, Harper Row. (out of print – pre-dates de Bono and others).

Orbiting the Giant Hairball: A corporate fool's guide to surviving with grace, Gordon MacKenzie.

A Whack on The Side of The Head, Roger von Oech, Warner Books.

Techniques of Structured Problem Solving, A. B. Van Gundy Jnr., Van Nostrand Reinhold.

Maverick! Ricardo Semler, Arrow. He pioneered very different way of setting up 'work'.

Emotional Intelligence, Daniel Goleman.

I'm OK You're OK, Thomas A. Harris, M. D. Arrow.

Appreciative Enquiry, Jane Magruder, Watkins & Bernard J. Mohr. Foreward by Richard Beckard & David Cooperrider, Jossey Bass- Pfeiffer.

Words That Change Minds, Shelle Rose Charvet, Kendall Hunt.

If Life Is a Game These Are the Rules, Cherie Carter-Scott, Hodder & Stoughton.

Useful books on innovation

Innovation and Entrepreneurship, Peter F. Drucker, Butterworth Heinemann.

Managing Innovation, Joe Tidd, John Bessant & Keith Pavitt, Wiley.

The Innovator's Dilemma, Clayton M. Christensen, Harvard Business School Press.

Winning Through Innovation, Tushman & O'Reilly (iii), Harvard Business School Press.

Copycats, Oded Shenkar, Harvard Business Press.

Useful books on leadership

The Leadership Challenge, Konzes & Posner, Jossey Bass.

The 48 Laws of Power, Robert Green, Joost Elfers.

The Politics of Management, Andrew Kakabadse, Nichols Press.

The Prince, Niccolo Machiavelli, Penguin.

The Mask of Command, John Keegan, Pimlico.

Managing the Unexpected, Karl E. Weick & Kathleen M. Sutcliffe, Jossey-Bass. (Copyright John Wiley & Sons).

Inside the Leader's Mind, Liz Mellon, Prentice Hall.

Useful books on strategy

Exploring Corporate Strategy, Gerry Johnson & Kevan Scholes, Prentice Hall.

The Strategy Process, Mintzberg, Quinn & Ghoshal, Prentice Hall.

The 5th Discipline, Peter Senge, Currency Doubleday, New York. (See the section on systems thinking.)

The Art of the Long View, Peter Schwartz, Currency Doubleday, New York.

The Art of War, Sun Tzu, Oxford University Press.

The Mask of Command, John Keegan, Pimlico.

War in European History, Michael Howard, Oxford University Press.

Clausewitz: A very short introduction, Michael Howard, Oxford University Press.

Scenario Planning – Managing for the Future, Gill Ringland, Wiley.

And finally, an insight into 'concentricity'. Quite apart from being a good read, this book is an early appreciation of how things, people and situations are often arranged concentrically.

The Inferno, Dante Alighieri, Signet.

Books on the meaning of things and people who have thought about certainty and uncertainty

Nicomachean Ethics, Aristotle, Translated by Terence Irwin, Hackett Publishing.

Commentaries on Living (first series), Krishnamurti, Quest Books. This is a collection of short essays concerning his encounters with people who have problems to solve. Each story provides a useful, sometimes quite deep, insight. Also you will notice that his style of being present in the moment is often used in published business papers.

Freedom from the Known, Krishnamurti, HarperCollins.

Consolations of Philosophy, Alain de Botton, Penguin. A pleasure to read.

A History of Western Philosophy, Bertrand Russell, Routledge. A good read.

The Empty Raincoat, Charles Handy, Arrow; *The Age of Unreason,* Charles Handy, Hutchinson; *Inside Organisations*, Charles Handy, Penguin. Almost all of his books are very well crafted and enjoyable to read.

Useful books on 'being'

Miracle of Mindfulness, Thich Nhat Hanh.

The Art of Being, Erich Fromm, Constable.

The Prophet, Khalil Gibran, Pan. This provides a useful antidote to cynical perception.

The Experience of Insight, Joseph Goldstein, Shambhala.

Tao Te Ching (The Book of the Way), ascribed to Lao Tzu, Translated by Stephen Mitchell, Kyle Cathie.

Everyday Tao, Deng Ming Dao, Harper.

Useful web links

Online video clips

Get your alternative lines of thinking from multiple sources. TED talks are excellent.

www.ted.com/ Suggested searches on the site: Ken Robinson; Dan Ariely; Michael Sandel; Dan Pink; Malcolm Gladwell on spaghetti sauce; Richard Branson's life at 30,000 feet. Capt. Charles Moore on the seas of plastic is stunning. See also Benjamin Zander's clip on music and passion, Alain de Botton on career crisis and Clay Shirky on cognitive surplus.

Who to avoid working for – basis of an HBR paper and a book, *The No Asshole Rule: Building a civilized workplace and surviving one that isn't.*

www.50lessons.com/sutton/ or see YouTube

www.youtube.com/watch?v=QAThL4TJfaA (A shorter link is http://bit.ly/k5YfsR)

Beliefs tested

See Michael Sandel and his Reith lectures at www.bbc.co.uk/programmes/b00kt7rg (A shorter link is http://bbc.in/kkOrk9) This site has four really good podcasts plus downloadable transcripts.

Leadership materials

There are lots of business leadership materials on www.BNET.com, the CBS interactive website.

Young entrepreneurs at Innocent making a difference with 70 percent of the information and seeking honest clarity to stop rubbish entering the decision process. This is a short four-minute clip from October 2010: www.bbc.co.uk/news/business-11551271. (A shorter link is http://bbc.in/mTdN3P)

This is a longer clip from 2007. It's fuzzy and lasts about 22 minutes: http://news.bbc.co.uk/1/hi/programmes/hardtalk/6225099.stm (A shorter link is http://bbc.in/jkB2Y6)

Other websites

The WVS Cultural Map of the World, written by Ronald Inglehart & Chris Welzel. This site shows an interesting map of cultural orientations. www.worldvaluessurvey.org/wvs/articles/folder_published/article_base_54 (A shorter link is http://bit.ly/kkU1dV)

Historical information and the Innocent Drinks alliance with Coke, see: www.innocentdrinks.co.uk/us/our_story/investment/ (A shorter link is http://bit.ly/jACySV) and www.innocentdrinks.co.uk/us/our_story/index.cfm. (A shorter link is http://bit.ly/lGqwBp)

References

1   *Capitalising on Complexity, Insights from the Global Chief Executive Officer (CEO) Study*, IBM, May 2010. Comments reproduced courtesy of IBM.

2   ibid

3   J. B. Harreld, C. A. O'Reilly, & M. L. Tushman, Dynamic capabilities at IBM: Driving Strategy into Action, *California Management Review*. Vol. 49 no. 4–Summer 2007 p 21-43.

4   I can recommend reading: Krishnamurti *Commentaries on Living* (first series), Quest Books and *Freedom from the Known,* HarperCollins. An essential step is to realise what we are "attached" to and why.

5   Bertrand Russell, *A History of Western Philosophy, Routledge*.

6   B. Hart & T. R. Risley, *Meaningful Differences in the Everyday Experience of Young American Children*, Brookes Publishing, 1995. See also a review of later findings here: T. R. Risley & B. Hart, 'Promoting early language development' in N. F. Watt, C. Ayoub, R. H. Bradley, J. E. Puma & W. A. LeBoeuf (Eds.), *The Crisis in Youth Mental Health: Critical issues and effective programs, Volume 4, Early Intervention Programs and Policies* (83-88). Westport, CT: Praeger, 2006.

7   *Capitalising on Complexity, Insights from the Global Chief Executive Officer (CEO) Study*, IBM, May 2010.

8   (See www.bing.com/videos/watch/video/bhutans-gross-national-happiness/6upbype A shortened link is: http://binged.it/kdqLzs) The idea of gross national happiness was coined by King Jigme Singye Wangchuck of Bhutan in 1972 and applies to country policy **ahead** of other mundane financial considerations.

9   Cherie Carter-Scott, *If Life Is a Game, These Are the Rules,* Hodder & Stoughton.

10 For the terms convergent and divergent thinking, see Liam Hudson – *Contrary Imaginations,* Penguin, 1967 and J. P. Guildford, *The Nature of Intelligence*, McGraw-Hill, New York,1967.

11 Stephen Reid, chapter on Creativity in Business in Exploring Techniques of Analysis and Evaluation in Strategic Management, V. Ambrosini, G. Johnson & K. Scholes, (eds) Pearson Higher Education, London & New York 1998. Also see S. P. Reid, *How To Think*, Pearson Higher Education, 2002 and S. P. Reid *High Performance Thinking Skill,* Permillion 2006.

12 S. P. Reid, *How To Think*, Pearson Higher Education, 2002.

13 S. P. Reid, *High Performance Thinking Skills,* Permillion, 2006.

14 In the earlier model, published in S. P. Reid, *How To Think*, Pearson Higher Education, 2002, I had only three realms. Since then I have extended realm 1 to

capture the idea of very high precision alongside people in realm 2 who believe in moderate flexibility, yet who remain quite 'grounded'.

15 Fons Trompenaars & Charles Hampden-Turner, *Riding the Waves of Culture,* Nicholas Brealey, 1997. Also see Fons Trompenaars & Charles Hampden-Turner, *Building Cross Cultural Competence: How to create wealth from conflicting values*, Wiley, 2000, 11.

16 Barry Johnson, *Polarity Management*, HRD Press, Inc., Amherst, Massachusetts, USA, 1992,1996.

17 Addition attributed by Barry Johnson to John Scherer, Centre for Work and the Human Spirit.

18 Douglas Stone, Bruce Patton & Sheila Heen, from the Harvard Negotiation Project, *Difficult Conversations: How to discuss what matters most*, Penguin Books.

19 Interview February 2011. These are the personal views and insights of John Chambers, a UK citizen.

20 Liz Mellon, *Inside the Leader's Mind*, Prentice Hall, 2011.

21 R. F. Baumeister, E. Bratslavsky, C. Finkenauer & K. D. Vohs. 'Bad is stronger than good', *Review of General Psychology*, 2001 (5), 323–370.

22 For more on mindfulness and inner calm I recommend you read the writings of Thich Nhat Hanh. Also read Lao Tzu, *Tao Te Ching: (The Book of The Way)*, translated by Stephen Mitchell, various publishers, and D. T. Suzuki, *An Introduction To Zen Buddhism*.

23 Interview, February 2011. These are the personal views and insights of John Chambers, a UK citizen.

24 Yuichi Shoda, Walter Mischel, Philip K. Peake, 'Predicting adolescent cognitive and self-regulatory competencies from preschool delay of gratification: identifying diagnostic conditions', *Developmental Psychology*, 1990, (26) 6, 978-986.

25 Keynote speech presented by Professor George Ainslie at the annual convention of the American Psychological Association at Chicago, IL, 22 August, 2002. 'The effect of hyperbolic discounting on personal choices' http://picoeconomics.org/Articles/APA.pdf (A shortened link is: http://bit.ly/knuxRP)

26 George Ainslie, 'Précis of breakdown of will', *Behavioral and Brain Sciences,* 2005 (28), 635-673.

27 Kathleen D. Vohs & Ronald J. Faber, 'Spent resources: self-regulatory resource availability affects impulse buying', *Journal of Consumer Research*, March 2007 (33).

28 George Ainslie, 'Uncertainty as wealth', *Behavioural Processes,* 2003 (64), 369-385.

29 *The Experience of Insight*, Joseph Goldstein. Shambala. Also see *Tao Te Ching (The Book of the Way)*, ascribed to Lao Tzu. Read also *Everyday Tao*, Deng Ming Dao.

30 www.bbc.co.uk/news/education-14003616 (A shorter link is http://bbc.in/q7IPqK)

31 Available from the Johnson & Johnson website.

32 www.fda.gov/ICECI/CriminalInvestigations/ucm213163.htm (A shortened link is: http://1.usa.gov/meKr4D) Refers to off-label promotion.

33 'Oregon sues Johnson & Johnson'. A web search on this phrase (see http://bit.ly/kLPits) scored several thousand hits on Google. For references take your pick. A quite detailed account of events is provided by a local blog here: www.oregonlive.

com/business/index.ssf/2011/01/oregon_sues_johnson_johnson_fo.html (A shortened link is: http://bit.ly/lCTsFN) whilst a shorter account appears on the Reuters website.

34   Search the web using key words: USA, Reuters, Congress, Phantom, McNeil and Motrin. Also try the same search and substitute 'fiercepharma.com' for Reuters in the search.

35   Regarding the impact of bad behaviours, see: W. Felps, T. R. Mitchell & E. Byington, 'How, when, and why bad apples spoil the barrel: negative group members and dysfunctional groups', *Research in Organizational Behavior*, 2006 (27), 175–222.

36   G. Labianca & D. J. Brass, 'Exploring the social ledger: negative relationships and negative asymmetry in social networks in organizations', *Academy of Management Review*, 2006 (31), 596-614. Runner-up: AMR Best Paper of 2006.

37   G. Labianca, & D. J. Brass, 'Extending the social ledger: correlates and outcomes of negative relationships in workplace social networks', Working papers. Department of Organization and Management, Goizueta Business School, Emory University, 2003.

38   A more complete account of Benjamin Franklin's 13 virtues and how he attempted to conduct himself accordingly can be had from a free copy of the original manuscript: www.gutenberg.org/ebooks/148 (A shortened link is: http://bit.ly/oGQoSq)

39   *Commentaries on Living* (first series), Krishnamurti, Quest Books. Notice the way each story begins with the author being present in the moment. Many of the stories speak of the bind of attachment and the freedom that comes from letting go. See also *Freedom from the Known*, Krishnamurti, HarperCollins.

40   See the reading list above on 'Being'. In particular, read *The Miracle of Mindfulness*, Thich Nhat Hanh.

41   Cited by Steven D. Levitt, Steven J. Dubner in *Freakonomics*.

42   Cited by Steven D. Levitt, www.freakonomics.com/2009/04/21/winner-loser-and-marijuana-pepsi/ (A shortened link is: http://bit.ly/nElcy5)

43   Interview, February 2011. These are the personal views and insights of John Chambers, a UK citizen.

44   Keith Oates, Deputy Chairman, Marks & Spencer Plc., *Innovation is Everybody's Business,* the UK Innovation Lecture, 27th February 1997, Dept. of Trade and Industry, 97/592.

45   N. Collier (2008) 'Marks & Spencer B: A case study'. In G. Johnson, K. Scholes & R. Whittington, *Exploring Corporate Strategy*, 8th Edition, Pearson Education, Harlow.

46   A review of 10 big flops is here www.independent.co.uk/news/business/analysis-and-features/was-abn-the-worst-takeover-deal-ever-1451520.html (A shortened link is: http://ind.pn/qKjmod)

47   Information abridged from the Dyson website here www.dyson.co.uk/insideDyson/article.asp?aID=storyofstruggleanddisType=anddir=andcp=andhf=andjs= (A shortened link is: http://bit.ly/oausmP)

48   Arthur Schopenhauer, *Parerga and Paralipomena,* published in 1851.

49   The reader should review this comment in the light of any other more recent developments. Editing note, June 2011: not long after cabin staff at British Airways

voted to end a long-running dispute, Virgin pilots overwhelmingly voted to strike for the first time in their history but subsequently decided to negotiate and called off the threatened strike.

50   Personal communication.

51   The Thomas Kilmann Conflict Mode Instrument (TKI) is owned by CPP, Inc., Mountain View, CA, US. See www.cpp.com for further details. It is available as a paper-based system or online through registered practitioners.

52   Douglas Stone, Bruce Patton & Sheila Heen, from the Harvard Negotiation Project, *Difficult Conversations: How to discuss what matters most*, Penguin Books.

53   Sue Canney & Karen Ward, *Leading International Teams*, McGraw Hill, 1999.

54   Download posted here: www.ashridge.org.uk/Website/IC.nsf/wFARATT/ Making%20Complex%20Teams%20Work/$file/Making_Complex_Teams_ Work_2001.pdf (A shortened link is: http://bit.ly/kGMrNQ)

55   Dan Ariely, 'How honest people cheat', *Harvard Business Review*, February 2008.

56   Dan Ariely, 'The end of rational economics', *Harvard Business Review*, July-August 2009.

57   Karl E. Weick & Kathleen M. Sutcliffe, *Managing the Unexpected*, Jossey-Bass, John Wiley & Sons, 2007.

58   *Capitalising on Complexity, Insights from the Global Chief Executive Officer (CEO) Study*, IBM, May 2010.

59   Geert Hofstede, *Culture's Consequences: International Differences in Work-Related Values*, Sage, Beverly Hills CA, 1980.

60   Geert Hofstede, GertJan Hofstede & Michael Minkov, *Cultures and Organizations: Software of the Mind, revised and expanded 3rd Edition*, McGraw-Hill, New York, 2010.

61   Also see valuable additions to Geert Hofstede's work from his son GertJan Hofstede www.gertjanhofstede.com/FAQ.htm (A shortened link is: http://bit.ly/ m2okiq)

62   Additional resources here: www.geerthofstede.com/ and www.geerthofstede.nl/ and www.geert-hofstede.com/geert_hofstede_resources.shtml (A shortened link is: http://bit.ly/kSEvmV)

63   Fons Trompenaars & Charles Hampden-Turner, *Building Cross Cultural Competence: how to create wealth from conflicting values*, Wiley, 2000, 11.

64   Fons Trompenaars & Charles Hampden-Turner, *Riding the Waves of Culture,* Nicholas Brealey, 1997.

65   Fons Trompenaars & Charles Hampden-Turner, *21 Leaders for the 21st Century*, see page 429. 73percent propensity of executives to reconcile vs. 35percent of managers.

66   *Personal communication*, Peter Woolliams, April 2011. For the latest information regarding the work of Fons Trompenaars, Charles Hampden-Turner & Peter Woolliams, see www.thtconsulting.com. Peter Woolliams also suggests Terence Brake's *Culture Prism*, which gives similar insights. See also Terence Brake, *The Global Leader.*

67   *Personal communication*, Peter Woolliams, April 2011.

68 Fons Trompenaars & Charles Hampden-Turner, *21 Leaders for the 21st Century*. See page 430.

69 R. P. White & P. Hodgson, *Relax It's Only Uncertainty!*, Pearson Education, 2001.

70 For the nine years to 2011, Duke Corporate Education (Duke CE) has been top of the FT global ranking for the delivery of corporate education programmes. Duke CE draws upon a wide network of international experts as associates, of which I'm proud to be one.

71 R. P. White, P. Hodgson & S. Crainer, *The Future of Leadership: Riding the corporate rapids into the 21st century*, Pitman Publishing, London, 1996.

72 R. P. White & P. Hodgson, *The Ambiguity Architect Assessment*, 1999, 2005. The Ambiguity Architect ®, registered 2000, is the property of Executive Development Group, LLC, Greensboro, NC, 27455-3012 USA. More information is available from info@edgp.com and www.edgp.com/ambiguity_architect.html (A shortened link is: http://bit.ly/mKThnY)

73 Personal communication.

74 A. D. Amar, Carsten Hentrich & Vlatka Hlupic, 'To be a better leader, give up authority', *Harvard Business Review*, December 2009, 87(12), 22-24. Also see hbr.org/2009/12/to-be-a-better-leader-give-up-authority/ar/pr (A shortened link is: http://bit.ly/j0njSe)

75 Ibid.

76 Study quoted by James O'Toole & Warren Bennis, 'What's needed next: a culture of candor', *Harvard Business Review*, June 2009.

77 'Only the Liberal Democrats are committed to scrapping tuition fees and opposing any attempt to raise them. We will phase out tuition fees over six years, starting by immediately scrapping final year fees for students doing their first degree.' In January 2010 he told the BBC '… tuition fees would be axed over six years. We will do it year group by year group starting first with final year students and working down over time.'

78 Higher education was managed by the department of business and led on a day-to-day basis by a Conservative minister.

79 See www.brainjuicer.com

80 John Kearon, The death of innovation, *Market Leader,* Quarter 4, 2010.

81 Vijay Govindarajan & Chris Trimble, 'Stop the Innovation Wars', *Harvard Business Review*, July/August 2010.

82 See a four-minute BBC clip from October 2010 at www.bbc.co.uk/news/business-11551271 (A shortened link is: http://bbc.in/mTdN3P).

83 Gifford Pinchot III, *Intrapreneuring*, Harper Row Publishers, New York, 1985.

84 Verified with Novozymes directly.

85 Oded Shenkar, *Copycats*, Harvard Business Press, 2010.

86 Interview, January 2011. These are the personal views and insights of Eric Peeters.

87 J. B. Harreld, C. A. O'Reilly, & M. L. Tushman, *Dynamic Capabilities at IBM: Driving Strategy into Action,* California Management Review. Vol. 49 no. 4 -Summer 2007 p 21-43

88 Clayton Christensen, *The Innovator's Dilemma*, Harvard Business School Press, 1997 and Harper Paperbacks, 2003.

89 Ibid.

90 Ibid., xii and xiii.

91 'The House That Jack Built', *The Economist,* September 16, 1999.

92 DYB.com, *The Economist*, 16 September, 1999.

93 Guido Jouret, 'Inside Cisco's search for the next big idea', *Harvard Business Review*, September 2009.

94 Also see blogs.cisco.com/borderless/subject_meet_the_cisco_i-prize_finalists_ rhinnovation/ (A shortened link is: http://bit.ly/juL6zk)

95 Personal communication with Tokyo Shoko Research, Ltd., Japan. Their article was originally written in Japanese and never released in English. They analysed close to two million companies in their database of companies from around the world. For further details look on the web for Wiki and 'List of oldest companies'.

96 'The enlightenment of Richard Branson'. Search via *Fastcompany* magazine for the article by Alan Deutschman, September 2006.

97 *The Mask of Command*, John Keegan, Pimlico. *War in European History* Michael Howard, Oxford University Press and *Clausewitz: A Very Short Introduction*, Michael Howard, Oxford University Press

98 Roger Steare has written a brief informative book on ethics entitled *Ethicability*®. First published in 2006, his book pre-dates the economic crash. *Ethicability*® is a UK-registered trademark of Roger Steare Consulting Limited.

99 Organizational Culture Inventory® (OCI®) registered to Human Synergistics International, USA.

100 J. Rust, *Giotto Manual*, Pearson Assessment, 1997. See also www.psychometrics. ppsis.cam.ac.uk/page/102/giotto.htm (A shortened link is: http://bit.ly/mmpBiP).

101 Christopher Jamison, the 'Abbot of Worth', lecture given on 11 November, 2008. www.operationnoah.org/node/117 (A shortened link is: http://bit.ly/jhxmC0).

102 See www.arup.com/Publications/The_Key_Speech.aspx (A shortened link is http:// bit.ly/o7idRP).

103 Interviews and correspondence March 2011 with Colin Harris, Head of UKMEA Infrastructure, Ove Arup.

Notes

Notes